Fuelling Economic Growth

Praise for the book...

'The IDRC's Research on Knowledge Systems programme, which is partly captured in the this book, was a unique exercise in practical learning and networking to fill the very real gaps on how partnerships can stimulate and create conditions for innovation in developing countries. Case studies like these can help de-mystify and make very practical, the enabling (and confounding) variables in the process of innovation. The authors and the editors are applauded for this work and its contribution to the global discourse on knowledge and its use.'
Adi Paterson, CEO designate of the Australian Nuclear Science and Technology Organisation, Member of the National Advisory Council on Innovation, South Africa.

'This book constitutes an important contribution to the understanding of the conceptual framework under which science and innovation have evolved in developing countries'
Carlos Aguirre-Bastos, Visiting Researcher, Austrian Research Center.

'The changing role of public and private sector funding for research is an important policy issue. This book presents findings concerning this and related policies based on analysis from a number of developing countries. The book is an important contribution to the policy debate and demonstrates the significance of IDRC support for such work on science, technology and innovation policy and practice.'
Fred Gault is former Chair of the OECD Working Group of National Experts on Science and Technology Indicators (NESTI).

'This is an important collection of research covering a critical central issue: the question of public–private sector relations in science and technology-based economic development. The book sheds light on an impressive range of countries and issues, translating detailed empirical analysis into practical policy advice. It represents a major contribution to the field of innovation-oriented development studies.'
Richard Isnor was formerly Director, Innovation, Policy and Science, IDRC, and is now Manager, NSERC-Atlantic Scientific Park, Canada.

*This book is dedicated to
the memory of Daniel Chudnovsky*

Fuelling Economic Growth
The Role of Public–Private Sector Research in Development

Edited by
Michael Graham and Jean Woo

International Development Research Centre
Ottawa • Cairo • Dakar • Montevideo • Nairobi • New Delhi • Singapore

Practical Action Publishing Ltd
25 Albert Street, Rugby, CV21 2SD, Warwickshire, UK
www.practicalactionpublishing.com

ISBN 978 1 85339 675 5

and the International Development Research Centre
P.O. Box 8500, Ottawa, ON, Canada K1G 3HP
www.idrc.ca/info@idrc.ca

ISBN 978 1 55250 416 1 (e-book)

© International Development Research Centre, 2009

First published 2009

All rights reserved. No part of this publication may be reprinted or reproduced or utilized in any form or by any electronic, mechanical, or other means, now known or hereafter invented, including photocopying and recording, or in any information storage or retrieval system, without the written permission of the publishers.

A catalogue record for this book is available from the British Library.

The contributors have asserted their rights under the Copyright Designs and Patents Act 1988 to be identified as authors of their respective contributions.

Since 1974, Practical Action Publishing has published and disseminated books and information in support of international development work throughout the world. Practical Action Publishing Ltd (Company Reg. No. 1159018) is the wholly owned publishing company of Practical Action Ltd. Practical Action Publishing trades only in support of its parent charity objectives and any profitsarecovenantedbacktoPracticalAction(Charity Reg. No. 247257, Group VAT Registration No. 880 9924 76).

Cover photograph with kind permission from
International Development Research Centre

Cover design by Practical Action Publishing Ltd
Indexed by Pindar NZ
Typeset by SJI Services

Contents

Figures	vii
Tables	viii
Acronyms and abbreviations	xi
Authors	xiii

1. Introduction — 1

2. Innovation and productivity: Argentine manufacturing firms in the 1990s — 5
   - Conceptual and methodological issues — 7
   - Innovation inputs and outputs — 10
   - Methodology and results — 17
   - Lessons learned and policy recommendations — 26

   Daniel Chudnovsky, Andrés López, and Germán Pupato

3. Research for policy development: Industrial clusters in South China — 39
   - Methodology — 40
   - Guangdong: A region developed in successive steps — 41
   - The logic of industrial development in Guangdong — 44
   - Innovation policy and innovation centres — 49
   - Case studies — 54
   - Lessons and results — 75
   - Conclusion: Toward a Regional Innovation System — 79

   Rigas Arvanitis and Qiu Haixiong

4. Partnerships for agroindustrial research and development in Costa Rica and El Salvador — 87
   - Activities and achievements — 88
   - Potential impact — 92
   - Constraints — 93
   - Conclusions — 93

   Frank Hartwich, Olman Quirós, and Jorge Garza

5. Public–private research, development, and innovation in Peru — 105
   - Methodology — 106
   - Results — 107
   - Research and technology institutions — 122
   - Case study: Technological innovation in copper hydrometallurgy — 130
   - Case study: Technological innovation to control the fruit fly in mango agriculture — 139
   - Lessons learned — 146

	Policy recommendations	147
	Juana Kuramoto and Máximo Torero	
6	Trends in research and development in Tanzania: Funding sources, institutional arrangements, and relevance	159
	Background	160
	Problem	160
	Objectives	161
	Conceptual framework	161
	Methodological framework	162
	R&D systems in Tanzania: An overview	164
	Industrial R&D system	167
	Health R&D system	168
	Research findings	169
	Industrial sector	178
	Health sector	183
	Comparative analysis	187
	Conclusion and policy recommendations	190
	Samuel Wangwe, Bitrina Diyamett, and Adalgot Komba	
7	Public–private partnerships in fish genetics research: The Philippine experience	193
	Project implementation and management	194
	Research methodology	195
	Research findings	197
	Effects of changing partnerships on genetic R&D	201
	Findings of tilapia R&D by public- and private-sector institutions	212
	Issues and recommendations	212
	Lessons learned	215
8	Learning by networking with multinationals: A study of the Vietnamese automotive industry	219
	Linking with foreign partners as a learning strategy	220
	Intellectual property rights: Pros and cons for learning	222
	Innovation: Developing country perspective	224
	Adapting the system of innovation approach	226
	Research questions	228
	Automotive industry in Vietnam	228
	Emergence of the motorcycle industry	229
	Automobile sector	233
	Learning in the automotive sector	235
	Case studies	246
	Observations and policy proposals	253
	Conclusion	258
	Tran Ngoc Ca	
9	Conclusion	263
Index		267

Figures

2.1	Stages in the innovation process	8
2.2	Distribution of innovative sales as a percentage of total sales (1998–2001)	14
3.1	A schematic presentation of the 'piling-up' of productive systems	42
5.1	R&D expenditures (as a percentage of GNP in 1997) of three groups of countries	108
5.2	1997 R&D expenditures (% of GNP) and GNP per capita	108
5.3	R&D expenditures (% GNP) and GNP per capita in 1997	109
5.4	Economic creativity and its components	111
5.5	A regional comparison of the availability of ICTs in 2000	113
5.6	The relative quality of third and fourth levels of primary education	117
5.7	Patent applications by residents and non residents (1990–1999)	118
5.8	Costs of infrastructure	121
7.1	Distribution pathways for genetically improved tilapia	205
8.1	Innovation system showing the dominant role of commercial interactions	227
8.2	Motorcycle sales in different market segments in Vietnam	230
8.3	Shares in the Vietnamese Motorcycle Market	231

Tables

2.1	Percentage distribution of firms according to size and nationality	11
2.2	Performance of firms between 1992 and 2001	12
2.3	Distribution of firms according to sector of production	13
2.4	Innovation and in-house R&D expenditures of firms that performed R&D	16
2.5	Innovation and in-house R&D expenditures (expressed in percentages) of firms that performed R&D	17
2.6	Cooperative links related to innovation activities during 1998–2001	18
2.7	The decision to undertake innovation activities and the intensity of innovation (summary of econometric estimates)	21
2.8	Innovative output (summary of econometric estimates)	23
2.9	Firm performance (summary of econometric estimates)	26
3.1	The three institutional settings that include the industrial clusters and the university that were studied	40
3.2	Characteristics of different models of interactive learning	45
3.3	Research innovation projects that linked Zhongshan University to enterprises	74
3.4	Main problems reported by innovation centres	78
5.1	Source of R&D expenditures	110
5.2	Competitiveness in the institutional environment (The Global Competitiveness Report 2001–2)	118
5.3	Indicators of infrastructure in Latin America	121
5.4	Achievement of specific roles by a sample of research and technology institutions (Mullin Consulting 2002)	123
5.5	Areas of specialization and locations of Technological Innovation Centres (PRODUCE, 2007)	124
5.6	Supply and demand by field of skilled labour 1996–98	127
5.7	Most important differences between innovative and non-innovative firms	131
5.8	Mango farmer associations	143
6.1	Trends in agricultural R&D expenditures, MAFS, Dar es Salaam	170

6.2	Trends in manufacturing GDP (1976 prices)	178
6.3	Funding for R&D at TIRDO	179
6.4	Funding for R&D at CAMARTEC	179
6.5	Summary of effective R&D projects	181
6.6	Allocation and use of funds at NIMR	184
6.7	Distribution of research funds to various activities (1994)	184
6.8	Expenditures on health R&D by NIMR	185
7.1	Genetic-improvement programmes undertaken by public-sector institutions	198
7.2	Mode of access to tilapia genetics-based fish products being distributed by breeding institutions under the Tilapia Science Centre	206
7.3	Distribution of users of genetically improved tilapia strain by gender	206
7.4	Access to technical advice	208
7.5	Awareness and main sources of information on tilapia-genetics technology	210
7.6	Adoption and use of tilapia-genetics technology by hatchery farmers	210
7.7	Operating revenues and R&D expenditures of non-profit private sector (GIFT Foundation)	211
8.1	Motorcycle production in Vietnam (1999–2004)	230
8.2	FDI in the Vietnamese motorcycle industry (1992–2001)	232
8.3	Performance of FDI firms in the automobile sector (up to 31 December 2002)	234
8.4	Years in which firms were established	236
8.5	Time lag (in months) between time of establishment of firm and production of parts	236
8.6	Types of firms that participated in the survey	236
8.7	Types of parts manufactured by domestic firms in the automotive sector	237
8.8	The first, second, and third most important capabilities required to enter the automotive parts market	238
8.9	Firm size in terms of number of workers during peak year	239
8.10	Proportion of sales that automotive parts contributed to total sales during peak year	239

8.11 Percentage of sales that go to FDI firms 240

8.12 Obstacles that firms experience in learning to make automotive parts 241

8.13 Contributions of various organizations to the learning processes of firms 243

8.14 Problems firms experienced when working with customers and vendors 243

8.15 Importance of different learning channels to automotive parts makers 245

8.16 Impact of policy issues on learning activities of firms 246

Acronyms and abbreviations

AIDS	Acquired Immune Deficiency Syndrome
ARS	Argentine Peso
CAMARTEC	Centre for Agricultural Mechanization and Rural Technology
CDM	Common Diagnostic Model
CENTROMIN	State-Owned Mining Firm (Peru)
CITEs	Technological Innovation Centres
CLANAE	National Classification of Economic Activities
CNC	Computer Numerical Control
CNY	Chinese Yuan
CONCYTEC	Consejo Nacional de Tecnología (Peru)
DFID	Department for International Development (UK)
FAC-CLSU	Freshwater Aquaculture Centre, Central Luzon State University
FDI	Foreign Direct Investment
FONCYC	Science and Competitiveness Fund
FSA	Farming Systems Approach
GDP	Gross Domestic Product
GET	Genetically Enhanced Tilapia
GMT	Genetically Male Tilapia
GST	GIFT Super Tilapia/GenoMar Supreme Tilapia
HIERRO	State-Owned Enterprise (Peru)
HVN	Honda Vietnam
IADB	Inter-American Development Bank
ICCA	Inter-American Institute for Cooperation on Agriculture
ICLARM	International Centre for Living Aquatic Resources Management
ICTs	Information and Communication Technologies
IDRC	International Development Research Centre
IFPRI	International Food Policy Research Institute
IHRDC	Ifakara Health Research and Development Centre
INCAGRO	Innovación y Competitividad para el Agro Peruano
INDEC	National Statistical Institute, Argentina
INGEMMET	Instituto Geológico Minero y Metalúrgico
INIA	Instituto Nacional de Investigaciones Agrarias
IPEN	Instituto Peruano de Energía Nuclear
IPRs	Intellectual Property Rights
IPS	Innovation, Policy and Science (Programme Area)
IRD	Institute for Research for Development

IRRI	International Rice Research Institute
ISNAR	International Service for National Agricultural Research
MAFS	Ministry of Agriculture and Food Security
MERCOSUR	Southern Common Market
MINERO	State-Owned Mining Firm (Peru)
MIT	Ministry of Industry and Trade
MNCs	Multinational Companies
NFFTC-BFAR	National Freshwater Fisheries Technology Centre, Bureau of Fisheries and Aquatic Resources
NIMR	National Institute for Medical Research
NORAD	Norwegian Agency for Development Cooperation
NSI	National Systems of Innovation
OECD	Organization for Economic Cooperation and Development
OEM	Original Equipment Manufacturing
PHP	Philippine Peso
R&D	Research and Development
RICyT	Inter American Network for Science and Technology
RoKS	Research on Knowledge Systems
S&T	Science and Technology
SENASA	National Service of Agrarian Sanitation
SMEs	Small- and Medium-Size Enterprises
SOEs	State-Owned Enterprises
STD	Sexually Transmitted Disease
SX-EW	Solvent Extraction and Electrowinning
TaCRI	Tanzania Coffee Research Institute
TaTEDO	Tanzania Traditional Energy Development and Environment Organization
TEMDO	Tanzania Engineering and Manufacturing Design Organization
TIRDO	Tanzania Industrial Research and Development Organization
TIS	Technological Innovation System
TRIT	Tea Research Institute of Tanzania
TZS	Tanzanian Shillings
UNU-INTECH	United Nations University-Institute for New Technologies
UP Visayas	University of the Philippines in the Visayas
USAID	United States Agency for International Development
VMEP	Vietnam Manufacturing and Export Processing Company
WDI	World Development Indicators
WIPO	World Intellectual Property Organization
WTO	World Trade Organization
ZURIGuD	Research Institute for Guangdong Development

Authors

Belen Acosta: Senior Research Associate, The WorldFish Center, P.O. Box 500, GPO 10670, Penang, Malaysia.

Rigas Arvanitis: Institute for Research for Development (IRD), Research Unit 'Savoir et développement', Bondy, France.

Daniel Chudnovsky (1944–2007): His co-authors, Andrés López and Germán Pupato, regret the passing of their friend, colleague, and mentor.

Bitrina Diyamett: Tanzania Commission for Science and Technology, Ali Hassan Mwinyi Road, Kijitonyama (Sayansi), COSTECH (Tanzania Commission for Science and Technology) Building, Dar es Salaam (www.costech.or.tz).

Jorge Garza: Principal Researcher, International Service for National Agricultural Research – International Food Policy Research Institute (IFPRI–ISNAR). Office at the Inter-American Institute for Cooperation on Agriculture (ICCA), San José, Coronado, Costa Rica.

Michael Graham: Science Editor, 2422 Fairmile Road, RR4 Kemptville, ON, K0G 1J0, Canada.

Qiu Haixiong: Guangdong Development Research Institute (ZURIGuD), Zhongshan University, Guangzhou, China (purigud@zsu.edu.cn).

Frank Hartwich: Project Advisor, IFPRI–ISNAR, ICCA, San José, Coronado, Costa Rica.

Adalgot Komba: Institute of Development Studies, University of Dar es Salaam, Dar es Salaam, Tanzania (www.ids.udsm.ac.tz).

Juana Kuramoto: Associate Researcher, Grupo de Análisis para el Desarrollo (Group for the Analysis of Development) (GRADE), Peru.

Andrés López: Director, Centro de Investigaciones para la Transformación (CENIT), Buenos Aires, Argentina (www.fund-cenit.org.ar) and Head of Department of Economics, Faculty of Economic Sciences, University of Buenos Aires.

Tran Ngoc Ca: Deputy Director, National Institute for Science and Technology Policy and Strategy Studies (NISTPASS), Ministry of Science and Technology (MOST), Vietnam.

Germán Pupato: PhD candidate, University of British Columbia, Canada, and formerly enrolled at Universidad de San Andrés, Argentina.

Olman Quirós: Principal Researcher, IFPRI–ISNAR, Office at The ICCA, San José, Coronado, Costa Rica.

Máximo Torero: Director, Markets, Trade and Institutions Division (IFPRI), Washington, DC, USA. This research was initiated while Mr Torero was Senior Researcher at GRADE.

Samuel Wangwe: Economic and Social Research Foundation, Dar es Salaam (www.esrftz.org).

Jean Woo: Programme Officer, Innovation, Policy and Science, IDRC, Ottawa, Canada.

CHAPTER 1
Introduction

Support for policy-relevant research on science, technology and innovation has always been a programme priority for the International Development Research Centre (IDRC). Initially, this support was provided through initiatives such as the Science and Technology Policy Instruments (STPI) project. In 2001, the Research on Knowledge Systems (RoKS) exploration supported a series of funding competitions focused on research designed specifically to support and inform policy development. The work supported by RoKS was a precursor to a larger programme commitment by IDRC to this programme area.

IDRC has continued to evolve and to apply the lessons learned from support to these RoKS projects. Building on these experiences, and furthering its commitment to understanding the role of innovation in development, the IDRC Board of Governors approved the creation of the new Innovation, Policy, and Science (IPS) programme in March 2005.

The IPS programme area focuses its research activities on supporting the development of science, technology, and innovation (STI) policies that aim to alleviate poverty in developing countries. IPS research also supports efforts to strengthen the evidence base for, as well as multi-stakeholder equity and involvement in, STI policy making processes at local, national, regional and international levels.

The programme area works to enhance research on questions of governance, public understanding, access and benefits associated with new transformative technologies in and for the South. It also seeks to enhance open and transparent processes that involve stakeholders in the development of new technologies in and for the South, and to improve knowledge of the impacts of science, technology and innovation. IPS-supported research addresses the social, environmental and economic impacts of science, technology and innovation policies from a Southern perspective.

IPS also provides a platform within IDRC for active representation within the Canadian research and science policy communities to ensure that international cooperation and development remain important priorities for Canada's research efforts. In pursuit of this objective, IPS supports new strategic mechanisms for strengthened and appropriate Canadian–Southern research partnerships that respond to research priorities of IDRC's Southern partners.

This book presents the outputs of the first series of RoKS-supported research projects stemming from the competitions. These projects addressed the fundamental changes that are taking place in the funding of research in the public and private sectors and looked at how these changes are affecting the development of effective public policy.

The RoKS competition was launched to 'support research on the changing balance between public- and private-sector funding of research, and its implications for developing country governments and research institutions.' The selection of this theme recognized the obvious global changes taking place in the environment for research and development. Particularly in the South, the need for scientific knowledge continues to expand as developing countries struggle to compete in an increasingly knowledge-intensive global economy and to confront new challenges ranging from HIV/AIDS to global environmental change. Yet at the same time, traditional sources of research funding – from national governments, international agencies, and the donor community – have stagnated and in many cases declined.

In part because of the drop-off of traditional sources of funding, the private sector has come to play an increasingly important role as a source of research funding. Globally, private-sector funding of research and development (R&D) now doubles the contribution from public-sector sources. This shifting balance between public and private sectors is not limited to the industrialized countries of the North. Particularly in the more industrialized Southern countries, shares of private-sector funding have risen dramatically, and frequently represent more than half of total resources for research and science.

The shifting balance between public and private sectors is by no means the only change in the environment for scientific research and innovation in the South. But changes in the balance of funding are an important marker of evolution in the nature of research systems in the South, and they have critical implications for public policy and the management of scientific institutions.

Unfortunately, our understanding of trends in research funding and their implications remains extremely limited. Official statistics remain sketchy, in many cases are of poor quality, and at best provide partial clues to the changes under way. Analysis of alternative policy instruments and institutional arrangements has been limited. As a result, evidence with regard to 'good practice' is frequently anecdotal. Perhaps most critically, there has been little opportunity to date to compare experiences across countries, or to engage in debate between the academic and policy-making communities.

The RoKS competition sought to develop a knowledge network to advance understanding of the shifting balance of public- and private-sector support to research for development. It was also envisioned that it would foster debate on possible policy responses at the institutional, national and international level. Within this context, research projects focused on one or both of these themes: trends in funding, performance, and management of research and development; and policy options to stimulate research and development in, and for, developing countries.

The individual chapters in this book are authored by researchers with a deep interest in the role that scientific and technological knowledge and local innovation must play in their countries' development.

Each chapter presents detailed specific case studies funded by the RoKS competition that include work from: Argentina; China; Costa Rica; El Salvador; Peru; the Philippines; Tanzania; and Vietnam. In chapter two, Daniel Chudnovsky, Andrés López, and Germán Pupato analyse innovation and productivity among Argentine manufacturing firms in the 1990s and summarize the lessons that have been learned in order to make policy recommendations. The third chapter takes us to China where Rigas Arvanitis and Qiu Haixiong take a detailed look at the development of industrial clusters in South China to better understand how policies have been developed and implemented to encourage innovation. They identify issues that have arisen and identify where policy changes may be required.

In chapter four, Frank Hartwich, Olman Quirós, and Jorge Garza examine partnerships that have arisen within agroindustrial research and development in Costa Rica and El Salvador. Their research shows how public–private partnerships have influenced agricultural and social development in Central America. In chapter five, Juana Kuramoto and Maximo Torero of Peru report on their work on research, development, and innovation. They examine the institutional policies for innovation, and for research and development in Peru, assess the effect of these policies on the performance of firms, and present case studies to be able to make policy-relevant recommendations.

In chapter six, Samuel Wangwe, Bitrina Diyamett, and Adalgot Komba look at the trends that have developed in funding, institutional arrangements, and the relevance of research and development in Tanzania to better understand how policy is influencing both public and private support to research and development. Their research suggests how such policy can be more relevant to socioeconomic development in Tanzania. In chapter seven, the WorldFish Centre in Malaysia reports on research it undertook to better understand the contributions of public–private partnerships to fish genetics research in the Philippines. Issues are identified and recommendations on how to improve future partnerships are presented.

The final case study found in chapter eight by Tran Ngoc Ca and his team looks at the Vietnamese automotive industry to better understand how learning has taken place at the national level, through the establishment of networks with multinational companies. This study demonstrates how companies were able to become active learners while working with their partners and identifies policy measures that support learning.

Each of the chapters stands alone as an independent study, but in sum they present a good summary of the work supported by the RoKS competitive grants programme. In publishing this volume, the IPS programme area of IDRC hopes to contribute to the understanding of how best to encourage the development of science, technology, and innovation policies that are relevant to the conditions and priorities of developing countries.

CHAPTER 2
Innovation and productivity: Argentine manufacturing firms in the 1990s[1]

Daniel Chudnovsky, Andrés López, and Germán Pupato

Abstract

This study analyses productivity among Argentine manufacturing firms in the 1990s, in particular the policies introduced to foster innovation in the private sector. The research was designed to better assess the costs and benefits of the tax-credit system for research and development activities, and the performance of the main industrial technology institution in Argentina. Several lessons are identified for policymakers: research and development investment is a fundamental determinant of the probability of successfully introducing innovations; technological flows increase the magnitude of innovation output; large firms are more likely to engage in innovative activities; and firms consider research and development activities to be valuable, even during recessionary times. The authors suggest that by extrapolating these findings, public policies geared toward promoting research and development should have positive results. They recommend removal of barriers that prevent small- and medium-size industries from engaging in innovation, and suggest the need for additional research on the relationships between domestic innovative efforts and the acquisition of technology, and the impacts of new policies designed to foster private innovation.

After the adoption of the Convertibility Plan and of a far-reaching programme of structural reforms in the early 1990s, Argentina's economy had periods of high growth in 1991–94 (interrupted by the Tequila crisis in 1995) and in 1996–98. In late 1998, the economy started to stagnate and there was a deep fall in GDP in 2001 and 2002. The country suffered the worst crisis of its history as a result of a banking crisis, a default on external debt, and a huge devaluation of the peso.

At the firm level, responses to these changes (in particular, trade and investment liberalization, which implied enhanced access to modern technologies and increased competition in the domestic market) were far from homogeneous. Although many domestic firms closed – this was especially the case among small- and medium-size enterprises (SMEs) – or were sold to foreign investors, others totally or partially abandoned production activities to become importers of foreign goods. In turn, large firms and most notably affiliates of transnational corporations (TNCs) performed better in the new market conditions.

In the post-reform scenario, it could be expected that manufacturing firms (either survivors or newcomers in the industry) would increase their investments in technology modernization to face the challenges of trade liberalization. This was what happened, as revealed by the first national survey on innovation activities in manufacturing firms (INDEC, 1998). In a context of booming sales and productivity, innovation expenditures (including R&D activities, acquisition of capital goods related to innovation activities, and expenditures in training, consultancies, engineering, and design) increased by almost 25% between 1992 and 1996.

Among the firms that augmented their innovation expenditures, the bias in favour of technology imports over domestic innovation expenditures that had traditionally characterized the conduct of Argentine manufacturing firms was, if anything, reinforced. In spite of an increase in in-house R&D and innovation expenditures, during the high-growth period, inputs from abroad – mainly capital goods imports and foreign direct investment (FDI) inflows – were the main source of technological modernization for the industrial sector.

During this period, manufacturing firms were active in introducing new product and process technologies. This was no surprise given the need to compete in a more open and deregulated economy and the technological lag that had accumulated during the previous decade when Argentina's economy was closed, stagnating, and highly volatile.

What happened when the growth cycle was over? In the adverse conditions that had prevailed since 1998, a severe reduction in innovation expenditures would be expected. This presumption was confirmed by the second national survey on innovation in the manufacturing sector (INDEC, 2003), which showed that as sales (as well as productivity and investment) sharply fell, innovation expenditures were drastically reduced between 1998 and 2001. Few firms introduced new technologies during this period, but in-house R&D activities did not fall, although they remained at modest levels.

A number of questions that arise from Argentina's experience are addressed in this paper: Did firms that introduced product and process innovations during that period perform better than those that stuck with their old technologies? Was the probability of introducing a new technology in the market enhanced by making innovation expenditures and by interacting with other firms and institutions (as suggested by the received literature)? Did in-house innovation activities have a different impact on the probability of becoming an innovator with regard to technology acquisition? Were both knowledge sources complements and substitutes in terms of the innovative processes of firms? What kinds of firms were more likely to engage in innovation activities and to launch innovations to the market (that is, what were the determinants of innovative behaviour among Argentina's manufacturing firms)?

To answer these questions, data from innovation surveys conducted by the National Statistical Institute (INDEC) were used. The conceptual framework and methodology were based on those used in the European Community Innovation Surveys (CIS).

The fact that innovation is a key element of a firm's performance is well established in developed countries. However, this is not always properly acknowledged in a developing country like Argentina. Moreover, firms, policymakers, and economists often believe that, even if it 'pays' to be an innovator, only access to foreign sources matter. They do not grant enough attention to the need to combine imported technologies with domestic and in-house innovation activities.

Our results show that innovators performed better than non-innovators in Argentina. Both technology acquisition and in-house R&D activities were crucial to becoming an innovator, which suggests that policies aimed at fostering both kinds of innovation activities should have a positive impact on the performance of domestic firms. Moreover, among the determinants of the probability of becoming an innovator, size is a key factor. Policies aimed at removing barriers that prevent SMEs from engaging in innovation activities should allow these firms to enhance their competitiveness.

Conceptual and methodological issues

Innovation surveys in the 1990s from the European Community and other countries, such as Canada, provided valuable information on the innovation process at the firm level. These have been emphasized in the chain-linked model proposed by Kline and Rosenberg (1986) and in the National Systems of Innovation (NSI) literature (Edquist, 1997). The rich information available from those surveys has also fostered new ways of doing research, such as applying advanced econometric techniques.

Innovation surveys supply data on among other things: innovation inputs other than R&D expenditures (e.g. industrial designs, training, licensing, and innovation-related fixed asset investments); the interactions that firms engage in during the innovation process; and the innovative output, estimated by the weight of new or significantly improved products and their resulting turnover at the firm level.

To analyse the information from these surveys, most researchers have followed the conceptual framework of Crepon et al. (1998) (the CDM model, see Appendix 2.1). In this framework, innovation is considered to be a process that is carried out with some specific inputs (R&D activities and acquisition of tangible and intangible technologies) and through interactions with other firms and institutions. The innovative process should lead to certain outputs, such as process innovations or sales of new (for the firms or for the market, but not necessarily for the world) or significantly improved products. In turn, innovators (i.e. those firms that have launched new or improved products or processes) are expected to perform better than non-innovators.

First, a decision is made on whether or not to allocate financial and human resources to innovation activities (Figure 2.1). Second, the amount of financial and human resources assigned provides a measure of the intensity of these activities at the firm level. Third, there is (or should be) an innovative output (process or product innovations) that should be related to innovation intensity[2] or to some other features of the innovation process (such as interactions with different agents and institutions of the NSI). Fourth, the firm's performance should be related to the innovative output.[3]

A number of variables are usually introduced to represent the probability of engaging in innovation activities and the intensity of those activities. These variables are used to control other aspects that could influence innovative output and the firms' performance. Among those variables are firms' size, ownership, export activity, labour skills, sector, profitability, and market power.

The performance of firms is captured through a variety of indicators, including labour and total factor productivity, profits, rates of growth of sales, total assets, and exports. The choice of indicators generally depends not only on research objectives but on data availability (see Kemp et al., 2003 and Kleinknecht and Mohnen, 2002 for surveys of the results of papers produced on this subject).

Available studies also explicitly account for features of the innovation process that may impact on the efficiency with which firms transform innovative inputs into innovative outputs. Because innovation is an interactive process, cooperation with other firms or universities, links with suppliers, and knowledge about customers are key issues.

It is useful to highlight some aspects of these innovation surveys, and the studies based on them, to understand the specific advantages and limitations of the adopted methodology. It is also important to adapt the CDM model to the reality of innovation activities in a developing country such as Argentina.

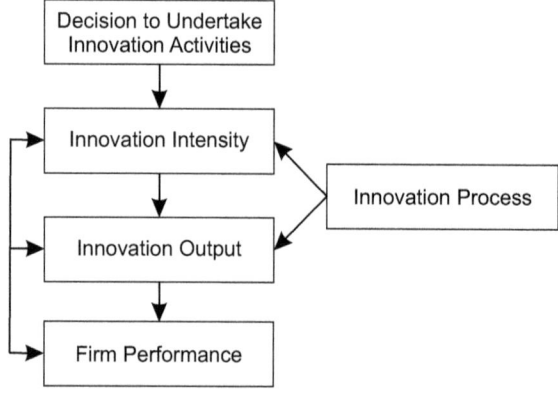

Figure 2.1 Stages in the innovation process
Source: Kemp et al., 2003

In most studies, innovation intensity is measured through R&D expenditures or employees, or by innovation expenditures as compiled in the innovation surveys. There are two important considerations. First, firms (especially SMEs) often make expenditures in informal innovation activities that are usually hard to estimate (because they are a byproduct of learning by doing processes, or firms do not know how the amount of monetary or labour resources are assigned to them because no dedicated department or team exists) but can be very relevant, especially in developing countries. Unfortunately, many of these activities are not captured in the available innovation surveys and the impact of these informal inputs is not taken into account.

Second, although it may be understandable that studies for developed countries do not take into account technology acquisition when measuring innovative inputs, this cannot be the case when analyzing the innovative behaviour of firms in developing countries. External sources of technology are, in general, more relevant than in-house innovation activities. Because Argentina's innovation survey includes questions on the acquisition of tangible and intangible technology, the respective flows can be included when measuring innovative inputs. It is also important to determine if external and in-house innovative expenditures are complementary or substitutes in such studies in developing countries.[4]

The innovative output of firms is often measured by the effect of new or significantly improved products on firms' turnover.[5] The main advantage of this indicator is the direct link between the innovation effort and commercial success. This procedure also has advantages over previous studies that employed patents, an indicator that has well-known limitations and is of little use in the Argentine case because manufacturing firms have relatively few patents.[6]

Measuring innovative output in terms of sales of new products has three main disadvantages: sectors have diverse product lifecycles, which should be adequately controlled to properly estimate innovative output; the variable is based on the respondent's own judgment (what is considered to be an innovation for a small firm might not qualify as such for a large firm); the influence of process and organizational innovations as innovative outputs (when they do not necessarily lead to new or improved products) is not measured.

In innovation surveys, the innovative output may consist not only of 'true' innovations but of products or processes that can be new for the firm but not for the industry (imitations). This is very important because in the case of developing countries most new products or processes are in fact imitations even when they are introduced through licensing agreements or foreign direct investment.

When interpreting the results, it is essential to remember the limitations of the data on which the analysis is based. In this study, sectoral characteristics were controlled; however, organizational innovations were not directly reflected in the output indicators used in the analysis.

Innovation inputs and outputs

Two datasets from Argentina were used in the descriptive statistics and econometric exercises. The first was based on matched information for 718 firms from the 1992–96 and 1998–2001 innovation surveys,[7] which were both designed in accordance with the methodologies suggested by the Oslo and Bogotá Manuals.[8] This information was complemented with a second dataset that contained information only from the second innovation survey (for 1,243 firms in 1998–2001). The second dataset contained data not available in the first survey, but that was still very important (e.g. information on sales of innovative products and links within the NSI). Although for the second dataset, panel-data techniques could not be used, the information it provided presented a more comprehensive analysis of the issues.

The majority (69%) of the enterprises surveyed in both datasets were founded before 1975 and survived the liberalization process in the early 1990s. Only 7% of the firms were created during the 1990s. Therefore, the majority of the firms were created during the import-substitution industrialization (ISI) period. However, more than 50% of the enterprises founded before 1975 changed ownership. These changes occurred mostly in the 1990s and generally involved the acquisition of indigenous firms by TNCs.

Small and domestic firms accounted for the majority of the 718 firms. Although large firms made up the smallest group, their numbers increased during the second period (Table 2.1). Because the database focused on the evolution of a given group of firms over time, this trend reflected the fact that manufacturing sales in 1998–2001 were, on average, larger than in 1992–96 (Table 2.2). Likewise, foreign-owned firms increased their participation in 1998–2001 by acquiring domestic firms (Table 2.1).

A firm was considered to be an innovator if it introduced new or radically modified products or processes (or both) during the periods under analysis. Although most firms (576 of 718, 80%) reported to be innovators in 1992–96, the number decreased notably during 1998–2001 (425 of 718, 59%) (Table 2.1). These figures may appear surprisingly high, but it is important to note that the Community Innovation Survey reported that 50% of European manufacturing firms introduced a product or process innovation during 1990–92 (Archibugi and Sirilli, 2000), a considerably shorter period than that covered by the Argentine surveys. Furthermore, the implementation of structural reforms in the early 1990s radically transformed Argentine industry, and firms were induced to adopt new strategies (including innovation) to survive.

Most of the innovative firms are both process and product innovators (Table 2.1). However, the relative weight of this group in our sample decreased substantially between 1992–96 and 1998–2001 (from 494 to 290 firms). Some of these firms became either only product or only process innovators in 1998–2001. However, the increase in these two subgroups was not enough to offset the reduction in the overall number of innovators during the recession period compared with the previous one (from 576 to 425 firms).

Table 2.1 Percentage distribution of firms according to size and nationality

	1992–96[a]				1998–2001			
	Large	Medium	Small	Total	Large	Medium	Small	Total
All surveyed firms	718 firms				718 firms			
Domestic	3.6	13.0	72.3	88.9	3.8	11.4	65.0	80.2
Foreign	2.4	3.5	5.3	11.1	4.5	6.8	8.5	19.8
Total firms	6.0	16.4	77.6	100	8.2	18.2	73.5	100
Innovators	576 firms				425 firms			
Domestic	4.2	14.8	68.1	87.0	4.5	14.6	55.3	74.4
Foreign	3.0	4.0	6.1	13.0	7.1	9.9	8.7	25.6
Total innovators	7.1	18.8	74.1	100	11.5	24.5	64.0	100
Process and product innovators	494 firms				290 firms			
Domestic	4.7	16.6	65.8	87.0	6.2	13.8	51.7	71.7
Foreign	3.2	4.0	5.7	13.0	8.3	11.0	9.0	28.3
Total innovators	7.9	20.6	71.5	100	14.5	24.8	60.7	100
Only product innovators	48 firms				63 firms			
Domestic	0	0	85.4	85.4	1.6	12.7	73.0	87.3
Foreign	2.1	4.2	8.3	14.6	3.2	4.8	4.8	12.7
Total non-innovators	2.1	4.2	93.8	100	4.8	17.5	77.8	100
Only process innovators	34 firms				72 firms			
Domestic	2.9	8.8	76.5	88.2	0	19.4	54.2	73.6
Foreign	0	2.9	8.8	11.8	5.6	9.7	11.1	26.4
Total non-innovators	2.9	11.8	85.3	100	5.6	29.2	65.3	100

[a] Firms were classified as small, medium, or large if their average total sales in 1998–2001 was less than US$25 m, between $25 and 100 m, or more than $100 m, respectively. A firm is considered to be foreign if its share of foreign capital is at least 10% of total capital.

Table 2.1 also shows that the group of innovators (and especially firms that were both process and product innovators) had a larger presence of large foreign firms. Furthermore, when these figures are compared between the two periods, it can be seen that these trends were reinforced throughout the 1990s.

Food and beverages, rubber and plastics, chemicals, textiles, and machinery and equipment account for more than half of the firms. Natural-resources intensive sectors account for almost one third of the firms, and R&D intensive firms are the least numerous. As expected, the weight of R&D and the scale-intensive sectors increases when the group of innovators is considered[9] (Table 2.3).

Although no information on the intensity of the innovative output was provided in the first innovation survey, these valuable data were available in the second survey. Figure 2.2 presents the distribution of the surveyed firms according to the intensity of their innovative sales.

12 FUELLING ECONOMIC GROWTH

Table 2.2 Performance of firms between 1992 and 2001

	1992		1996		1998		2001	
	Avg[a]	%[b]	Avg[a]	%[b]	Avg[a]	%[b]	Avg[a]	%[b]
All surveyed firms								
Total labour[c]	100		93.1		91.0		79.8	
In terms of total employees								
Sales[d] (ARS 000)	100		127.3		137.3		121.6	
Growth rate (%)[e]	–		27.3		7.8		–11.5	
Skilled labour (%)	7.4	83	8.1	84	18.4	92	19.2	92
In terms of total sales (%)								
Exports	13.9	44	14.9	60	16.5	51	19.4	54
Imports	13.6	64	14.9	73	17.5	62	14.6	60
Investment in capital goods	7.2	77	8.5	76	7.1	69	7.2	60
Innovators								
Total labour[c]	100		94.3		109.2		96.4	
In terms of total employees								
Sales[d] (ARS 000)	100		130.4		145.7		130.0	
Growth rate (%)[e]	–		30.4		11.7		–10.8	
Skilled labour (%)	7.5	87	8.3	89	20.2	96	21.4	96
In terms of total sales (%)								
Exports	13.4	49	14.8	67	16.2	64	18.0	67
Imports	13.9	71	15.4	80	16.4	76	14.6	74
Investment in capital goods	7.2	82	8.5	82	6.0	82	4.3	75
Product and process innovators								
Total labour[c]	100		94.5		112.3		100.5	
In terms of total employees								
Sales[d] (ARS 000)	100		128.8		154.6		138.0	
Growth rate (%)[e]	–		28.8		20.1		–10.7	
Skilled labour (%)	7.6	89	8.4	90	21.1	97	22.7	97
In terms of total sales (%)								
Exports	12.5	50	14.4	68	15.6	67	18.1	70
Imports	14.1	72	13.9	81	16.3	81	14.3	78
Investment in capital goods	6.1	84	6.2	83	6.0	85	4.6	77
Only product innovators								
Total labour[c]	100		103.5		201.7		151.9	
In terms of total employees								
Sales[d] (ARS 000)	100		129.3		121.9		103.7	
Growth rate (%)[e]	–		29.3		–5.8		–14.9	
Skilled labour (%)	8.1	77	8.7	79	17.8	92	18.0	92
In terms of total sales (%)								
Exports	12.6	52	14.2	60	9.4	51	11.1	57
Imports	13.3	67	18.0	73	15.2	65	14.9	62
Investment in capital goods	7.2	69	14.7	69	5.2	78	3.0	68
Only process innovators								
Total labour[c]	100		81.5		104.3		95.0	
In terms of total employees								
Sales[d] (ARS 000)	100		163.0		172.2		157.9	
Growth rate (%)[e]	–		63.0		5.6		–8.3	
Skilled labour (%)	5.6	79	6.1	82	18.6	97	19.1	99

	1992		1996		1998		2001	
	Avg[a]	%[b]	Avg[a]	%[b]	Avg[a]	%[b]	Avg[a]	%[b]
In terms of total sales (%)								
Exports	33.5	35	24.3	53	23.3	64	23.0	64
Imports	10.2	53	35.4	76	17.8	67	15.4	65
Investment in capital goods	24.3	74	34.8	85	6.4	74	3.9	74

[a] Calculated for firms that reported a positive value of the respective variable.
[b] Percentage of firms that reported a positive value of the respective variable.
[c] The values in 1990 are taken as 100 and the other three years are expressed in relation to the 1990 value (Exchange rate: ARS 1.00 = US$0.31).
[d] Excluding sales of goods produced by third parties.
[e] Calculated with respect to the previous period.

Table 2.3 Distribution of firms according to sector of production

	Sector (CLANAE[10] classification)	All firms		Innovators (1992–96)		Innovators (1998–2001)	
		No.	%	No.	%	No.	%
Scale intensive	Rubber and plastics	46	6.4	38	6.6	32	7.5
	Common metals	24	3.3	20	3.5	18	4.2
	Metal products	39	5.4	30	5.2	19	4.5
	Machinery and equipment	59	8.2	53	9.2	42	9.9
	Radio and TV equipment	9	1.3	8	1.4	8	1.9
	Vehicles	31	4.3	30	5.2	22	5.2
	Other transport equipment	10	1.4	6	1	2	0.5
	Scale	**218**	**30.4**	**185**	**32.1**	**143**	**33.6**
Labour intensive	Textiles	67	9.3	47	8.2	25	5.9
	Clothing	15	2.1	10	1.7	7	1.6
	Leather and footwear	13	1.8	11	1.9	10	2.4
	Publishing and printing	38	5.3	32	5.6	18	4.2
	Furniture	27	3.8	19	3.3	12	2.8
	Labour	**160**	**22.3**	**119**	**20.7**	**72**	**16.9**
R&D intensive	Chemicals	75	10.4	65	11.3	55	12.9
	Electrical machinery	24	3.3	22	3.8	17	4
	Medical instruments	10	1.4	7	1.2	6	1.4
	R&D	**109**	**15.2**	**94**	**16.3**	**78**	**18.4**
Natural Resources intensive	Food and beverages	144	20.1	114	19.8	83	19.5
	Tobacco	1	0.1	1	0.2	1	0.2
	Wood	21	2.9	9	1.6	5	1.2
	Paper	21	2.9	18	3.1	13	3.1
	Petroleum	6	0.8	6	1	5	1.2
	Fabricated and non-ferrous minerals	38	5.3	30	5.2	25	5.9
	Natural resources	**231**	**32.2**	**178**	**30.9**	**132**	**31.1**
Total		**718**	**100**	**576**	**100**	**425**	**100**

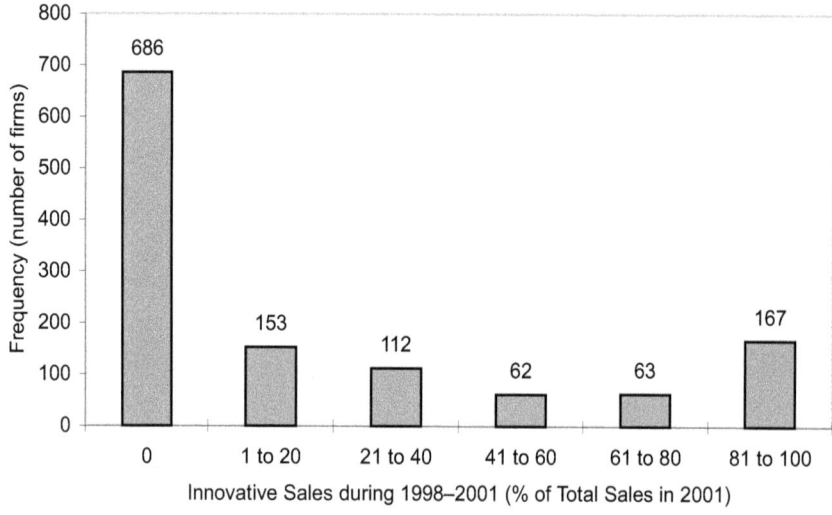

Figure 2.2 Distribution of innovative sales as a percentage of total sales (1998–2001)

Of the 1243 firms, 557 (45%) reported a positive level of innovation output during 1998–2001.[11] This group of firms reported that 52% of their total turnover in 2001 was innovative sales, but the dispersion of values is large. For example, the 167 highly innovative firms (30% of total innovators) had an innovative output during 1998–2001 that amounted to more than 80% of their total turnover in 2001. However, 153 innovators (27% of this group) reported innovative low output intensities that ranged from 1% to 20% of total sales in 2001. Finally, 686 firms (55% of the firms surveyed) declared no innovative sales during this period (therefore, they are non-innovators).

Performance of firms

Considering the evolution of labour productivity (measured by sales per employee), it is clear that between 1992 and 1998 surveyed firms experienced a period of high growth (37%); whereas, the opposite occurred during 1998–2001 (–11.5%). Notably, growth rates were markedly higher for innovators (45.7% during 1992–98) and their decline was slightly less severe (–10.8% during 1998–2001) when compared with the whole sample (Table 2.2).

Total employment in surveyed firms decreased throughout the 1990s (Table 2.2). However, in the case of innovators, employment in 1998 was higher than in 1992. Workforce reduction reached 20% for all surveyed firms (comparing 2001 with 1992), but amounted to only 3.6% in the case of innovators.

The weight of skilled labour in total employment increased without interruption throughout the 1990s, from about 7% to almost 20%. The increase was larger for innovators than for the whole sample. A similar trend is visible for export and import coefficients (except in 2001 for imports, a consequence of the economic crisis). Whereas a higher than average proportion of innovators participated in foreign trade, their export and import intensities did not differ from the average of all surveyed firms.

The number of firms reporting investments in capital goods decreased notably in 2001: 77% of the surveyed firms reported positive investments in 1992 but only 60% did so in 2001. Although innovators were more prone to acquire capital goods when compared with the average, unexpectedly, the intensity of their investments was lower (relative to their sales) in 1998 and 2001 than for the sample as a whole.

Expenditures on innovation activities

After increasing in 1992–96, the number of firms engaged in innovation activities (i.e. firms with positive innovation expenditures) decreased markedly (from 59% to 45%) during 1996–2001 (Table 2.4). Furthermore, among these firms, the intensity of total expenditures on innovation activities decreased to 3% of total sales in 2001 from the maximum of more than 4% that was reached in 1996.[12] This pattern was observed for both innovators and non-innovators.

The intensity of in-house R&D expenditures for firms that perform R&D increased considerably after 1996, even during the recession (Table 2.4). This trend holds for innovators and for the whole sample, and it is also observed in the sample of 1,243 firms (Table 2.5). Furthermore, the share of firms that perform R&D increased from 22% in 1992 to 28% in 2001. This figure is substantially higher among innovators, in particular, among product and process innovators (Table 2.4).

Technology-acquisition expenditures (which, for the sample of 718 firms, included technology transfer and investment in capital goods related to innovation activities) fell to 2.82% of total sales in 2001 from 4.26% in 1998. Furthermore, after a substantial increase in 1992–96, the proportion of all firms that invested in technology acquisition decreased sharply (from a peak of 45% in 1996 to 31% in 2001). However, this decrease was lower among innovators (50% of the firms in this group reported positive expenditures in technology acquisition in 2001, and 53% did so in 1996). Based on the dataset for 1,243 firms, expenditures can be broken down into tangible and intangible technology inputs,[13] either imported or locally acquired (Table 2.5). Expenditures in technology external to the firms decreased significantly during 1998–2001 among both innovators and non-innovators. This trend is particularly visible in the case of (domestic and imported) tangible technology (Table 2.5). Considering the intensity of expenditures, imported capital goods are still, by far, the most important source of technology acquisition for manufacturing firms in Argentina. Investments in imported technology are higher than in domestic technology in the case

Table 2.4 Innovation and in-house R&D expenditures of firms that performed R&D

		1992		1996		1998		2001	
		Avg.[a]	Firms (%)[b]	Avg.	Firms (%)	Avg.	Firms (%)	Avg.	Firms
All surveyed firms (718)	R&D	0.89	22	0.83	29	0.86	25	0.94	28
	Technology acquisition	4.99	28	4.22	45	4.26	33	2.82	31
	Total	3.93	46	4.08	59	3.91	45	3.04	45
Innovators	R&D	0.89	27	0.84	35	0.87	40	0.93	45
	Technology acquisition	5.03	33	4.10	53	4.29	50	2.79	50
	Total	3.93	55	4.00	69	4.00	68	3.06	70
Product and process innovators	R&D	0.87	29	0.80	37	0.93	49	0.95	53
	Technology acquisition	4.87	36	4.18	55	4.26	51	2.97	51
	Total	3.91	57	4.14	72	3.99	72	3.13	73
Only product innovators	R&D	0.89	19	0.94	29	0.80	35	1.08	40
	Technology acquisition	6.40	23	3.77	35	4.19	43	2.42	40
	Total	3.99	44	2.92	60	3.96	60	3.20	60
Only process innovators	R&D	1.80	12	1.93	15	0.26	13	0.35	17
	Technology acquisition	7.49	15	2.73	35	4.47	54	2.35	54
	Total	4.39	32	2.84	50	4.07	63	2.61	67

[a] Averages measure expenditures as a percentage of total sales and are calculated for firms that reported a positive value for the respective variable.
[b] Percentage indicates percentage of firms that reported a positive value for the variable.

of tangible technology in both 1998 and 2001; whereas, the opposite occurs with regard to intangible technology. Furthermore, the share of firms that declared innovative expenditures from domestic sources is larger than for those that acquired technology from foreign sources (this is true both for innovators and for non-innovators). This suggests that even if firms invest more intensely in the acquisition of foreign technologies than in domestic ones, domestic technologies seemingly have a higher level of diffusion.

Expectedly, more firms undertake R&D and technology-acquisition activities among innovators than among non-innovators. However, there are no relevant differences in the relative intensity with which firms in both groups resort to the different sources of technology (Tables 2.4 and 2.5).

Cooperative links

The second survey also provided information on cooperative links related to innovation activities undertaken by manufacturing firms during 1998–2001. Manufacturing firms have, primarily, engaged in cooperative links with

Table 2.5 Innovation and in-house R&D expenditures (expressed as percentages) of firms that performed R&D

			1998		2001	
			Avg.[a]	Firms (%)[b]	Avg.	Firms (%)
All surveyed firms (1,243)						
In-house R&D			0.84	25	0.97	27
Technology acquisition	Imported	Tangible	4.03	21	2.15	19
		Intangible	0.61	10	0.82	12
	Domestic	Tangible	2.52	34	1.7	35
		Intangible	0.94	37	0.86	43
Total expenditures in innovation activities			4.52	51	3.15	54
Innovators (557 firms)						
In-house R&D			0.90	46	1.02	47
Technology acquisition	Imported	Tangible	3.73	32	2.09	28
		Intangible	0.57	15	0.89	17
	Domestic	Tangible	2.19	52	1.59	53
		Intangible	1.13	57	0.97	64
Total expenditures in innovation activities			4.55	77	3.35	80
Non-innovators (686 firms)						
In-house R&D			0.53	7.3	0.75	9.8
Technology acquisition	Imported	Tangible	4.66	12	2.27	11
		Intangible	0.68	6.1	0.7	7.1
	Domestic	Tangible	3.26	19	1.95	20
		Intangible	0.53	21	0.65	26
Total expenditures in innovation activities			4.47	31	2.78	33

[a] Averages measure expenditures as a percentage of total sales and are calculated for firms that reported a positive value for the respective variable.
[b] Percentage of firms that reported a positive value for the respective variable.

domestic sources (Table 2.6). This fact is especially clear in the case of research and training institutions.

In general, innovators were markedly more involved in cooperative links than non-innovators. This was valid for every type of link considered, irrespective of whether it was domestic or foreign. Suppliers were the most important source of cooperation employed by non-innovators, for both domestic and foreign links. Although this was also the case for foreign links among innovators, they were primarily engaged with research and training institutions when domestic partners were considered. Government agencies (domestic and foreign) were, by far, the least widespread source of cooperation among manufacturing firms.

Methodology and results

Within the framework of the CDM model, this section analyses the innovation activities and performance of Argentine manufacturing firms during 1992–2001. The econometric exercises are primarily based on matched information

Table 2.6 Cooperative links related to innovation activities during 1998–2001

Type of institution	Domestic links (% of firms)	Foreign links (% of firms)
All surveyed firms (1,243)		
Research and training institutions	41.7	9.8
Suppliers	44.5	24.7
Clients	33.8	14.6
Other firms	38.1	13.4
Government agencies	6.4	0.8
Firms of the same group	22.4	15.0
Innovators (557 firms)		
Research and training institutions	56.7	15.8
Suppliers	54.9	37.2
Clients	43.3	22.4
Other firms	51.2	21.0
Government agencies	9.7	1.6
Firms of the same group	29.8	21.0
Non-innovators (686 firms)		
Research and training institutions	29.4	5.0
Suppliers	36.0	14.6
Clients	26.1	8.2
Other firms	27.6	7.3
Government agencies	3.8	0.1
Firms of the same group	16.3	10.1

for the 718 firms from both innovation surveys. This dataset collects information from the subset of firms sampled in both surveys (out of a total of 1,639 firms in 1992–96 and 1,243 firms in 1998–2001).

These estimates are not subject to sample selection (attrition) issues that would arise if the available data were not representative of the population of manufacturing firms. Because the innovation surveys in Argentina were not designed or intended to follow the behaviour of firms over time, but to obtain a representative sample from the universe of manufacturing firms in the Argentine industry, the decision to include or exclude firms from the survey was made randomly.

By considering the group of firms common to both surveys, panel-data techniques could be used in the econometric exercises. Otherwise, this would have been impossible because the data on innovative output were not reported on a year-by-year basis, but only once for the period covered by each survey. Fixed effects in panel-data analysis are sector specific and not firm specific, as is the usual practice in econometric studies.[14] In general, the independent variables in our dataset do not present enough time variation to allow their effects on the dependent variables to be estimated separately from a firm-specific fixed effect.[15]

Econometric results based on the cross-section of 1,243 manufacturing firms from the second survey of innovation are also presented. The advantage of this second dataset is that, although it does not allow the use of panel-data techniques, it contains information about the intensity of the innovative output, extramural technology acquisition, and cooperation links that is not available in the panel of 718 firms.

Estimation strategy

A two-tiered model was used to analyse the first two stages of the CDM model using the panel data of 718 firms.[16] This model allowed the decision to engage in innovation activities, and its intensity, to be explained by different mechanisms. This was particularly appropriate for the Argentine case because a large proportion of the surveyed firms did not undertake innovation activities (41% in 1996 and 55% in 2001, see Table 2.4).

In this model, the first tier was whether or not the firm decided to invest resources in innovation activities. This was analysed by estimating and comparing pooled and fixed-effects Logit estimators.[17] The dependent variable was a dummy that identified the group of firms that reported a positive innovation input (expenditures in either R&D, technology acquisition, management, or engineering and industrial design) in each period under analysis. The second tier determined the intensity of this investment. This stage was estimated by standard fixed- and random-effects analysis that used only the subsample of firms with positive expenditures in both periods.[18] The intensity of innovation activities was measured by the natural logarithm of the yearly average of total innovation expenditures in each of the two periods under analysis (in terms of total employees in 1996 and 2001, respectively).

Regarding the third stage of the CDM model, the dataset of 718 firms enabled an analysis of the determinants of the probability of successfully introducing new (or improved) product or process innovations. The objective was to look for differences not only among innovators and non-innovators, but also among different kinds of innovators. Therefore, the innovation-output indicator was a categorical variable that classified firms as: only product, only process, both product and process, and non-innovators for each of the two time periods covered by the dataset. For this stage, the estimated econometric model was a multinomial Logit because, unlike the first stage of the CDM model, the dependent variable had more than two possible (unordered) outcomes.

Finally, the fourth stage involved a fixed- and random-effects estimate of the impact of the innovative output on the performance of the firms, as measured by the natural logarithm of the total sales of products per employee[19] in 1996 and 2001, respectively.[20]

Panel-data estimates were complemented and compared with econometric exercises for a cross-section of the 1,243 manufacturing firms from the second survey of innovation. In this case, the first three stages were estimated by two standard sample-selection models. The final stage involved the ordinary least squares (OLS) estimate of the impact of innovative output on the performance of the firm.

The estimate using this second dataset involved five dependent variables. The first stage of the CDM model required a dummy variable to be defined to distinguish between firms that had not incurred positive innovation expenditures in 1998–2001. Second, the intensity of innovation expenditures was measured by the yearly average of innovation expenditures (relative to total employment in 2001) during the analysed periods. In the estimate of the third stage of the CDM model, a firm was considered to be an innovator if it reported positive sales of new or significantly improved products introduced during 1998–2001. The magnitude of this variable (measured in terms of employees in 2001) defined the intensity of the innovative output in the fourth stage of the CDM model. Finally, the performance of the firm was measured by sales per employee in 2001.[21]

With respect to the explanatory variables used in the econometric estimates, innovation inputs were classified into R&D and technology acquisition in the panel-data analysis. Firms were also divided into continuous and noncontinuous R&D performers.[22] Using the cross-sectional data of the second innovation survey, the technology-acquisition investment could be further divided into tangible or intangible and imported or domestic expenditures. These activities were captured by a dummy variable equal to one if expenditures were positive (in 1992–96 or 1998–2001).

In every stage of the estimates from both datasets, control variables were included (e.g. size, labour skills, physical capital, foreign ownership, exports, and whether the firm was independent or belonged to an economic group). An index that considered total employees and sales was used as a proxy for firm size. Labour skills and physical capital were proxied by the average number of technical and professional employees and investment in capital goods, respectively, in terms of total employees in each period. The dummy variable for foreign ownership was one if nonresident investors owned more than 10% of a firm's equity capital.[23] To capture the effects of export activity on the dependent variables, a dummy variable, equal to one, was included if the firm exported during the period considered.[24]

The surveyed firms were classified into four groups (labour, scale, R&D, and natural resources) to control for differences in the availability of technological opportunities (see Table 2.3).[25] Finally, the information available in the cross-section of the 1,243 firms allowed differences in the firms' innovation processes (e.g. interactions or cooperation links with foreign or domestic government agencies, clients, suppliers, universities, and competitors) to be controlled using dummy variables in the first three stages of the CDM model.[26]

Decision to undertake innovation activities and the intensity of innovation

The initial step of the estimate identifies the determinants of the first two stages of the CDM model: the decision to undertake innovation activities and the intensity of these activities at the firm level. Table 2.7 summarizes qualitative information on the estimates.[27]

Table 2.7 The decision to undertake innovation activities and the intensity of innovation (summary of econometric estimates)

Panel of 718 firms[a] (1992–2001)			Cross-section of 1,243 firms (1998–2001)		
Explanatory variable	Probability of positive innovation expenditures[b]	Intensity of innovation expenditures[c]	Explanatory variable	Probability positive innovation expenditures	Intensity of innovation expenditures
Size	+	−	Size	+	0
Tsize	+	+	Group	0	0
Group	0	0	Skills	+	0
Skills	+	+	Exports	+	0
Exports	+	+	Foreign	+	0
Foreign	0	0	sectRN	0	0
TsecL	0	0	sectRD	+	0
TsecESC	0	0	sectESC	0	0
TsecRN	+	0	NSIcif		0
time01	0	0	NSIpro		0
			NSIcli		0
			NSIother		+
			NSIgroup		0
			NSIgob		0
			EXcif		0
			Expro		+
			Excli		−
			EXgroup		+
			Exother		+
			EXgob		0

[a] + or − correspond to the sign of an estimated coefficient (statistically significant at 10%). See Appendix 2.2 for definitions of the variables. Cooperative links are classified into domestic (NSI) and foreign (EX).
[b] Results from the Fixed-effects Logit estimate.
[c] Results from standard fixed-effects estimate.

The estimate from both datasets shows that firm size is a relevant explanatory variable in the first stage.[28] In other words, larger firms are more prone to be engaged in innovation activities. This may be because, among other determinants, it is more difficult for smaller firms to finance innovation expenditures, and this asymmetry is reinforced in times of macroeconomic instability.

The panel-data analysis suggested that the relationship between the intensity of innovation expenditures (second stage of the CDM model) and firm size was not constant over time. It was negative during 1992–96 but positive in 1998–2001.[29] Therefore, although larger size implied lower innovation expenditure per employee during 1992–96, the changes in the economic environment that affected all firms in the following period caused this effect to be reversed (so that larger firms were associated to higher innovation intensities). Expectedly, the panel-data estimate supported the hypothesis that labour skills and exports had a positive and significant impact in both of these stages of the CDM model (Table 2.7). This was not the case for the dummy variable representing foreign ownership, which increased the chances of undertaking innovation activities (only in the cross-sectional estimate) but did not affect the intensity of expenditures for a firm already engaged in those activities. The dummy variable, being part of a group, did not affect any of these stages of the CDM model.

Cooperative links are a part of the innovation process that might influence the technological behaviour of industrial firms. In general, the econometric exercises using the cross-sectional data for the 1998–2001 period revealed that domestic relationships of cooperation do not have a significant impact on the magnitude of the innovation effort (the exceptions are links with other firms or consultants). However, as shown in Table 2.7, cooperation with different foreign sources seems to have a positive impact on that variable (links with foreign suppliers seem to be especially important in this regard). A surprising exception is relationships with foreign clients (negative and significant coefficient).

In general, the 1998–2001 data did not provide evidence of different technological opportunities among the four technological sectors considered (after firm size, skills, and exports were controlled). The exception was firms operating in R&D intensive branches, which are the most prone to undertake innovation activities. Although fixed-effects estimates using the panel data for 1992–2001 did not allow technological-sector variables to be included (because they were constant over time), their interaction with the dummy variable for time revealed that firms operating in the natural-resource sector were more likely to initiate innovation activities during 1998–2001.

Innovative output

The innovative-output indicators in the panel of 718 firms are dummy variables that estimate the probability of introducing new products or processes during the years covered in the innovation surveys. This information was complemented using the cross-sectional data for 1,243 firms that provided firm-level information on the intensity of the innovative output (measured by sales per employee in 2001 that were related to new or improved products introduced during 1998–2001).[30] A summary of the estimates obtained from both sets of data is presented in Table 2.8.[31]

Following the CDM model, the main focus of this section was on determining the impact of different innovation activities on the innovative-output indicators. Innovation inputs were classified as intramural (continuous and noncontinuous) R&D and external technology acquisition.

First, the estimates revealed that in-house R&D performers had a greater probability (compared with non-R&D performers) of having a positive innovative output. This effect became larger if the firm was a continuous R&D performer. This robust result held both in the panel and cross-sectional datasets.[32] This means a firm that performs continuous R&D activities is more likely to introduce innovations than a firm that performs R&D discontinuously.

Technology acquisition had a positive and significant effect on the probability of becoming an innovator – this was true for the three types of innovators considered (see Table 2.8). However, the estimates supported the hypothesis that technology acquisition had a smaller impact on the likelihood of introducing both product and process and only product innovations than R&D expenditures (particularly when R&D was performed as a continuous activity).[33] The opposite was true for only process innovations. This result reflects the fact that the main component of technology acquisition is tangible technology, which is a key source of process innovations in the manufacturing industry.

Although performing R&D did augment the chances of becoming an innovator (i.e. of having positive innovation output), it also increased the relative likelihood of both product and process, and only product innovations compared with only process innovations.[34] Interestingly, unlike R&D activities, technology acquisition seemed to be a 'neutral' innovative input because,

Table 2.8 Innovative output (summary of econometric estimates)[a]

Panel of 718 firms[b] (1992–2001)				Cross-section of 1243 firms (1998–2001)		
	Innovator type					
Explanatory variable	Both product and process	Only product	Only process	Explanatory variable	Probability of positive output	Intensity of innovation output
Size	+	0	+	Size	+	+
Group	0	0	0	Foreign	0	0
Skills	0	0	0	Group	0	0
Exports	+	+	+	Skills	0	0
Foreign	–	0	0	Exports	+	0
RDc	+	+	+	RDc	+	+
RDnc	+	+	0	RDnc	+	0
TechAcq	+	+	+	TDinc	0	+
time01	–	–	–	TMinc	0	+
secRD	0	0	0	TDdesin	0	0
secESC	+	0	0	TMdesin	0	0
secRN	0	0	0	Cif	+	0
				Pro	+	0
				Cli	0	0
				Grouplink	0	+
				Other	+	0
				Gob	0	0
				sectRN	0	0
				sectRD	0	0
				sectESC	0	+

[a] + or – correspond to the sign of an estimated coefficient (statistically significant at 10%). See Appendix 2.2 for a definition of the variables included in this table.
[b] Results from multinomial Logit estimate (non-innovators is the comparison group).

although it increased the possibility of having any type of innovation output, it did not significantly affect the relative likelihood of the different output classes.

Based on the available cross-sectional information for 1,243 firms, R&D investment had a positive impact on innovative-output intensity for innovators only if it was continuous (Table 2.8). Although expenditures on tangible technology (acquired either domestically or abroad) had a positive and significant effect on the intensity of innovative sales, intangible technology seemed statistically insignificant.

The magnitude of the estimated coefficients provided information on the impacts of each variable. The results suggested that the impact of imported tangible technology was about three times larger than the estimated effect for continuous R&D expenditures (this means that for a continuous R&D performer, each peso invested per employee in imported tangible technology will yield an innovative output three times larger than for each peso invested per employee in R&D). The small coefficient associated with domestic tangible technology indicated a minor economic impact of this variable. Intangible technology inputs had no impact on the innovative output of the firms.

To capture substitution or complementarity effects among R&D and the different kinds of extramural technology sources on the innovation-output intensity, the usual practice is to include interaction terms between those variables in the econometric regressions (Hu et al., 2003). Using this methodology with the cross-sectional data, no general evidence was found to support these effects.[35]

The estimate suggests that although R&D investment is a fundamental determinant of the probability of successfully introducing innovations (but a moderate factor in output intensity), extramural (in particular, tangible) technological flows contribute significantly to the magnitude of the innovative output if the firm is an innovator. This result could be interpreted as evidence of a complementary effect between R&D and extramural technological flows that differs from the link usually considered in the literature. However, this interpretation demands further research.

To obtain the econometric results from the two sets of data, controls for size, labour skills, exports, group, and foreign ownership were included. The size of the firm had a positive effect on the probability of having an innovative output, particularly with respect to both product and process and only process innovations (Table 2.8). Furthermore, the cross-sectional results showed that size had an increasing impact on the intensity of the innovative output.

Quite unexpectedly, the econometric results from both sets of data suggested that labour skills did not have statistical significance in this stage of the estimate. Export activity only impacted the probability of having an innovative output. The dummy variable for being part of a group impacted neither on the probability nor on the intensity of the innovative output. The negative coefficient associated to the dummy for foreign ownership in the multinomial Logit estimate suggests that foreign firms were less likely to introduce innovations (although this difference was statistically significant for both product and process innovations).

Regarding sectors, firms operating in the scale-intensive sectors appeared to have a higher likelihood of introducing both product and process innovations. In turn, firms in these sectors also seemed to have the highest innovation intensity when compared with firms operating in other sectors (as revealed in the cross-sectional estimates).

The results from the cross-sectional data (Table 2.8) also showed that cooperative links had heterogeneous impacts on the innovative output of manufacturing firms in Argentina. Interactions with research and training institutions, suppliers, and other firms had a significant impact only on the probability of launching new products, not on the intensity of that activity. The opposite occurred when cooperation was undertaken within firms belonging to the same group. Links with clients or government agencies had no impact on the innovation output.

Finally, as expected (given the hostile domestic economic environment), the panel-data results for the dummy variable for time showed that during 1998–2001, firms were less likely to have a positive innovation output (i.e. to become innovators).

Firm performance

Based on the cross-sectional data (Table 2.9), the OLS regression of sales per employee on the intensity of innovative output (both measured in 2001) yielded a positive and significant effect.[36] The fixed-effects estimate using the panel data for 1992–2001 revealed that the dummy variables for the different types of innovative output had the (positive) expected sign, although high statistical significance was attained only for both product and process innovators (see Table 2.9). The overall picture is that being an innovator (in both product and process) had a direct benefit for manufacturing firms in Argentina: it contributed to improved labour productivity during the period under analysis.

As expected, the negative sign associated to the dummy variable for time indicated that manufacturing firms attained smaller productivity levels in 1998–2001 than in the previous period. Also, proxies for labour skills, physical capital, export activity, and size had a positive impact on productivity based on the estimates using both datasets.

Being part of a group, and foreign ownership, were significant explanatory variables in the panel dataset, which indicated that foreign firms were more productive than domestic firms. Finally, the cross-sectional data estimates suggested that firms operating in the natural-resource sector had the highest productivity, followed by those in the scale and R&D intensive sectors.[37]

Table 2.9 Firm performance (summary of econometric estimates)[a]

Panel of 718 firms[b] (1992–2001)		Cross section of 1,243 firms (1998–2001)	
Explanatory variable	Firm productivity	Explanatory variable	Firm productivity
Only product	0	vinntotL	+
Only process	0	Exports	0
Both product and process	+	Skills	+
Size	+	Group	0
Skills	+	Size	+
Ikprodum	+	Foreign	0
Foreign	+	IKprom	+
Group	+	Iprod98	+
Exports	+	sectRN	+
time01	−	sectRD	+
TsecRN	0	sectESC	+
TsecESC	0		
TsecL	0		

[a] + or − corresponds to the sign of an estimated coefficient (statistically significant at 10%). See Appendix 2.2 for definitions of the variables in this table.
[b] Results from standard fixed-effects estimate.

Lessons learned and policy recommendations

The findings of this study are mostly in line with those reported in the literature:

- Innovators perform better than non-innovators, both during periods of high growth and recession.
- Innovation activities (including both in-house R&D and technology acquisition) and links with other agents (especially suppliers) enhance the probability of becoming an innovator.
- Although R&D investment is a fundamental determinant of the probability of successfully introducing innovations, extramural (in particular, tangible) technological flows significantly increase the magnitude of the innovative output, if the firm is an innovator.
- Large firms are more likely to engage in innovation activities and to launch innovations to the market. Exporting is also positively associated with both variables. Human skills influence both the decision to innovate and the intensity of the innovative effort.

An important lesson from our findings is that in spite of low R&D expenditures in Argentina's manufacturing industry, firms consider R&D activities to be part of their routines and a valuable asset to be preserved even during bad times. Our results suggest they do so for good microeconomic reasons. R&D contributes to becoming an innovator and to achieving higher productivity levels than competitors who do not innovate. Therefore, public policies geared to R&D promotion should have positive results in terms of the overall productivity of the manufacturing sector.

It is very relevant to take into account that continuous R&D efforts have an impact on the intensity of the firms' innovative output; whereas, discontinuous expenditures do not. Therefore, discontinuing in-house R&D activities would have a negative impact on the results of these activities. This fact reminds us of the importance of considering that firms also learn to innovate and that this learning must be a continuous process to be effective. Policies aimed at stimulating R&D activities should aim to integrate these activities into the routines of the firms, not just foster specific projects.

The smaller the firm, the lower the probability that it will undertake innovation activities or become an innovator. Therefore, small firms are at a disadvantage against large firms due to factors that prevent them from engaging in those kinds of activities. The fact that size was positively associated with the level of innovation expenditure suggests that small firms may be even more harmed during recessions. The removal of the obstacles that may prevent SMEs from engaging in innovation activities is a key area for policymakers.

To learn more about the determinants and impacts of the innovative behaviour of Argentine manufacturing firms, and the impact of this behaviour on the performance of firms, the following issues are important areas of research:

- Because the number of firms that consider themselves to be innovators seems to be quite high, more research is needed on the scope and quality of the innovations introduced by Argentine manufacturing firms.
- Because many firms that stated they had been engaged in innovation activities were not innovators during the period under analysis, it would be interesting to learn why this happened. Possible reasons include: innovation activities may have longer-term results (and therefore those firms should become innovators in the future); some firms may have failed to get commercially successful innovations; or the firms obtained results that were not translated into product and process innovations but that are useful for other purposes.
- Several firms stated they had introduced innovations, but had not performed any of the innovation activities included in the surveys. This casts some doubt on the scope and quality of the innovation indicators, but it could be explained by other factors. The innovations could be the result of innovation expenditures undertaken before 1992. It is also possible that there are activities that were not covered in the surveys that may also lead firms to become innovators. Furthermore, the literature and our econometric results show that innovation activities are not the only determinants of innovations.
- The obstacles to the innovation process that affect SMEs should be examined. Special attention should be paid to the role of access to finance.
- Although some links within the NSI are relevant to the innovative process of firms, it is important to learn more about the precise nature

and impact of these links. In particular, the different roles of domestic and international links should be considered.
- More research is needed on the relationships between domestic innovative efforts and the acquisition of technology. With regard to the acquisition of technology, research is needed on the relationships between tangible and intangible technology inflows, and between foreign and domestic inflows.
- During the period under analysis, a number of policies were introduced to foster innovation activities in the private sector. Learning about the impact of these policies would be relevant to assess and, eventually, to improve.
- Finally, given the fact that in our study innovators have a better employment record than non-innovators, it is important to quantify the impact of the introduction of new products and processes on employment. It would also be relevant to learn to what extent export performance can be explained by the intensity of innovation inputs and outputs.

Endnotes

1. This article is an edited version of a longer report. The full version can be downloaded from either the CENIT or RoKS websites. The econometric advice of Walter Sosa Escudero from the Universidad de San Andrés and the research assistance of Ariana Sacroisky and Hernán Seoane are greatly acknowledged. The data were provided by the National Statistical Institute (INDEC) through a special agreement. We are grateful to Jorge Souto from INDEC for his cooperation in this regard.
2. Undertaking innovation activities is not the same as being an innovator, and an innovator does not always needed to have innovative expenditures. For example, Crepon et al. (1996) report that only 20% of the near 10,000 manufacturing firms in their sample that did some research in 1989 innovated between 1986 and 1990; whereas, only 74% of all innovators performed some R&D. At least a part of these differences may arise from innovation activities that are not captured in R&D indicators.
3. To deal with the feedback loops from firm performance to innovation inputs and outputs, and with the correlation of error terms of each equation that may be reflecting non-observed variables or firm-specific effects, several studies based on the CDM model estimate all the stages simultaneously.
4. The study by Hu et al. (2003) in China explicitly accounts for these specific features of the innovative process in a developing country.
5. Binary variables that indicate whether products or process innovations have been accomplished are usually used when this indicator is not available.
6. According to INDEC (2003), 98 firms registered 317 patents in 1998–2001. About only 10% of the innovators obtained patents.

7. These firms account for 29% of sales, 27% of employment, and 24% of exports of the manufacturing sector in 1992–1996. For 1998–2001, the figures were 27%, 20%, and 19%, respectively.
8. OECD (1997) and RICYT (2001).
9. The classification of sectors into scale, labour, R&D, and natural-resources intensive was developed by Pavitt (1984) and later adapted by Guerrieri and Milana (1989) and Guerrieri (1992).
10. National Classification of Economic Activities.
11. This percentage of innovators is not strictly comparable to the 59% figure mentioned for the dataset of 718 firms. The reason is that the former considers product innovators (to calculate the importance of innovative sales); whereas, the latter also includes process innovators. A comparable figure can be obtained from Table 2.1, where the number of product innovators is 353 (adding both product and process, and only product), which is equivalent to 49% of the 718 firms considered.
12. Total innovation expenditures include, in addition to R&D and technology acquisition, management, engineering, and industrial-design investments related to innovation activities.
13. In this dataset, technology acquisition has a broader definition than in the matched dataset because more information is available. Tangible technology includes capital goods and hardware investments related to innovation activities. Intangible technology consists of external R&D, software, technological licences, training, and consulting expenditures related to innovation activities. This information is only provided by the second survey, together with the percentage of those technological inflows that came from foreign sources. Data on inflows from foreign sources allows intanglible and tangible investments to be further divided into domestic and imported expenditures.
14. The sector variable used in the fixed-effects regression was based on the classification of sectors presented in Table 2.3 (21 sectors from the CLANAE, the National Classification of Economic Activities).
15. In fact, when firm-specific fixed effects were included in the estimates presented in this study, although in most cases the sign of the coefficients did not differ with the sector-specific fixed-effects estimates, statistical significance at conventional levels was not attained.
16. An alternative to this model is the Heckman sample selection model (see Wooldridge, 2002 for further details). Nevertheless, its adaptation to panel data entails a substantial computational cost. Furthermore, the Heckman model presents no clear performance advantages with respect to the two-tier model, at least for cross-sectional data (see Leung and Yu, 1996).
17. In general, the estimated pooled and fixed-effects Logit coefficients agreed on the sign and significance of the explanatory variables. Therefore, in the presentation of the econometric results no distinction is made between these models, except for the few cases of disagreement.
18. Nevertheless, the results are based on the fixed-effects estimate because the Hausman test rejected the hypothesis that differences in the estimated coefficients from both models were not systematic (p-value is 0.0000).
19. Excluding sales of goods produced by third parties.

20. As with the second stage of the CDM model, the reported results are based in the fixed-effects estimate because the Hausman test rejected the null hypothesis of random effects (p-value is 0.0001 in this case).
21. The three continuous dependent variables (innovation expenditures, innovative output, and productivity) are measured in natural logarithms. The dummy variables (probability of having innovative expenditures and being an innovator) are used in the selection equations of the sample-selection models applied to the first and the third stage of the CDM model.
22. A firm was considered to be a continuous R&D performer (in 1992–96 or 1998–2001) if it reported positive R&D expenditures in every year of the period.
23. The reported results were not significantly altered if this dummy variable took the value one when foreign ownership was either 51% or 100% of the firm's capital.
24. Please contact the authors to obtain additional details on the measurement of the variables.
25. As an alternative to this classification, the regressions were also estimated using the 21 industrial sectors described in Table 2.3 as controls for technological opportunity. Although not reported here, the estimated coefficients of the variables of interest are robust to either specification.
26. In the estimate of the third stage of the CDM model, the distinction between foreign and domestic links was avoided only because it would have consumed too many degrees of freedom in the regression; therefore, the estimates would have lost statistical significance.
27. Details of the economic results can be obtained from the authors.
28. Throughout this section we characterize a variable as 'statistically significant' if the p-value of its associated coefficient is smaller than 10%.
29. This result was obtained by comparing the magnitudes of the estimated coefficients associated to size and to the interaction between the time dummy and size variables in the fixed-effects estimate. As well, in the cross-sectional data, size had an insignificant statistical impact on innovation expenditures.
30. Therefore, this indicator captured the intensity of process innovations only indirectly (through their effect on the development of new products).
31. Details of the economic results can be obtained from the authors.
32. The only exception was that noncontinuous R&D expenditure did not appear to have a significant impact on the odds of obtaining a process-innovation against no-innovation output.
33. This result was obtained by comparing the magnitude of the estimated coefficients for the R&D-activity and technology-acquisition variables.
34. This result is true both for continuous and for discontinuous R&D expenditure.
35. This result is generally true when technological flows are measured either as continuous or dummy variables or as continuous or sporadic R&D performers.
36. In the cross-sectional OLS regression on productivity, the performance observed in 1998 was included as an additional regressor. This provided a simple way to account for (unobserved) historical factors that may have

caused differences among the firms' performances in 2001, which would have been difficult to account for in other ways. For example, it is possible that some unobserved factors at the firm level that affected productivity in 1998 continued to do so in 2001. If some of them happen to be correlated with the intensity of the innovative output, it would be unlikely to obtain unbiased estimates of the impact of the latter on productivity without including the lagged dependent variable. In fact, the positive and significant coefficient associated with the lagged productivity variable indicates that these unobserved factors are important determinants of productivity and that better performance in 1998 contributed to better performance in 2001.

37. Details of the economic results can be obtained from the authors.

References

Archibugi, D. and Sirilli, G. (2000) The direct measurement of technological innovation in business, in Innovation and enterprise creation: statistics and indicators. *Proceedings of Conference held at Sophia Antipolis, France*, 23–24 November, European Commission, Luxembourg.

Benavente, J.M. (2002) *The role of research and innovation in promoting productivity in Chile.* (http://emlab.berkeley.edu/users/bhhall/EINT/Benavente.pdf)

Crepon, B., Duguet, E., and Kabla, I. (1996) Schumpeterian conjectures: a moderate support from various innovation measures, in Kleinknecht, A. (ed.) *Determinants of innovation: the message from new indicators.* Macmillan, London.

Crepon, B., Duguet, E., and Mairesse, J. (1998) Research, innovation and productivity: an econometric analysis at the firm level. *National Bureau of Economic Research* (NBER) Working Paper No. 6696, Cambridge.

Duguet, E. (2002) *Innovation height, spillovers and TFP growth at the firm level: evidence from French manufacturing.* (http://ideas.repec.org/a/taf/ecinnt/v15y2006i4-5p415-442.html)

Edquist, C. (ed.) (1997) *Systems of innovation: technologies, institutions and organizations.* Pinter, London.

Galia, F. and Legros, D. (2002) Complementarities between obstacles to innovation: empirical study on a French data set. Paper presented at the *DRUID Summer Conference 2003* on Industrial dynamics of the New and Old Economy: who is embracing whom? (http://www.druid.dk/uploads/tx_picturedb/ds2002-606.pdf)

Guerrieri, P. and Milana, C. (1989) *L' industria italiana nel commercio mondiale.* 2nd edn, Mulino, Bologna.

Guerrieri, P. (1992) Technology and trade performance of the most advanced countries. *Berkeley Roundtable on the International Economy*. Paper BRIEWP49 (http://repositories.cdlib.org/brie/BRIEWP49)

Hu, A., Jefferson, G., and Jinchang, Q. (2003) *R&D and technology transfer. Firm-level evidence from Chinese industry.* (http://people.brandeis.edu/~jefferso/REStat%20RD%20technologytransfer.pdf)

Hu, A. and Jefferson, G. (2003) *Returns to research and development in Chinese industry: evidence from enterprises in Beijing.* (http://people.brandeis.edu/

~jefferso/CER,%20RD%20-%20Hu%20-%20Jefferson%2024%20May%202003.pdf)
INDEC. (1998) Encuesta sobre la conducta tecnológica de las empresas industriales argentinas, *Serie Estudios*, No. 31, Instituto Nacional de Estadística y Censos, Buenos Aires.
INDEC. (2003) Segunda Encuesta Nacional de Innovación y Conducta Tecnológica de las Empresas Argentinas, *Serie Estudios*, No. 38, Instituto Nacional de Estadística y Censos, Buenos Aires.
Janz, N., Lööf, H., and Peters, B. (2003) *Innovation and productivity: a cross-country comparison between Germany and Sweden.* (www.zew.de/en/publikationen/publikation.php3?action=detailandnr=1858)
Jefferson, G., Huamano, B., Xioajing, G., and Xiaoyun, Y. (2002) *R and D Performance in Chinese Industry.* (http://elsa.berkeley.edu/~bhhall/EINT/Jeffersonetal.pdf)
Kemp, R., Folkeringa, M., De Jong, J., and Wubben, D. (2003) Innovation and firm performance. *SCALES (Scientific Analysis of Entrepreneurship and SMEs)*, Research Report No. H200207.
Kleinknecht, A. and Mohnen, P. (eds) (2002) *Innovation and firm performance. Econometric explorations of survey data.* Palgrave, New York.
Kline, S. and Rosenberg, N. (1986) An overview of innovation, in Landau, R. and Rosenberg, N. (eds) *The positive sum strategy: harnessing technology for economic growth.* National Academic Press, Washington.
Lööf, H. and Heshmati, A. (2002a) Knowledge capital and performance heterogeneity: a firm-level innovation study. *International Journal of Production Economics*, 76(1), 61–85.
Lööf, H. and Heshmati, A. (2002b) *On the relationship between innovation and performance: a sensitivity analysis.* (http://ideas.repec.org/a/taf/ecinnt/v15y2006i4-5p317-344.html)
Lööf H., Heshmati, A., Asplund, R., and Naas, S. (2002) Innovation and performance in manufacturing industries: a comparison of the Nordic countries. *SSE/EFI Working Paper Series in Economics and Finance* No. 457. (http://swopec.hhs.se/hastef/abs/hastef0457.htm).
Leung, S.F. and Yu, S. (1996) On the choice between sample selection and two-part models. *Journal of Econometrics*, 72(1–2), 197–229.
Mairesse, J. and Mohnen, P. (2003) R&D and productivity: a reexamination in light of the innovation surveys. Paper presented at the *DRUID Summer Conference 2003* on Creating, Shearing and Transferring Knowledge, The Role of Geography, Institutions and Organizations, Copenhagen, Denmark.
OECD. (1997) *The measurement of scientific and technological activities. Proposed guidelines for collecting and interpreting technological innovation data. Oslo Manual*, Organisation for Economic Co-operation and Development, Paris.
Parisi, M.L., Schiantarelli, F., and Sembenelli, A. (2002) *Productivity creation and absorption, and R&D: Micro evidence for Italy.* (http://fmwww.bc.edu/ec-p/wp526.pdf)
Pavitt, K. (1984) Sectoral patterns of technical change: towards a taxonomy and a theory. *Research Policy*, 13(6), 343–373.
RICYT. (2001) Standardization of indicators of technological innovation in Latin American and Caribbean countries. *Bogotá Manual*, La Red Iberoamericana de Indicadores de Ciencia y Tecnología, Buenos Aires.

Van Leeuwen, G. (2002) Linking innovation to productivity growth using two waves of CIS. *STI Working Paper* 2002/8, Organisation for Economic Co-operation and Development, Paris.

Van Leeuwen, G. and Klomp, L. (2001) *On the contribution of innovation to multifactor productivity growth.* (http://econpapers.repec.org/article/tafecinnt/ v_3A15_3Ay_3A2006_3Ai_3A4-5_3Ap_3A367-390.htm)

Wooldridge, J.M. (2002) *Econometric analysis of cross section and panel data.* MIT Press, Cambridge.

Appendix 2.1 Studies based on the CDM model (Mairesse and Mohnen, 2003)

Study	Individual Data	Endogenous variables	Estimate method	Other comments
Crepon et al. (1998)	France 1986–90	R&D, patent (or share of innovative sales), labour productivity	ALS (Adaptive Least Squares)	Censored data for R&D
Duguet (2002)	France 1986–90	Radical innovation, incremental innovation, TFP growth	FIML Logit for innov., 2SLS or GMM for TFP growth	Separate estimate for various technological opportunities
Galia and Legros (2002)	France 1994–96	R&D, innovation output, training, quality, profitability	ALS	Censored data for R&D and training, dichotomous data for quality; allows for feedback effects
Janz et al. (2003)	Germany and Sweden 1998–2000	Innovation expenditures/employee, innov. sales/employee, and sales/employee	FIML for gen. Tobit on innov. expend., other equations by 2SLS with correction for selection bias	Censored data for innovation expenditures; feedback effect from productivity on innov. output
Van Leeuwen and Klomp (2001)	Netherlands 1994–96	Innovation input (R&D or innov. expend.), innovation output, productivity (in levels or growth rates)	OLS, 3SLS limited system, or 3SLS full system (with or without correction for selectivity)	Productivity measured by revenue per employee or value added per employee; feedback effect from revenues on innov. output
Van Leeuwen (2002)	Netherlands Panel data from CIS2 and CIS2.5	R&D, innovation output, growth in revenue/employee	FIML gen. tobit for R&D or innovation output; separate FIML for growth of revenue/employee with correction for selection bias	Dynamic model for 1994–96 or pooled model for 1994–96 and 1996–98; innov. output measured by new sales or by new and improved sales.
Benavente (2002)	Chile	R&D, patent (or share of innovative sales), labour productivity	ALS	Censored data for R&D
Lööf and Heshmati (2002a)	Sweden	Innov. expend./employee; innovative sales/employee; and value added/employee	FIML for generalized Tobit on innov. expend., other equations by 2SLS with correction for selection bias	Also estimated with only radical innovations; productivity estimated in levels and growth rates; feedback effect from productivity on innov. output

Study	Individual Data	Endogenous variables	Estimate method	Other comments
Lööf et al. (2002b)	Sweden	Innov. expend./employee; innovative sales/employee; and labour productivity	FIML for gen. Tobit for innov. input, other equations by 3SLS with correction for selection bias	Labour productivity measured as innov. sales/employee or value added/employee; feedback effect from productivity on innov. output
Lööf et al. (2002)	Finland, Norway and Sweden 1994–96	Innov. expend./employee; innovative sales/employee; and labour productivity	FIML for gen. Tobit for innov. input, other equations by 2SLS and 3SLS with correction for selection bias	Estimates for all innovations and for radical innovations; feedback effect from productivity on innov. output
Jefferson et al. (2002)	China Panel data 1995–99	R&D, share of innovative sales, productivity (or profitability)	Separate estimate of each equation by OLS and IV	Square term on innovative sales
Parisi et al. (2002)	Italy, Panel data 1992–94 and 1997–95	Labour productivity growth, product innovation, process innovation. Product and process innovations estimated by Logit or conditional Logit, product growth estimated by IV		
Hu and Jefferson (2003)	China (Beijing area) 1991–97	R&D, output, and profit. Individual and SURE estimate of 2 or 3 equations with correction for selection bias		

Appendix 2.2 Definition of variables used in the econometric regressions[a]

Variable	Definition
Innovation expenditures (Iginn)	Yearly average of total expenditure in innovation activities during 1992–96 (1998–2001), per employee in 1996 (01) (measured in log)
Innovative sales (vinntotL and Ivinn when measured in log)	Sales in 2001 accounted by new or improved products developed during 1998–2001, in terms of total employees in 2001 (measured in logarithm when regressed in the innovative output intensity equation)
Sginn	Dependent dummy variable in the selection equation for innovation expenditures. Equal to one if the firm reported positive innovation expenditures throughout 1998–2001
Sinn	Dependent dummy variable in the selection equation for innovative sales. Equal to one if the firm reported positive innovative sales in 2001
Productivity in 2001 (lprod)	Sales of own products per employee (log)
Productivity in 1998 (lprod98)	Sales of own products per employee in 1998 (log)
Size (insize)	According to the legal definitions currently in place in Argentina (mostly for purposes of defining whether a firm has, or does not have, the right to take advantage of some policy instruments aimed at SMEs) to include firms in different size segments, we have used the following formula: $$I = \left(10 \times \frac{Emp}{Emp^*} \times 10 \times \frac{Sales}{Sales^*}\right)^{\frac{1}{2}}$$ Emp = total employees; Sales = total sales; Emp* = 300 employees; and Sales* = $18 million
Foreign (FDI10)	Dummy equal to one if foreign capital share is equal or greater than 10%
Skills	Average share of technical and professional labour between 1998 and 2001
Investment in capital goods (Ikprom and Ikprodum)	Average investment in capital goods between 1998 and 2001, in terms of total employees in 2001. Ikprodum is a dummy equal to one if Ikprom is positive
Group	Dummy equal to one if the firm is part of a group
Exports (expo)	Dummy equal to one if the firm exported in the period considered
Research and development (R&D)	Yearly average during 1998–2001 per employee in 2001
RDdummy	Dummy equal to one if the firm reported positive R&D expenditures during 1998–2001
RDc	Dummy equal to one if the firm reported positive R&D expenditures in every year during the period considered
RDnc	Dummy equal to one if the firm reported non-continuous R&D expenditures during the period considered
RDRDdummy	Interaction term between R&D and RDdummy
RDRDcont	Interaction term between R&D and RDc

Variable	Definition
Technology acquisition (GexMpd)	Dummy equal to one if the firm reported positive Technology acquisition expenditures during the period considered
Domestic tangible technology (TDinc)	Yearly average during 1998–2001 per employee in 2001
Domestic intangible technology (TDdesin)	Yearly average during 1998–2001 per employee in 2001
Imported tangible technology (TMinc)	Yearly average during 1998–2001 per employee in 2001
Imported intangible technology (TMdesin)	Yearly average during 1998–2001 per employee in 2001
RDTMinc	Interaction term between R&D and Imported tangible technology
RDTMdesi	Interaction term between R&D and Imported intangible technology
RDTDinc	Interaction term between R&D and Domestic tangible technology
RDTDdesi	Interaction term between R&D and Domestic intangible technology
Clients (cli)	Dummy equal to one when firm reports cooperation links with clients during 1998–2001
Suppliers (pro)	Dummy equal to one when firm reports cooperation links with suppliers during 1998–2001
Research and training institutions (Cif)	Dummy equal to one when firm reports cooperation links with such institutions during 1998–2001
Government agencies (gov)	Dummy equal to one when firm reports cooperation links with government agencies during 1998–2001
Other firms (other)	Dummy equal to one when firm reports cooperation links with consultants and other firms during 1998–2001
Group links (Grouplink)	Dummy equal to one when firm reports cooperation links with firms of its group during 1998–2001
SectRN	Dummy equal to one if the firm belongs to the natural resources intensive sector
SectRD	Dummy equal to one if the firm belongs to the R&D intensive sector
SectESC	Dummy equal to one if the firm belongs to the scale intensive sector
SectL	Dummy equal to one if the firm belongs to the labour intensive sector
Time01	Dummy variable for time

[a] This classification was developed by Pavitt (1984) and later adapted by Guerrieri and Milana (1989) and Guerrieri (1992).

CHAPTER 3
Research for policy development: Industrial clusters in South China[1]

Rigas Arvanitis and Qiu Haixiong

Abstract

> *This research study analyses the development of industrial clusters in three institutional contexts in South China to better understand how policies have been developed and implemented to encourage innovation. The authors trace the growth of private enterprises within these clusters, and note that this growth was assisted by local governments and by links with foreign companies, which were instrumental in upgrading networks of suppliers and bringing in foreign expertise. The research shows that innovation centres have begun to create networks of enterprises, improve innovation capacities, and enhance communication with universities and research centres. In some districts, local government policy has promoted innovation centres, especially during difficult economic times, when a need for better quality and higher priced products made sense in China. As such, the innovation centres were mainly oriented toward servicing the local industry, rather than maintaining a competitive edge. The research team concludes that 'marketized' research centres have a greater probability of success than innovation centres because they base decisions on selling products.*

Since 1999, China has actively promoted innovation policy to reinforce the technological capabilities of smaller firms, while continuing to promote larger multinational firms. At the same time, public research centres have undergone rapid 'marketization',[2] which has transformed many former public engineering research centres into enterprises. It is much too early to assess this strategy, but the speed with which private firms and collective enterprises have acquired, adapted and promoted new products, and new productive processes, is remarkable. Moreover, the information technology (IT) sector has grown at an unexpectedly rapid rate, and has become the main sector for investment and technological development.

This project used empirical evidence to describe the links between scientists and non-scientific clients in different institutional contexts in Guangdong Province. It had three objectives:
- to investigate the innovation system for research and development (R&D) in the South of China;

- to understand the dynamics of the relationships between research units and the non-research technological users in different social, economic, and institutional contexts (content of the links, motives, resources, and incentives); and
- to promote the creation of a pool of excellence on science and technology policy by providing an empirical basis to policymakers.

The institutions that were studied were located in three different institutional settings: Zhongshan University (City of Guangzhou); the industrial districts of Xiqiao (City of Nanhai) and Dachong (Zhongshan City); and a large industrial district producing motorcycles in Pengjiang (City of Jiangmen). Also, an industrial cluster that had no innovation centre (in Dongguan), but an important industrial base, was studied (Table 3.1).

Methodology

The Research Institute for Guangdong Development (ZURIGuD) of Zhongshan University studies social and economic problems in Guangdong. Local authorities see technological development and innovation as important and have expressed the need for new policies. To support policy development, research was required on the dynamics of industrial and technological development inside firms, and on the role of R&D and innovation in Guangdong.

Field research for a small project in the industrial cluster of Shuikou, Kaiping, which specializes in the plumbing industry, was conducted in

Table 3.1 The three institutional settings that include the industrial clusters and the university that were studied

Setting	Example	Context	Activity
Technology or 'innovation centre' focused on local industry	Xiqiao (Nanhai) textiles innovation centre; Dachong (Zhongshan) furniture innovation centre	Local industry	The centres provide service to local companies, mainly SMEs. Some centres also provide patterns for new products (e.g. moulds and patterns for textiles).
R&D unit servicing productive units of an industrial group	Pengjiang (Jiangmen) motorcycle R&D centre	National and global industrial corporation	Provide designs requested by production units, or in response to demand.
University undertaking research and linked to production units	Zhongshan University (Guangzhou)	National research system and its local implementation	Research collaboration and support for activities with high knowledge content (e.g. environmental monitoring). Also, common research laboratories with world-class companies.

January 2000 and March 2001. This was followed by research on the dynamics of the industrial clusters and the links among knowledge providers in the South of China. This research project was a complement to on going research by ZURIGuD on industrial clusters.[3] The ZURIGuD team focused on the roles of innovation centres, intermediate organizations (such as local associations of industrial firms), and enterprises in the industrial cluster. This project was designed to use qualitative analysis, a type of research relatively new to our team, and to include the active participation of students. Specific interview guides were designed to gather information on: origins and evolution of the innovation centres or institutions; sources of funding and the management of resources; flows of knowledge from academic institutions; relationships with enterprises; and incentives.

The students participated in the fieldwork, and in some cases, stayed quite a long time in the industrial districts to gain a better understanding of the situation. As the project progressed, more importance was given to the role of industrial clusters in the Guangdong region and the newly created 'innovation centres', because they were becoming sites of technological development. Project staff also participated in debates on how to modify the structure of the innovation centres and refurbish their policy tools. Cooperation as advisors to local authorities has been quite successful, and the local government of the Municipality of Nanhai, as well as the Province of Guangdong, provided partial support to our activities and access to the innovation centres. This exceptional situation allowed our research to focus on the role, context, and future of these innovation centres.

Guangdong: A region developed in successive steps

The development of Guangdong, and all China for that matter, is the result of successive steps to build a new economic environment. Guangdong received three successive waves of investment.[4] The first phase of expansion industrialized the countryside because initial reforms were aimed at that sector. The ability to grow and sell products outside the state planning system led to a rapid rise in agricultural production. In the early 1980s, profits from the sale of agricultural produce were massively invested in rural enterprises, the so-called 'township and village enterprises' (*xiangzhen qiye*). This growth lasted 6 years (1983–88). The investments were a boon for the local authorities and the most adept rural inhabitants. They found themselves in quite exceptional circumstances, given the absence of any competition and the existence of a large unsatisfied demand. This new economic opportunity permitted the development of an 'economy out of the plan' (Naughton, 1995).

The early 1990s saw the arrival of 'foreign' investments, mostly from Taiwan, Hong Kong, and overseas Chinese. In 1994, foreign direct investment (FDI) represented 20% of overall investment. In 2001, foreign investment from Hong Kong, Macao, and Taiwan continued to represent 18% of total investments (CNY158 bn)[5] and 47.5% of foreign investments (CNY55 bn) in

Guangdong Province. During this phase, two-thirds of the foreign investments were in the hands of small- and medium-sized firms from Hong Kong and Taiwan. These firms used labour-intensive production to assemble imported parts that they exported to international markets. This system received the blessing of local officials because it provided them with great decision-making powers. These firms did not represent direct competition to either the China-based township and village enterprises or private- or state-owned enterprises. However, they improved the trade balance and increased employment and incomes. Moreover, demands from the poorly paid labour force were directed to the low-quality products of the communal- and the state-owned enterprises. These enterprises continue to profit from growth in domestic demand. It also explains why these enterprises survived despite producing goods that were in many ways outdated. The Asian crisis of 1997 led to reduced orders being placed with Chinese enterprises, and slowed (relatively) this form of FDI.

The third phase of development began with the arrival of FDI from industrialized countries (e.g. the United States, Japan, and Europe). The Chinese government reacted extremely quickly and adopted a range of measures to attract this foreign investment. The huge campaign in favour of entry into the World Trade Organization (WTO) became the main objective of official policy. Since 1997, investment in real estate has increased rapidly, and large cities have become showcases of China's growth. Events, such as the Beijing Olympic Games in 2008 and the Shanghai Universal Exhibition in 2010, provide additional appeal to international investors. This increase in international investment has also triggered capital inflows from Taiwan and Hong Kong, which continue to be an important part of the overall FDI in China. These waves of investment can be thought of as a 'piling up' of productive systems (Figure 3.1).

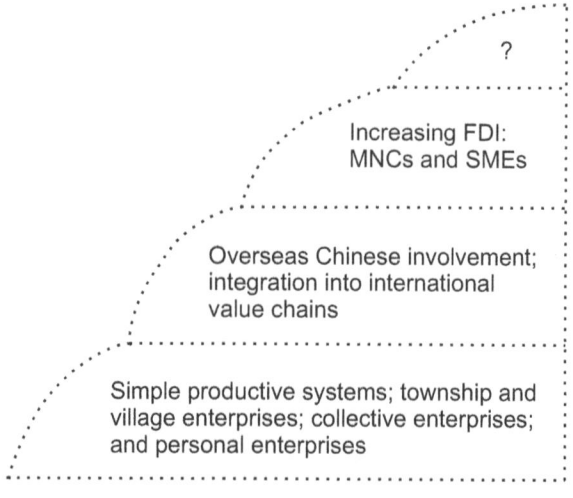

Figure 3.1 A schematic presentation of the 'piling-up' of productive systems

The first productive system includes township and village enterprises. These enterprises were established in the early 1980s and operated as private companies. However, for ideological reasons, they were officially registered as collective enterprises. They worked with raw materials, employed low-cost labour, and concentrated on various sectors of production, which they quickly dominated. At the same time, the larger collective enterprises that were already in place started to operate as 'private' firms (e.g. Yueqing in Shuikou Township, Guangdong Province). Starting as a tap manufacturing plant, Yueqing modernized and produced a myriad of small plumbing firms. Consequently, Shuikou Township is now the site of a whole industrial sector, and Yueqing is one of many new enterprises. Many other enterprises followed a similar path throughout China. Well-known brand names (e.g. Legend, TCL, Haier, Konka, and Galanz) arose with the first phase of expansion and prospered because their status as collective enterprises gave them access to public funds.

A second type of production system is evident in enterprises established during the second wave of investment from Taiwan and Hong Kong. Industries that produced textiles and clothing, electronics, and electrical household goods were relocated to the Pearl River Delta. Although these enterprises share features with the first wave, they have some unique characteristics. First, the investors not only established the enterprises; they brought with them their own networks of suppliers and customers. The Taiwanese and Hong Kong enterprises, established to take advantage of low production costs, were backed by more than 30 years of experience in supplying multinational companies. In addition, they had their own ways of doing business, to which the entrepreneurs from Guangdong were quick to adapt. Second, they brought with them more complex production techniques, even in the case of less sophisticated industries like shoes, clothing, and basic electrical goods. However, they profited from low labour costs and adapted to local conditions by making less use of intensive technologies. Third, these overseas Chinese established strong ties with mainland officials and local government bodies. They also included the local power structures in their operations in a much more intense way than local entrepreneurs. More effectively still, local authorities appealed to these firms to help strengthen technological development and launch technical education initiatives (e.g. practical demonstrations, technical training, and apprenticeship schemes). In some cases, innovation centres were created to promote technological innovation and to provide technical know-how to enterprises in a particular sector of production. In the industrialized world, such centres are usually organized by the chambers of commerce or public education bodies. In China, they were achieved by the joint enterprises to which the foreign partners brought both expertise and markets.

In the Pearl River Delta area, these FDI-dependent enterprises, which were owned by foreign capital, employed an estimated 30 million workers from the most impoverished inland provinces of China. The foreign enterprises have made good use of this continuing supply of low-cost labour. They have turned the whole area into one huge factory (Ruffier, 2006) with local concentrations producing various products. Shunde is the main manufacturing centre in China for electrical household goods; Ronggui the largest centre in the world for air-conditioning units; Shaxi is centre for leisure wear; and Humen (Dongguan) a centre for clothing (Qiu, 2001: 234). By the end of the 1990s, this system had reached its limits, but it continued to coexist with other production systems.[6]

The third wave of investment in Guangdong was provided by industrialized countries, which installed 'third generation' systems of production that were more directly piloted by foreign firms. Four hundred of the largest global firms have investments in China. The world's leading manufacturers of telecommunications and oil-industry equipment, cars, and machine tools have set up their own production networks in China. Often focused in the Shanghai region, the foreign firms begin by setting up small offices and then establishing production sites. Foreign investors no longer only seek to establish manufacturing plants; they hope to develop a market in China.

Unlike the systems of production established under the first two waves of investment, these firms have no difficulty using efficient managerial techniques and establishing organizational structures geared toward their production goals and markets. Potential difficulties arise solely from their social environment. Future legal and institutional setting will be decisive for these 'third generation' systems of production. The foreign investors who back these firms are relying on the complete opening of the Chinese economy in accordance with international agreements. It is still too early to make a full assessment of this third wave, and of the eventual outcome of the superimposition of these three different systems of production. At the time of this research, these new systems of production were still at a preliminary stage, and the foreign firms were just beginning to perceive the problems any enterprise encounters when it first establishes operations (see Richet et al., 2001; Verillaud, 2001). Even foreign firms that were already established were finding it difficult to make any profit. For a foreign firm, everything is more expensive in China – land purchases and building costs, installations, employee recruitment and training, communications with headquarters, relations with government offices handling labour and the environment, and commercial dealings with suppliers. In many cases, it is more expensive to set up an integral system of production than to collaborate with a local supplier.

The logic of industrial development in Guangdong

Enterprises were the main actor of industrial development in Guangdong; therefore, our research framework placed technological learning by enterprises at the centre of the research. Technological learning is the main process by which an enterprise acquires and develops a technology and its productive processes (Pirela et al., 1993; Arvanitis and Villavicencio, 1998; Arvanitis, 2000; Arvanitis and Vonortas, 2000). Learning inside an organization creates the basic internal capabilities of the enterprise (i.e. the workshop, the production line, the engineering or R&D departments, and the complementary departments such as maintenance, sales, marketing, and finances). But these internal structures must create external links through which experiences with new products, new processes, and new management procedures can be acquired by the enterprise. This *external learning* is acquired by *interacting* with clients, providers, and many socioeconomic actors (e.g. authorities, engineers, and experts). For developing countries, international technology transfers are a very frequent form of external interaction.

The literature that has grown on technology transfers in the last 10 years has been enriched by the perspective of 'user-provider'. However, the knowledge transfers that take place between a foreign client and a local enterprise are often not considered, although they should be seen as an essential form of technological learning. In developing countries, a large part of relating to new technology is based on technology transfer. Instead of focusing on the legal status of technology transfers, which brought the debate to a dead-end (Ruffier, 1996), the types of arrangements that can be made between buyers and sellers of technology should be examined. Guangdong presents many opportunities to study interactions of enterprises with their productive environments.

Technological learning in companies in Guangdong

Arvanitis and Zhao (2003) present six case studies that highlight relations of companies with foreign clients. Four models of learning were identified through these case studies. An important part of the learning comes from the client, who inspects the processes, provides blueprints, and pushes the provider to achieve high quality. The client is the provider of the technology, and the providers of the products are the users of the technology: the user-provider relationship is the inverse of the common understanding of the expression 'user-provider'. Various types of external links, or interactive learning, are summarized in Table 3.2.

Table 3.2 Characteristics of different models of interactive learning

Interactive learning	Main characteristics
OEM model	Dominated by FDI, the company is inserted in the value chain. Stable relations and regular and long-term commitment to client. Strong productive learning and design capabilities. No original design, no capacity to innovate strongly in models because the brand is the one that decides.
Contracted provider	Unstable relation to client. Strong local competition. Can be private or collective enterprise. Emphasis on quality control and productive processes.
Joint venture (subsidiary or affiliate)	Mainly internal learning. Transnational circuit inside the firms. Very stable relation.
Large local producer (OEM and provider under contract)	A mix of stable and unstable relations. External learning, emphasis on quality control, productive processes, and innovative products.

Original equipment manufacturing (OEM) is what made Taiwan famous. Particularly well suited to a globalized industry, the international brand gives productive orders. The local factory exploits low labour costs and ensures high quality control. R&D is not done unless it serves the purposes of the brand. The brand company makes higher margins and exploits its decisive advantage: access to markets. But this market access has no meaning if low cost is not maintained by the local producer. Taiwanese producers, after 1990, understood the full advantage they could get from coming to mainland China (Guiheux, 2002). Hong Kong investors came to Mainland China for the same reason, and transformed Hong Kong into an industrial desert (obliging HK to focus on a strategy to develop shipping, transport, logistics, financial and other services, and tourism) while providing the Pearl River Delta with the impetus for industrial development.

The most common type of arrangement in Guangdong is a contracted provider, a case well illustrated by the Shuikou industrial cluster (Arvanitis, 2001; Sun and Xu, 2002; Arvanitis, 2004a). This is a medium-range solution for companies looking for very cheap providers (e.g. the faucet and plumbing industry and all traditional industries). Difficult access to the international market obliges local companies to accept the conditions imposed by the foreign client. In fact, the local companies do this very gladly because they seek foreign clients. 'Our clients are our teachers', said one manager. Through these contacts with international clients, companies access higher quality models and improved quality. Sales to foreign markets also return better prices and make ISO (International Standards Organization) or similar certification easier. Companies become contracted providers for foreign clients not so much because they want to export, but because they must if they are to gain access to more products, better designs, higher quality, and better processes.

Joint ventures (JVs) were once thought to be a panacea. They were supposed to bring money and technology to Asia, mainly China and Vietnam. Vietnam today is experiencing a considerable fall in investments and China has instituted legislation to promote FDI in different forms. Foreigners are usually uncomfortable with JVs and most foreign companies now want to become wholly owned foreign enterprises because the law authorizes this new possibility. The partnership is a forced one, not a chosen one, and whatever the benefits, they are always seen with suspicion. There are great variations in JVs. Technologies usually flow well, and there is an important flow of know-how, as would be the case of any subsidiary of a transnational firm. However, there are no efforts that are genuinely local and independent. All decisions depend on the internal structure of the transnational or the foreign partner.

A mixed model would appear to be ideal, but it is not frequently observed. Dachangjiang (motorcycles) or Jinling (electro-domestics), both companies in Jiangmen, are two exemplary cases. They both attained technological capabilities and are simultaneously producing their own products and products under OEM arrangements with foreign clients. They are both dominant clients and contracted providers. They have a long-term strategy for technological development, depend on rapid changes in local markets, act in very open and competitive markets, and have some more specialized and less competitive markets. Other large companies in China (e.g. Haier, TCL, Konka, Legend, and Fenghua) are probably similar in their pattern of development in the electro-domestic and electronics industries. A mixed model of learning means that these companies have learning strategies based on technological development and high standards of production, not exclusively on commercial and management aspects. These companies will never cut costs at the expense of investment. They develop collaborative R&D with outside sources of knowledge. The mixed model is efficient if it permits a company to offer lower costs to a client who, in exchange, offers entry to foreign technologies. Moreover, learning companies under this mixed model seek technologies and markets in foreign countries. This explains why more and more Chinese companies invest in productive or research facilities in foreign countries, although they seem not to be leaders in technology.

Arvanitis et al. (2006) report on the effects of different types of interactions on technological learning. Although theories on technological learning must take advantage of work on technological development (Tidd et al., 1997), they must also consider the particularities of corporate organization in China (Richet and Huchet, 2000). Companies have a strong capability to incorporate new technologies (Huchet, 1999), but they frequently have more difficulties competing in international markets if they are not linked to a foreign client who acts as a provider. Corporate strategies are not always successful in producing a coherent technological and economic strategy (Zhao, 2006). Moreover, technology is mainly provided through strong relations with clients who become the main sources of this technology (Arvanitis and Zhao, 2003).

Future challenges for Guangdong

The 'miracle' of South China industrialization seems to be based on a specific economic phenomenon: the creation of enterprises *de novo* in an environment in which close collaboration with foreign partners was made easy by specific policies (e.g. economic zones and promotion of FDI). Guangdong's development has relied on basically unskilled labour in productive units funded by foreign capital. Local entrepreneurs created companies using the same logic, but their difficulty was how to obtain productive technologies. Today, they are being forced to upgrade their technology. Very low labour costs do not provide sufficient incentives for firms to invest heavily, and there are signs of serious difficulties due to very intense price competition between companies.

Due to rapid growth, local markets seem particularly crowded, and already strong competition is being accentuated. These conditions are reflected in the strategy put forward by the provincial government of Guangdong. Not only will companies face strong competition; regions will also compete to keep companies. Guangdong Province has now become more expensive than other regions. Competition between regions can be expected to grow to attract new FDI. The current model is thus reaching its limits. Although problematic because of scarce access to funds, growth in size seems necessary if companies want to maintain high technological abilities. In this context, companies are seeking special considerations from local governments, not just economic support, but also many other concessions.

Local authorities in Guangdong never directly fund a business. Rather, they work on enhancing the image of the city by providing support for commercial fairs and by promoting and publicizing the city outside the region. They also work to improve infrastructure and recently developed innovation centres, maintain close relations with companies, and provide easier access to foreign clients, which can be seriously affected by local authorities (e.g. visas, authorizations, imports, and exports). Some more direct relations probably exist between the financial office and specific companies. However, these are likely personal relations that in some cases are promoted by local government officials (with great care, because corruption is heavily punished).

Technological upgrading is essential and will dictate whether an enterprise survives or dies. Many small companies rely on their foreign client to upgrade their technology. Up to a certain point, the stability of this relationship will depend on internal learning and the strategic capability of the company. Can Guangdong, and China in general, manage the large array of competing learning models? There is no sign to be either overly pessimistic, or extremely optimistic.

Until very recently, there were no specific policies to promote enterprises in the Guangdong region. This is why we qualify development in Guangdong as 'spontaneous' development of companies. Given China's planning experience, this spontaneous development is of paramount importance to both local actors and authorities. Everyone in the industrial cities of Guangdong considers that private drive, with strong autonomy from the state, is the main engine of growth. Local entrepreneurs are proud of their independence, although they welcome collaboration with local authorities. Under these conditions, it is difficult to engage in processes that involve public knowledge but require private funding. Public–private partnerships will be difficult to establish.

The clustering process

The OECD (1999) and the World Bank see clusters as a sort of new panacea to industrial development, mainly because clusters abound in those areas of Asia where industrial development has been rapid (Mahmood and Singh, 2003). In a conference organized by ZURIGuD in April 2004, many examples of industrial clusters in Malaysia and Thailand were presented.[7] However, comparisons that go beyond a simple correlation between rapid growth and cluster formation are needed. Cluster dynamics must be reinserted into the general process of industrialization that is ongoing in these countries. Based on the work of Guerrieri and Pietrobelli (2002), three types of clusters can be defined.

The first and most important cluster is the *Marshallian cluster*, which is named after Alfred Marshall who introduced the concept of an industrial district in 1876. It consists of a location of many small firms in the same industry. The concept has been used in many cases, mostly in the 1970s to describe the light industry in Tuscany (Italy), also known as the 'Third Italy.' Authors who have studied this type of cluster emphasize the role of long-term socioeconomic relationships among local firms, which involve trust and a blend of collaboration and competition. These relationships contribute to the 'industrial atmosphere' first underlined by Marshall.

The second type of cluster, the *hub-and-spoke cluster*, refers to a situation where one or more firms (usually large) within a region act as a hub of the regional economy. Suppliers and related activities spread around them as spokes of a wheel. It is a hierarchical relationship. Automobile industries usually are organized in this way, where the car constructor has all its providers surrounding it in the same region.

The third form of cluster is a *state-anchored cluster* (or satellite platform). These clusters are 'anchored' to a region by a public or non-profit entity, such as a military base, a university, or the concentration of government offices. Government policy plays an important role in the development of these clusters. Examples in Europe are the technological park in Sophia-Antipolis in France (Dalla Pria, 2004) and the development of nanotechnologies in Grenoble (France).

These are theoretical categories, and in practice, clusters are combinations of different sized companies that exhibit changes over time (Jastrabsky, 2004). As we will see in the conclusion, these three categories are not very clearly distinguished in Guangdong. Moreover, more thought is required on the formation of clusters and their integration into international value chains, because most theorizing on industrial clusters was done when international value chains were rather limited.

Innovation policy and innovation centres

Innovation policy attracted the attention of many scholars (Gu, 1999; Suttmeier and Cao, 1999; Liu and White, 2001; Cao, 2004; Huang et al., 2004) as the new technological landscape emerged in China (Sigurdson, 2002). These studies go hand-in-hand with the recent effort by the Chinese government to define an innovation policy beyond classic science and technology (S&T) policy – a drive that was predicted and recommended (IDRC, 1997). The government of Guangdong also tried to integrate this new orientation into its policy for technology (Guangdong Office of Science and Technology, 2002).

Innovation policy in China

In August 2001, the tenth 5-year plan (2001–6) was launched. Its stated objective in science and technology was to 'establish an efficient innovation system, with enterprises as the main location of the source of innovation. Government forces are necessary, but at some point they must give way to market forces'. This launch was the logical conclusion of a course of events that began in 1999 with the National Convention on Innovation in Beijing. Since then, innovation has been the buzzword in S&T policy.

Although 'innovation policy' was not located under a specific authority in China, a complex of activities and policies taken together can be considered instruments of innovation policy (Arvanitis, 2004b). These can be grouped into five categories: creation of science and technology development parks and high-technology (high-tech) zones; support to specific enterprises with high potential for technological development; 'marketization' of research centres; creation and support of industrial clusters; and creation of 'innovation centres'.

Creation of S&T development parks and high-tech zones

Hong et al. (2004) noted that there were 85 high-tech zones, 32 mid-sized economic and technology zones, and 58 university science parks. The five special economic zones (SEZs), of which the most famous is Shenzhen, which was created in Guangdong in 1980, should be added to this count. SEZs are all located on the coast, from Dalian in the North to Zhanjiang in the South, and were created to attract foreign capital. Guangdong hosts three of these SEZs (Shenzhen bordering Hong Kong, Zhuhai bordering Macao, and Shantou), which buffer these former foreign colonies that are hubs of commercial and maritime transportation. As a result, the disequilibrium between the Chinese hinterland and the coastal cities was accentuated. This led to a policy known in China as the 'Drive to the West', which promoted heavy infrastructure in the less endowed provinces in the north-west of China.

However, even more industrial zones appeared and local 'economic and technological development zones' (*jinji jishu kaifa qu*) were created in every part of the country – from urban buildings housing small software companies to larger national technology zones that covered a vast and growing geographic area. This expansion made Chinese policy less clear to investors and was denounced for the loss of arable land. Since 2004, the central government has tried to address this situation, which now involves as many as 12,300 industrial clusters. Most of these are vast, lucrative real estate operations that responded to incentives launched by the central government, mainly the Torch Programme (1988) – 'Windows Opening to the Outside World'.

These large high-tech zones function less as a tool for technology policy than as a magnet for foreign investment and large national investments. Local authorities are proud to show the abundance of new companies in these large, clean, healthy industrial zones. However, they have little influence on the strategies of the companies, their links to other companies, or their integration into the industrial set-up of their province. The dynamic of the high-tech zones is thus not directed by local authorities but rather determined by the companies themselves. An evaluation of these high-tech zones is needed. However, one measure of their success is the number of companies and the amount of investment: high-tech companies accounted for about 12% of the value of gross manufacturing output in China and invested CNY31.4 bn in R&D, which is 24.4% of the gross expenditure on R&D and 40% of business expenditure on R&D (MOST, 2004).

Support to specific enterprises with potential for technological development

This includes various forms of direct support not usually reported under statistical headings: direct funding; tax-relief measures; non-tax support, such as facilities for installation and other administrative facilities; and public procurement of products from these enterprises. These measures usually include strategic (like satellites and electronics for military use) and 'sensible' areas (such as the production of anti-retroviral drugs for AIDS). In the case of strategic areas, military orientations are important, or as the 863 Programme[8] announced: 'the combination of military and civil uses of science'.

Locally, small- and medium-size enterprises (SMEs) can receive this kind of support, but not usually in the form of direct financial support. Support usually includes helping enterprises get authorizations and assistance: visas for travel abroad; licences for exports and imports; invitations to workshops and meetings; help in making contacts with foreign clients; promotion of training for engineers and entrepreneurs; assistance with environmental facilities; and assistance with payments for land to install a workshop. Most of the measures are dealt with on a case-by-case basis and focus either on infrastructure or on facilitating contacts with authorities.

Policy measures are specifically oriented toward high-tech firms under Programmes 863 (since March 1986) or 973 (since 1996). Support to high-tech companies has effectively created technological resources. However, there has been no evaluation of these policy measures. To some extent, they have been successful because they gave birth to enterprises (mainly collectives) that are now engaged in R&D and technological development (Sigurdson, 2002).

The 'marketization' of research centres

'Marketization' of research centres is a vast programme to privatize the old public research institutes. This programme has received little attention from external observers, but some Chinese researchers have noted profound changes (Kong, 2003; Tang, 2003). Research centres now must be viable financially without public support. They must transform into enterprises that sell products. This policy was successful, in part, because many of the centres were related to large public corporations and had market knowledge. Moreover, they were able to easily find markets because Chinese client enterprises found it easier to buy products than to engage in research collaboration or technological alliances. This privatization has continued through years of successive reforms of the engineering and research centres that belong mainly to ministries of large state-owned enterprises (Gu, 1999). Over time, more initiative has been given to the research centres. What is new today is that this reform affects not only large public enterprises, but research centres related to specific ministries, like agriculture and forestry, and the Academy of Science.

Creation and support of industrial clusters

The creation of industrial clusters is a basic aspect of industrial policy in China. Most of these districts exist when the policy is announced. The industrial cluster appears because of the initiative of entrepreneurs, usually workers who were employed by a public company in this location. At the end of the 1990s, in Guangdong and Zhejiang, where clusters were common and economically strong, the authorities understood that they needed to support the clustering process to avoid overcrowding of the industrial sector, harsh competition, and degeneration of the entrepreneurial spirit. Most clusters that are supported by the government are located in traditional industries.

They resemble the Third Italy clusters in many aspects: autonomous growth; traditional industry; and later support by the government. However, there are differences in terms of management and clients. The companies in the Italian industrial districts provide highly specialized products of high quality in relatively small quantities, with competition based on quality and specificity of products. In China, the clusters service a large market, where competition is based mostly on price for low-quality products. More rarely, some of the industrial districts are organized around an industry that makes intensive use of human resources and provides products to international clients, like the *maquiladoras* companies in Mexico and Central America (these companies are called *san lai yi bu* in Chinese). Entire industrial districts, like Qingxi in Dongguan, have been created on this basis. However, some qualification is necessary. *Maquiladoras* enterprises were mostly inserted into the strategy of a large industrial group, mainly located in the United States or Japan. The industrial clusters in electronics in China were second-tier industries, which serviced some companies, usually from Taiwan or Hong Kong, and were providers to American or Japanese international groups. The presence of overseas Chinese in the Guangdong region facilitated this process.

Creation of 'innovation centres'

This is probably the most original policy measure implemented in China. Innovation centres are located inside an industrial cluster and support SMEs. Among their objectives, links with research activities in universities and public research institutions have been paramount. They participate directly in the modernization of enterprises within the industrial cluster and are well adapted to local industrial conditions.

Innovation is more than rhetoric in Chinese S&T policy. Among the priorities of the National S&T Plan, innovation is the primary objective. Questions could be asked about why there is this strong perspective and how this orientation affects all other scientific activities. However, innovation is a national objective implemented locally in every part of China. Guangdong is not an exception; it has been the site of experiments in every aspect of China's national innovation policy.

Guangdong has been particularly active in providing experience to policymakers in Beijing. Before the 1999 National Conference on Innovation held in Beijing, the Department of Science and Technology of Guangdong Province had already initiated local government intervention in technical innovation centres. In 1998, the Department launched the project 'Experimental units of technical innovation in specialized towns in Guangdong Province'. Each town that was specialized in one product had to create a 'platform' for the promotion of technical innovation – an innovation centre for each specialized town. An appropriation of CNY300,000 by the Department of Science and Technology was supplemented by other funds from local governments to provide initial funding for these technical innovation centres (ICs). This was the beginning of measures geared at technical innovation by local governments. Today, 50 industrial clusters participate in technological innovation pilot locations organized by the Department of Science and Technology.

Research and development in Guangdong

The Chinese government is responsible for most basic R&D funding. Nonetheless, 'funding amounts are not high enough to allow research structures to engage in large projects in the long term; research structures coexist without any previous selection and with a lack of initiative' (Guangdong Office of Science and Technology, 2002). Local governments usually fund little basic research. This is considered an advantage because the central government structures are more dedicated to basic research, which allows innovation and technology-related research to be conducted by local research structures. Guangdong follows Beijing, but is ahead of Shanghai in terms of R&D spending (Guangdong Office of Science and Technology, 2002: 78). Although Beijing and Shanghai have better diffusion channels, research in Guangdong is characterized by strong ties to enterprises. In 2001, overall spending for research in Guangdong was CNY13,423 million, or 1.27% of GDP (more than the national mean) (Guangdong Office of Science and Technology, 2002: 65). Enterprises contributed up to 88% (CNY9,520 m) of this spending on research in 2000 and 90% in 2001 (CNY11,370 m). This is exceptional because enterprises in China, in general, spend little on R&D. In Guangdong, 1.4% of revenue was spent on R&D in 1991 and 1.6% in 2001. Guangdong had 2,733 research and technology organizations[9] in 2001, and the City of Shenzhen has profited the most from rapid growth in the number of research organizations. Shenzhen now has 521 R&D organizations, and 91.7% are inside enterprises.

Of the 1,453 research centres in the Province of Guangdong, 979 are located inside enterprises (67%). In 1998, 23% of the large enterprises (national or foreign) had their own R&D centre. This figure grew to 43% in 2000. In 2001, 85% of small- and medium-size collective enterprises 'operating in technical fields' had an R&D unit. In 2001, of the CNY25.6 bn invested in S&T in Guangdong, 71.4% came from enterprises in the province. In 2001, large- and medium-size enterprises invested CNY9.45 bn, which was CNY4.17 bn more than in 1997.

In 2001, of the 4,082 high-technology products developed in the province, 62.8% were developed in collaboration with enterprises, universities, and research centres (Guangdong Office of Science and Technology, 2002: 73–4). The report does not provide specifics on the type of collaboration involved.

The number of patent applications has grown very impressively in Guangdong.[10] However, many of the patents are not for inventions but rather for designs and utility models. Moreover, foreign companies tend to patent inventions; whereas, Chinese companies tend to patent utility models and designs. This means the core technologies are still in the hands of the foreign companies, and most of the revenues from patents in core technologies enter the accounts of foreign companies (Cao, 2004).

Finally, there is a strong deficit in education in Guangdong as compared with other provinces because the province does not have enough universities and lacks strong S&T structures (Guangdong Office of Science and Technology, 2002). It is a priority of the local authorities to strengthen the educational level in Guangdong and to provide additional resources for universities and other educational centres.

Case studies

Three case studies were undertaken to examine the main issues and problems with the policy of innovation centres in the Pearl River Delta. In addition, an industrial cluster with no innovation centre and Zhongshan University were studied.

Mahogany furniture cluster, Dachong, Zhongshan

Dachong, in the municipality of Zhongshan,[11] is an industrial district that specializes in mahogany furniture. There are more than 300 enterprises, with the larger ones employing 400–500 workers. The innovation centre acts as a technical centre and has good relationships with universities and research centres on specific technical questions. The innovation centre tries to modernize production, improve knowledge, and enhance the quality of production from the enterprises. Its objective is to become 'a platform for the diffusion of innovation among enterprises'.

The economic situation in this industrial cluster was characterized by local actors as 'not good'. The market is no longer a 'sellers market,' where it suffices to produce and sell. Enterprises are more conscious of the need to improve the quality of their products and to specialize. The authorities, and many enterprises, want to enhance production standards and quality norms, and more generally, the overall quality of the enterprises. There are also plans to market a 'Made in Dachong' brand as a sign of guaranteed quality levels. The situation of Dachong is common to most of the industrial districts in the Pearl River Delta, which experienced rapid and relatively easy growth until the late 1990s. Since then, competition among enterprises has increased and new products are harder to copy.

The industrial cluster

Dachong, a district of 28,000 permanent residents and more than 30,000 immigrant residents, also known as 'Longdu', is located in the south-west of Zhongshan, Guangdong Province. Dachong specializes in the production of mahogany furniture and jeans, and per capita income is CNY5,000.

The wood industry is not native. It originated, in the late 1970s and early 1980s, when immigrants from Zhejiang came to work in small workshops owned by individual families. In 1993, there were about 300 mahogany furniture enterprises with more than 30,000 employees. Their output accounted for 60% of the national output (according to the officials interviewed), which makes it the largest manufacturer of mahogany furniture in China. Since 1999, the Party Committee and the government of Dachong have treated the mahogany furniture industry as a 'key characteristic industry', and it has become an activity of special interest for local authorities.

The chamber of commerce

The Dachong Chamber of Commerce, established in 1994 at the request of Zhongshan General Chamber of Commerce and promoted by many manufacturers,[12] is one of the earliest business organizations established in Zhongshan. Until then, market issues had been the responsibility of the Private Enterprises Office of the local government.

With the growth of the mahogany furniture industry, the Chamber of Commerce created a subordinate 'Joint Association of Mahogany Furniture' in 1997. This association accounts for 70% of the workload of the Chamber of Commerce. The government provided the Chamber of Commerce with 3,335 m^2 of land, which was sold mainly to affiliate enterprises. Other resources of the association include stores, with an area of more than 800 m^2, that have become permanent rights-and-interests property of the association. The Chamber of Commerce also promoted the creation of businesses for insurance, transportation, and tourism. The Dachong Chamber of Commerce now has more than 180 affiliate enterprises, among which are 105 mahogany furniture enterprises, 69 clothing manufacturing enterprises, and 10 enterprises in hardware and plastics.

The innovation centre

The innovation centre was established in 2001 by the local government of Dachong City (with an initial investment of CNY1 m). Additional financial support was received from the scientific committee of Zhongshan City (CNY300,000) and the Department of Science and Technology of Guangdong Province (CNY500,000). The local government donated land for the offices and has covered equipment and salary costs since establishment of the centre. As well, the scientific committee, the office of technical control, and the commercial association for mahogany furniture, all from Dachong City, have become part of this centre. The real leader of this centre is the local government, which has provided all funds and human resources and promoted its technical programmes.

The objective was to create an efficient network among enterprises, universities, and research centres. It was called a 'technical innovation system', and was designed both to provide support and services to small and medium enterprises in the city and to link the local government, the industrial association, and the enterprises.

The innovation centre analyses difficulties faced by mahogany furniture enterprises, diffuses technical solutions, and trains specialized employees. Other actions include: organizing training sessions, exhibitions, and other means to promote the newest information about techniques and management; establishing direct relationships with institutes, research centres, and specialists in China; and improving cooperation and communication among enterprises in the Dachong area. The centre provides both free and paid services.

The innovation centre has addressed three technical problems of the mahogany furniture industry: improving the drying process for the wood used in making furniture; promoting better designs for products; and improving the quality of paints and coatings to comply with environmental standards. The centre believes these are the main obstacles to expansion of the market and improvement of quality.

To address the problem of drying the wood, the centre bought and developed a computerized monitoring system. Three enterprises were interested in using the system, and they were each charged CNY50,000. Solutions to the other two problems were given free of charge to encourage the use of new technology and methods. In the near future, the centre plans to offer all services for a fee and to offer assistance with ISO certification.

The innovation centre has established contacts with universities and research centres to tackle these technical problems. The computerized system for drying timber was developed in association with the Guangzhou

Energy Research Centre of the Academy of Science (Zhongguo Ke Xueyuan Guangzhou Nengyuan Yanjiusuo). This system allowed enterprises to obtain the necessary certificates to enter markets in Northern China. This is an expensive system with high investment fees, and services are not free. In addition, some enterprises invested in their own drying systems. During an interview, the director of the innovation centre, Mr Xie, noted that initially the local government refused to invest the CNY30 m necessary to build a common system. This meant the centre either had to wait for the enterprises to grow rich enough to invest themselves, or convince the local government to invest. Even if the local government invested in that system today, the director is not sure the enterprises would use it: 'we cannot afford to have such capital losses in the future.'

The second major technical development was the design of new models. With an initial investment of CNY200,000, the centre signed a contract with the Forestry Institute of South China (Zhongnan Lin Xueyuan) to develop new products. This institute had one year to provide the innovation centre with eight new models for four series of furniture. The institute was also responsible for developing manufacturing techniques and for providing technical support to the enterprises. Some models have already been produced and used by the enterprises.

The third development was the use of environmentally friendly paints. An initial investment of CNY380,000 was made with the Institute of Chemistry and Environment of the Xi'an University of Transport (Xi'an Jiaotong Daxue Huanjing yu Huagong Xueyuan) to develop a paint specific for mahogany furniture. This project is just starting, and product trials are ongoing. If this project is successful, it would allow the Dachong enterprises to sell 'green products' and to lower the time and cost of production.

The innovation centre has also promoted exchanges with specialists and established a policy to attract them. In 2001, during the 'first research session on the development of the mahogany furniture industry in China', the innovation centre selected 14 specialists as consultants in production, sales, R&D, and management. In collaboration with the local government, the research centre on Chinese Traditional Furniture of the Forestry University of Beijing (Beijing Linye Daxue Zhongguo Chuantong Jiaju Yanjiusuo) established a department in Dachong to encourage professors and researchers to collaborate. The innovation centre plans to form an information and communication network with the Forestry University of Beijing and the South China Forestry University.

The innovation centre has also concentrated on publicity to establish a 'Made in Dachong' brand. It encourages enterprises to participate in commercial fairs and exhibitions. For example, in 2002, it helped some enterprises go to the 'Dongguan Chinese and International Furniture Exhibition', the 'Shenzhen Furniture Exhibition', and the 'Changsha Centre of China Cultural Festival of Furniture'. This effort is common to both the mahogany furniture industry and the garment industry, which is also quite strong in Dachong. The plan is for the mahogany furniture industry to become a leader throughout China by expanding its services and networks to SMEs outside Dachong.

Some issues

This case is typical of small industrial enterprises in the South of China. The industry in Dachong grew from craft work in wood, not from the creation of an industrial sector with previously well-established industrial markets and criteria. Companies in Dachong have, with some exceptions, low investment capacity and low technical skills in their employees and managers.[13] There are several pressing issues.

Changing market: Competition has increased during the last few years, and the links between the producers and the market have changed. For the Hong Xiqian company, it is more difficult to sell because all factories now have direct relationships with their clients.

> Before, in Dachong, the sector was flourishing. The lorries were in front of your door, waiting for products, we just had to produce and all was sold. Today, supply and demand have changed; the market is no longer good, so we have to improve the quality. Now that quality is improving, and prices are dropping, 95% of the commercial firms from Shenzhen and Dongguan, which export to Taiwan, have come back to Dachong (Hong Xiqian).

The activities of the innovation centre are accepted mainly because of this change.

Overlapping responsibilities: There are overlaps in the responsibilities of the local government, the innovation centre, and the industrial association. The director of the innovation centre is also the vice-director of the economic department in the local government and president of the commercial association. This was presented as an advantage. Before the innovation centre was established, the industrial association was in charge of all commercial and technical problems faced by the enterprises. The idea of creating an innovation centre came from the fact that the association did not have the appropriate means to resolve specific technical problems. Finally, the very active director of the innovation centre is to be credited for its positive results.

Different demands: The enterprises and the innovation centre must find a durable way to work together. The innovation centre has few *direct* relations with enterprises. Hong Xiqian said that if they have a technical problem, they do not go directly to the innovation centre but rather to the commercial association or the local government director. Hong Xiqian has established a technical department to design furniture with its own designers. On the contrary, Hexin takes the designs offered for free by the innovation centre and adapts these designs according to their production. Although these two companies seemed satisfied with the technical help provided by the innovation centre, the demands made by the enterprises are diverse and quite specific to their own situation.

High cost of technical development: Most companies find it difficult to engage in technical development because of high costs:

> I know this [automation dry equipment] is a good thing, which can improve product quality, shorten production time, and enlarge the market. However, when can I get return on such a high cost? For example, a stove costs two or more million CNY. For us, the most urgent thing is sales, for example in the Beijing market, where distributors control the sales network. They buy our products, put their brand on them, and sell them as their own. In such cases, we can only take about one tenth of the profit (Interview at Gush Enterprise, Dachong).

The problem of copying: Companies want to see improved protection of property rights and measures to fight copying. 'We develop our models very slowly, and after we show the new products, we are sure they will be very quickly copied. Now we have a new model, but we cannot sell it because it was copied with poorer, cheaper materials' (Hexin). Copying may appear to be a common problem in China, but in this industry copying is a new threat. In fact, the craft (before rapid industrialization) was based on specific craftsmanship, a know-how that is difficult to copy. The wood industry in Zhongshan was developed by Zhejiang immigrants who knew the woodworking craft. As production of furniture has become an industrial process, copying has become a very real threat. This issue is new and difficult for the innovation centre.

Few relationships between enterprises: The companies have few relationships and little cooperation. The only relations occur during the meetings of the industrial association, of which, now, practically all enterprises are members. When Hong Xiqian was established, it registered as a member. It participates in all events, such as trips, loans, anniversaries, market analysis, and meetings. Some of the activities promoted by the association are common issues, such as the possibility of an insurance policy: 'For example, if we have to rent a lorry, and this lorry has a problem, an accident, or lose the products, what can we do? But the association has enough money to be a guarantor, and this reassures us to sell and send more products' (Hong Xiqian).

Textile industry cluster, Xiqiao, Nanhai

Xiqiao is an industrial area in Nanhai District that specializes in textile production. The Xiqiao textile cluster is a typical success story in the Province of Guangdong. Xiqiao is composed mainly of SMEs. It is one of the four top textile-producing sites in China and has a long history in textiles. As early as the Jiaqing period in the Ming Dynasty, it was granted the title of 'hometown for textiles' and produced silk that was famous throughout the nation. Today, Xiqiao has 1,670 enterprises that include weaving mills, dye works, textile print factories, clothing firms, and two chemical-fibre factories. The labour force is 137,000, of which 60,000 are in the textile industry.

Production of textiles represents half of the total industrial production of Xiqiao. Enterprises mostly produce fabrics (1,265 factories with an annual production of about 1 billion metres of fabrics). There are also printing factories (56 printing and dyeing factories; 11 dyeing factories; and 6 fabric printing factories); garments producers (25 manufacturers without their own brand); and about 2,800 small trading companies. Labour is not well developed and this creates difficulties because the enterprises alone cannot master all techniques.

In the 1990s, after unprecedented expansion, the textile industry revealed many competitive problems. Most companies seemed to lack funds, 'overused' machines and equipment, and were creating virtually no new products. To rescue this traditional industry, the local government developed policies under the banners 'support the strong, the big, the outstanding' and 'support the advanced, help the backward, and promote the medium.' The idea was to help companies renew their equipment, upgrade their technologies, obtain better patterns for textile weaving, and achieve better access to information. The local authorities devised two instruments: the 'southern textile industry information network' and the 'southern technological innovation network'. Both initiatives were located inside a newly created technology development centre.

The innovation centre

At the beginning of 1997, the Xiqiao District Government and the China Textile Information Institution established a non-profit institution to develop new textile patterns and provide technical support. The government raised CNY200 m to introduce and run a high-level computer-aided design (CAD) system from Korea to make Jacquard weaving designs. It also hired experts to develop new products and provide technical services. The pattern-making department was created in May 1998, and has developed several thousand new patterns. Using CAD to make the patterns has greatly reduced the cost of technical development and information collection. Companies acquired a wider range of products and quality was greatly enhanced. Some larger enterprises in this district have already established their own pattern-making units.

The information centre also developed a web-based network. The 'South Textile Information Network' provides SMEs with information on supply and demand and with guidance on e-commerce and business on the Internet (business to business). The network gathers information on trends in both domestic and overseas textile markets and helps enterprises develop new products to match market demand.

In 1998, the government wanted enterprises to improve their technical innovation because the market, due to sudden overproduction, had become a 'buyers' market. The local government also wanted to further develop the textile industry because the market had been fluctuating greatly, and that government was convinced that, alone, the enterprises would not be able to improve their production. In 1999, an innovation centre was added to the textile pattern centre established in 1997.

The Xiqiao government invested CNY70 m to expand the centre into a 'South Technology Development Centre of Guangdong', which combined the information network and the CAD service. It also monitors contacts with scientific research institutions and intermediary organizations. The whole system, which is called the 'Xiqiao Textile Innovation Network', has three levels. The core level is the technology innovation system, which covers the main activities of the centre, and includes the CAD company, engineering technology research, and the Guangdong Textile Material Engineering and Technical Development Centre. All activities are designed to enhance machines and equipment and provide new products to the industry. The middle level is the innovation services, which includes the Xiqiao South Textile Information Network, the Nanhai Productive Force Promotion Centre (Xiqiao Branch), and other independent professional services. These groups sell services related to information, sales, purchasing, and financial capital to many SMEs. The periphery level is the service system (in Chinese, the social service system), which provides both training and contacts with higher education institutions, scientific research organizations, and professional training departments. Contacts are maintained with Donghua University, the National Institution for Scientific Information on Textiles, the Hong Kong Productivity Bureau, the Guangdong Textile College, and Qinghua University.

In 2000, Xiqiao was included in the first batch of 'Experimental Units of Technological Innovation for Specialized Towns', a programme conducted by Guangdong Province. The technical centre was given responsibility to act on behalf of the whole textile industry in the province, and was granted the title of 'Technology Research and Development Centre for Textiles of Guangdong Province'. The centre is an example of how to promote innovation in specialized zones of small and medium enterprises.

Some issues

In 2001, to establish the pattern-making centre, the government invested CNY4 m to buy equipment and pay employees, and then invested CNY73 m to build the new main office building for the innovation centre. In 2003, more than 50 employees worked in this innovation centre, which is one of the largest of its kind in the Pearl River Delta. This exceptional case merits close attention.

Success in modernizing SMEs: The local government continues to offer financial support to the centre for new equipment and projects. In theory, the local government follows the motto 'you get rich, I develop'. But in fact, the innovation centre and the enterprises depend on the government: 'We had already become a technical incubator for a few dozen enterprises, let's say a hundred enterprises. The large ones could do R&D alone and buy a CAD model, as we did…these enterprises could also establish a R&D system, like us…' (Mr Pan, Innovation Centre).

The innovation centre's main task appears to be to modernize small- and medium-size traditional enterprises. It must also modernize itself by improving its technical level and operations. As in Dachong, the activities of the innovation centre are: to test and diffuse techniques; to train its own employees and the workers in the enterprises; to encourage enterprises to participate in exhibitions and fairs; and to spread information about new managerial methods and new techniques. The industry's innovative capability has been strengthened by tracking new clothing fashions throughout the world. In the last 3 years, the centre has created nearly 800 new products, and 30–40% of the new textile products in Xiqiao are based on patterns and models developed by the innovation centre. In the process, the creative capability of the enterprises themselves has been strengthened. Most textile factories have gradually come to realize the importance of technological innovation and human resources. Over the past 3 years, more than 1000 professional technicians have been attracted to Xiqiao enterprises in product development and process engineering. Some enterprises have even begun to set up their own R&D or design units. Finally, the production structure has also changed. The proportion of fabric used for clothes, decorative cloth, and industrial cloth has changed from a ratio of 95/3/2 in 1997 to 53/42/5 today. The transformation from pure fibre to mixed textiles, cotton, raw edge, and sackcloth has been achieved. Xiqiao cloth has completed the transition from low-quality products to higher quality ones. The mean price of cloth per metre has risen by 15–20%, and the clothing fabrics and decorative cloth produced in Xiqiao are of the highest quality in China and have won awards for quality and design.

Links between local enterprises and other institutions: Close collaboration with educational institutions, such as the Institute of Fine Arts, Guangdong Province, are now common. The centre invites professors and students to help develop modern designs and acts as a bridge between students and entrepreneurs: 'When there is an exhibition by the newly graduated students, we (the innovation centre) send enterprise bosses to attend' (Mr Pan, Innovation Centre). Collaboration with universities is also seen as mutually beneficial. The centre plans to enlarge its influence to the national level by establishing a national research centre. The centre has already developed close collaboration with the University of Zhejiang. The centre was also impressed by the work of a research centre in Shanxi Province that specializes in cotton fabrics and wants to develop with it a national series of seminars on new techniques in fabrics making. Mr Pan encourages participation in industrial design competitions because they provide opportunities to advertise products.

Public or private? The status of the centre is unclear. Is it a private institute or a government body? What are its links with the commercial association? What is the decision-making power of the innovation centre? This uncertainty seems to be an obstacle rather than a benefit. The innovation centre is quite independent from the local government, but its directors are selected and nominated by the government and many things are decided by local government officers.

The Technology Centre in Xiqiao (the inner circle of the innovation system) is responsible for its profits and losses, its employees and finance, and it pays rent to the innovation centre. Although it is an autonomous organization (very much like an enterprise), it is not totally independent because the innovation centre provides it with contracts and tasks and has administrative responsibilities for the technical centre. And although the technical centre has direct commercial relations with enterprises and autonomously manages its resources, it is still part of the innovation centre.

> For people outside our structure, we are one department of the innovation centre, but, economically speaking, we alone manage our resources. We do not have to ask the innovation centre for that...The organization of our department allows us to manage our services according to our own objectives, each department has its own concrete business plans, but we act in the name of the innovation centre...Management, outgoing and incoming are separated, and nobody meddles...We collaborate only in technical fields, or when we need to renew equipment (Mr Rong Lan, Director, Department of Pattern Printing).

One difficulty relates to staff. Most management personnel were initially recruited from the public sector, but personnel are neither civil servants nor private-sector employees. Their salaries are fixed, without bonuses or penalties. In future, this needs to be clarified, especially in light of the high demand for professionals, and the high turnover that exists in the Guangdong region. The innovation centre team recognizes that government employees cannot resolve their problems, because they do not have the necessary economic and market competence.

Another difficulty is that the government has the last word in meetings with private partners. Mr Liang, the manager of a large company, shows scepticism about the power of the commercial association:

> During the meetings of the association, we have no right to take a decision without the approval of the government. For example, if we want to organize travel, we have to discuss it with the government, so we do not have any rights. The secretary of the association in the Light Industrial and Textile Special District and the secretary of our association are from the government...Associations have very low utility. The only thing the government can do is gather you together and give you a name (Mr Liang, Deyao Textile Industrial Ltd.).

The government itself is conscious of these difficulties. In an official document issued by the Province of Guangdong:

Accelerating the separation of government and trade association...related departments in the government must be separate from trade associations in operations, human resource, etc. They must not work together. Government employers cannot take a post in managing the trade association. Government officials who act as association leader must resign within two years (Suggestions on Further Transferring Government Functions and Fostering the Industry Institute: 2–3).

The privatization of research centres is a general trend in China and Guangdong. The Xiqiao innovation centre is scheduled to become a 'private centre', which would then sell services for higher fees. However, its services to SMEs would then become too expensive. This issue is the most important aspect facing today's centres. The products and services developed by the innovation centre are a non-profit public service. The new weaving patterns are sold to the local private and privately owned enterprises for CNY300, which is considered below cost.

Diversity of techniques and insufficient competence: Important problems include the lack of software development and technical knowledge. There are few specialists, and the technicians' level of knowledge is low. Because of high turnover, imitation and copying of products is very common. The enterprises themselves do not develop and design products, they make products according to orders from clients (a common feature for all industrial sectors). Also common are a lack of marketing and little knowledge of the market: 'In this industrial sector, the mastery of techniques is different, for example, than in the motorcycle sector. The more you produce one component, the more you learn how to produce it perfectly. But, with textile materials, selecting, dyeing, and mastering the techniques is very hard...' (Mr Xiong, Secretary, Nanhai Textile Association, and Director, Office for Diffusion of Information, Committee of the City of Xiqiao).

Relations between companies and innovation centres: Interviews with managers of Xiqiao enterprises point to some lack of confidence and trust between the main partners. The reasons are numerous: companies do not feel the need for technical enhancement; companies say they do not need the centre because they have their own R&D structure; there is a lack of confidence because the centre is a public-sector entity; and lack of specific competence at the centre in relation to the enterprise. Here are some examples.

Mr Huang owns a small enterprise, which has been selling textile fabrics since 1994, and has also produced garment fabrics for a few years. It is located in the Light Industry and Textile cluster. He regrets that he invested in production because the economic situation is bad. For him, there are no benefits from the cluster in Xiqiao because there is no particular specialization. This feeling is shared by other managers in Xiqiao.

> Now we do not have a lot of technical relationships. In Xiqiao, there are not a lot of enterprises producing garment fabrics and one of the reasons it is difficult to prosper is that there are few enterprises and no incentives to

open one...This district is too small in comparison with Hangzhou, Wuxi, and Changzhou, which are well-developed. Here in Guangdong, you just have Xiqiao, but with too disparate textile specializations. In Guangdong, the textile industry has not been seriously developed, not like the situation in Zhejiang Province (Mr Huang, Light Industrial and Textile Special District).

Nonetheless, Mr Huang has technical links with the innovation centre. He asks for help with pattern-design techniques and with printing his material. He is also a member of the commercial association and travelled with the group to the Wenzhou exhibition (one of the largest in China).

Even if relationships with the innovation centre are difficult to create, they can evolve over time and with experience. For example, here is the story of Mr Li, Manager of Hongye Textile Factory, and his relations with the commercial association:

> In 1995, I became a member of the association...people of this district in medium and large enterprises must enter this association to have common activities, such as participate in exhibitions, and go outside for visits. In fact, I entered this association quite unconsciously, it was like a worker entering a workers association...but I now participate actively in the activities. Before, there were few activities, just once or twice a year. In 2001, the association began to send faxes to us to announce exhibitions or travel, but before I did not go. You know, I am quite old minded, at first I did not trust these sort of things. After I saw that the effects of these activities were great, I decided to go there.

Managers also point to high turnover of enterprises and workers.

> SMEs always have the same problem, despite 20 years of reform; they still do not have real high-skilled managers. Except those very few who followed me during these 10 years, all my managers have left. Having someone stay 3–5 years in the same enterprise is extraordinary (Mr Liang, Deyao Textile Industrial Ltd.).

Difficulties are also encountered in competing with textile districts in the provinces of Zhejiang and Jiangsu. According to the interviews, the managers believe it is important to lower taxes, to educate and keep skilled workers, and to imagine a commune-leading brand.

Deyao, Mr Liang's company, is a large enterprise. Mr Liang is also the vice-chairman of the business association in Foshan, Nanhai. His enterprise was established in 1990. It produces industrial materials, jeans, and accessories for women.[14] It has its own design department. Deyao has no linkages with other enterprises. Mr Liang admits that the absence of collaboration with other large enterprises is a problem, although he does not explain why he has refused collaboration:

...maybe the capacities of other people do not follow the development of the enterprise, but between managers of large enterprises, the collaboration cannot last more than two years, we have to stop...The fact that we just use our own capacities to develop is not working. Sooner or later we will have to change.

Mr Liang says he cannot collaborate with the innovation centre because he has his own R&D department, and the innovation centre is not able to help large enterprises: 'SMEs can use the services of the innovation centres, but not the large ones. It is because the development of products for large enterprises exceeds CNY10,000 or 20,000. The innovation centre cannot support projects worth CNY100,000 or 1 million. It would be too risky...it just cannot do that.'

Another company states the same argument (Mr Mo, Manager of Fengli Textile Company):

No, we do not need to collaborate with the innovation centre...we have our own capacities. The innovation centre does its job, we do our own. I do not say it has no use, I say we do not need to participate in its work... the innovation centre has no particular products, it does not even think how to develop the market, it just gives techniques...I think the job of the innovation centre is to give reports to the government, to prove to the government that it is doing something.

A large variety of issues arise from the existence of this large innovation centre and the quite large industrial cluster. Our impression was that the innovation centre's development logic was rather different from the industrial logic. The industrial enterprises act as though the innovation centre is of little interest. They develop their own design and development capabilities and have little interest in links with other enterprises or institutions. Nonetheless, the innovation centre has helped create better conditions for industry and attracted higher skilled labour to the city.

Motorcycle area in Pengjiang

Pengjiang, Jiangmen City, is an ancient industrial base for machinery and hardware. Once a large trading city, it has become one of the largest motorcycle production sites in China. The motorcycle trade started in Pengjiang in the late 1980s and early 1990s. In 1991, Dachangjiang Corporation was founded and became the first manufacturer of motorcycles in Pengjiang. Since then, the industry has developed rapidly and the marketing network has been improved. Pengjiang was given the title 'Professional Motorcycle Manufacturing Area in Guangdong', and became one of the officially recognized industrial clusters in the province. The Dachangjiang Corporation created an R&D centre that services the corporation and all Suzuki-related branches in China.

The industrial cluster

The motorcycle industry plays a central role in Pengjiang's economy. The production value of motorcycles reached CNY2.87 bn in 2001, and accounted for 38% of total industrial production (CNY7.55 bn). Production of accessories was about CNY0.7 bn, and exports of motorcycles accounted for 39% of total production. Presently, Pengjiang has three factories manufacturing motorcycles (Dachangjiang Corporation, Dihao Motorcycle Corporation, and Yunbao Corporation) and about 30 motorcycle accessories enterprises. Dachangjiang Corporation is the leader in motorcycle manufacturing in Pengjiang and also a major market. There were 602 distributors of motorcycles and accessories at the end of 2001. It includes the largest market for motorcycles in the Pearl River Delta, the Shuanglong Professional Motorcycle Market, which was built in 1992 and includes 160 shops with an annual turnover of CNY 1.5 bn.

Pengjiang began to import motorcycles after Chinese policy reforms in the 1980s.[15] Foreign enterprises developed this production. Dachangjiang Great River Group was established in 1992 as the largest state-owned commercial enterprise specialized in motorcycle imports. Its output accounted for 70% of the production of motorcycles in Pengjiang (46,000 units worth CNY2.66 bn in 2003). Its gross assets are estimated at CNY2 bn with seven affiliated enterprises. With an annual output of one million motors and one million motorcycles, it is one of the four largest motorcycle-making enterprises in China. One of its three brands is the famous Haojue, a popular and robust 125 cc motorcycle.

Another large firm is Huayi Group (interviewed in 2003). This enterprise specializes in the production of spare parts for motorcycles, principally frames and moulds (60% of the South China market). Established in September 2000, it imports most of its equipment and raw materials. Another large enterprise, Minglong Group (interviewed in March 2002), imports motorcycles, specially the 'Guangyang', produced by Honda and by a Taiwanese enterprise based in Taiwan and in Changsha and Changzhou cities.

Dachangjiang has depended on Suzuki, and still depends on it, for techniques, management, investments, and international sales channels. The Huayi Group, which is quite new in this sector, wants to expand from the Chinese market to the international market, and is convinced that it can do so within 3–5 years. It is thus possible that competition will become stronger in the near future.

Dachangjiang (Great River) Group

Dachangjiang developed rapidly. From 1992 to 1997, annual output increased by an average of 143% each year. Gradually, Dachangjiang built a test station and assembly lines to make cushions, shock absorbers, engines, and whole motorcycles. In 1998, Dachangjiang's output became the tenth largest in China: 240,000 motorcycles, with a production value of CNY1.4 bn. Gradually,

Dachangjiang attracted many suppliers who were eager to cooperate. It set up several factories in Jiangmen, and the Jiangmen Machinery (Axletree) Company began to produce motors for Dachangjiang. The light industry in Jiangmen can also produce other kinds of accessories. About 30 accessory factories in Pengjiang became suppliers for Dachangjiang. Presently, the supply network includes more than 400 accessories suppliers that supply 80% of the accessories in a motorcycle and 70% of the total cost. The network has expanded far beyond Pengjiang to cover many other areas in China (e.g. Chongqing, Jiangzhe, and Guangdong). Engines are mainly made by Dachangjiang's subordinate enterprise, Wangjiang Lingmu (Suzuki) Motor Limited Company. Dachangjiang, which benefits from technology support from the Japanese Suzuki Corporation, has created its own R&D team.

Apart from key accessories, all other parts are mostly outsourced. Generally, accessories with the same specifications are produced under a 'multi-supplier' system – two or three companies supply the accessories at the same time. This multi-supplier system guarantees quality, improves delivery time, and maintains a competitive market. The multi-supplier system increases the competitive pressure on the suppliers.

The motorcycle industry demands a large work-force. The assembly of one motorcycle includes more than 1,000 accessories. What a single enterprise can do by itself is very limited. Therefore, the construction of the accessory-supply network for the core enterprise is very important (as is the case in the automobile industry).

In the beginning, it was the accessory producers who supported the industry's development. They offered a steady source of accessories for its motorcycles. At first, accessory production was not the firm's specialty. Many supplying factories were ahead of Dachangjiang in production technology and specialized in certain parts. When Dachangjiang matured and achieved production scale and competitiveness, it promoted its own providers. The change took place about 1998. By then, Dachangjiang had distinguished itself in China's motorcycle industry. Technology R&D took a stronger position inside the company. In 1998, it cooperated with the Japanese Suzuki Corporation and set up Dachangjiang Precise Machine Ltd., which focused on research, development, and production of engines, and is now known as one of the most modern engine producers in Asia with world-class equipment and assembly line. The company maintains close cooperation with the Japanese Suzuki Corporation, and in 2002, it built a large R&D centre. Dachangjiang maintains a rather high percentage of accessory outsourcing (about 80% in recent years). According to our research, the proportion of Dachangjiang's outsourcing represents at least 30% of the final product, and over 80% of the sales of the providers.[16]

Some issues

What structures the industrial space in Pengjiang is the suppliers' network for the large enterprises. This has immediate influence on neighbouring companies:

> Our neighbour was a factory, called Zongyi. It was ready to collapse, but its equipment was still there. Dachangjiang has its own engine factory, but it has a reputation of producing only the best, so [if it produced] low quality engines that would be with [the same] high costs. It is the reason why we have now an arrangement with Zongyi; we buy some engines from them. For technical matters, we send technicians to this factory to control the process (Mr Shi Yan, Manager, Dachangjiang Technical Centre).

Large enterprises, such as Dachangjiang and Huayi, have built a nation-wide network that includes both retail and wholesale agents and agents to sell spare parts. Dachangjiang alone has a network of more than 30 commercial agencies, and works with more than 40 manufacturers. These enterprises attach importance to marketing strategies, regularly study market trends, and try to adapt their production to the needs of the consumers. For example, they developed a small motorcycle for men and another one for women, with specific colours and designs:

> We have some regular and very important clients. Our largest client buys about 20% of our production, so we send a specialist there to provide help services, if there are some quality problems with our products, we are always ready to help resolve problems, we offer the spare parts, they assemble them...The degree of trust you share with your client depends on the way you complement one another, but for us the question if we can trust the client does not exist anymore, because there are so many years, we know each other very well. The only question is whether they can produce all the things we need or not' (Mr Rong Dexiong, Vice-Manager, Huayi Group).

Large enterprises have some links with universities and research centres in technical fields, but no relationships in management fields. Dachangjiang sends people directly to Japan to be trained, and once a year, it organizes training classes. Its R&D centre has relationships with the University of Tianjin and projects for undergraduate students at the University of Wuba. The Huayi Group organizes special meetings with other motorcycle enterprises because it finds it useful to understand the problems and assets of the entire sector. This group also has relations with the University of Wuba for design purposes. The Minglong Group has its own test centre to monitor all the motorcycles it sells and to test the products of its suppliers. All large enterprises agree on the lack of highly specialized workers. They expect the local government to invest more in training and education.

Faced with increased competition in the motorcycle industrial sector and market saturation, enterprises are not willing to declare a price war, but compete rather in quality and marketing. In 2002, from January to November, 800 enterprises in Guangdong went bankrupt and closed. Managers said that the crisis began in 2000. In the past, it was possible to sell more than 200 vehicles per month. Now if an enterprise sells more than 40 vehicles that is good. The Minglong Group chose to cut profits and reinvest in improved production and increased advertising. Dachangjiang counts on innovation to maintain its economic growth. The Huayi Group wants to develop a quality brand. In terms of future prospects, here are the thoughts of Mr Shi Yan, Manager, Dachangjiang Technical Department:

> After China enters WTO, the most important problems this sector will have to face are management, quality, and certification. Just with certification, 80% of the enterprises will be eliminated. From this point of view, it is the most incredible sanctions this sector will have. In fact, violation of rights and copyright are very hard.

These enterprises must also deal with the better quality and know-how of enterprises in other provinces. For Mr Shi Yan, from Dachangjiang: 'it is not that Guangdong people are stupid, but that, in Jiangsu and Zhejiang provinces, people are particularly smart, because they have accumulated years of experience'. Mr Rong Dexiong, from Huayi Group, also said that motorcycle production in Guangdong Province is not bad but cannot be compared favourably with the best production of Chongqing: 'A cluster has to be successful, if it is not successful, it cannot attract other enterprises in its territory. The work force is quite sufficient here, but we have a lack of high skilled workers, as in technical skills…'

An area with no innovation centre: Qingxi, Dongguan

Because of its importance in the Pearl River Delta, it is interesting to look at Qingxi, in Dongguan Province, which has 77 companies involved in information technology (IT) and electronics. Here, there is no innovation centre and most of the industry was developed by foreign capital, mainly from Taiwan (23%), Hong Kong (8%), and other countries (32%). A large number of companies (35%) are *san lai yi bu*[17] and there is only one collective enterprise. Most companies in Qingxi were established between 1984 and 2002, and, on average, have existed for fewer than 9 years. The enterprises are quite large: 82% had more than 100 employees, and of these, 41% had between 101 and 500 employees. Similarly, 20% had capital of more than of CNY50 m, and 36% had between CNY10 and 50 mn. Smaller enterprises (capital of less than CNY10 m) accounted for 44% of the total. This distribution is quite representative of the local area. Almost 40% of these enterprises established their factory outside Qingxi. Linkages are sparse between companies inside the Qingxi cluster: more than half (56%) of the enterprises spend less than 5% of their budget for spare parts with their Qingxi partners. Enterprises that spend more than a quarter of their total spare-parts expenses locally represent only 8.4% of these enterprises. Most of these enterprises buy spare parts from foreign enterprises or joint ventures. Finally, about a third (38%) of these enterprises have established a suppliers network for spare parts with Qingxi collective enterprises, but this represents a small part of the output of these enterprises.

The main reasons for coming to Qingxi are low-cost resources (labour, water, and electricity), the proximity of harbours and the port of Hong Kong, and transportation facilities. However, most enterprises are not satisfied with the economic environment. They feel the local government should offer better conditions in terms of electricity supply, security, accommodation, and schools. Foreign capital enterprises feel insecure in China because they are unsure of administrative costs and taxes, and worry about payments from their Chinese clients. The technical level of companies is quite low, even in quality control. Foreign-owned companies generally have higher technical skills than the Chinese enterprises in the industrial cluster, which are often 'family managed' or 'individual managed' enterprises.

Foreign-owned companies control the more basic parts of the process, but have transferred some of the R&D to China: 'All the structure of R&D has been transferred from Taiwan to Qingxi, and we operate an OEM process. The main objective of our new R&D department is to improve the techniques of production, especially for products for Samsung or Sony' (XG electronics). However, the most complex R&D remains in the country of origin:

> R&D is divided in two parts. The first one, involving difficult or high technology levels and know-how, is done in Taiwan. In Qingxi, we do the second part, the one with simple techniques and crafts. We have 20 employees in the R&D department. In Taiwan, they only have 5 or 6 employees, but they do the highest technology work (CA electronics).

Another common arrangement is that: 'technical development remains in Japan; in Qingxi we have all the equipment to test the quality, and technicians come from Japan' (Siguo Electrical Lines). The less technically developed 'just transform the raw material, the design and development of products is done in Hong Kong' (Cheng Xiang Electronics).

Industrial associations

Although there is no innovation centre, there are three associations of enterprises in Qingxi: one for Taiwanese enterprises (since 1990); one for Hong Kong enterprises (since 1998); and one for Chinese enterprises. They were established with no help from the local government of Qingxi. The government did provide support by offering offices for free, but it limits its actions to help the enterprises. In 2003, the Taiwan association had 245 members, and the Hong Kong association 109 members. Half the members of both associations are enterprises specialized in IT. The other half produce many different products, from electroplating to gloves and umbrellas. However, the influence of these associations among enterprises is not strong. The Chinese commercial association of Qingxi was established by the government under the leadership of the main commercial association of Chinese collective enterprises in Dongguan City. This association controls 32 villages, and by August 2003 had established 25 local branch associations. However, these associations are not acting as an innovation centre.

The Qingxi government has made many efforts to attract enterprises. It published a guide for investment, offered services to enterprises willing to invest, created well-equipped industrial parks, and renovated the city centre. The government has also helped enterprises to hire specialized workers from other cities, or provinces, by: facilitating administrative obligations (they provide a *hukou*, a local working and living permit that must be approved by the police and is compulsory in China); obtaining loans for housing; and developing cultural and sports activities. One of the main problems for Qingxi is that high-skilled workers, and even whole enterprises, often move to bigger cities, such as Shenzhen, Suzhou, and Shanghai, where employees can live more comfortably and find modern equipment and cultural life.

One enterprise suggested the need to create a training body and placement office. This issue is critical for highly skilled personnel:

> Today the main R&D structure is in Taiwan, and the R&D structure for production technology is in Shanghai. In Qingxi, we just do the production. In Shanghai, they have a high technology cluster, because workers come from there, and have been there a long time. In Dongguan, most of the workers come from outside and the turnover is high, maybe because they earn money very quickly and then go away. So, in the R&D units of the company, to attract employees, they attach importance to long-term development in Shanghai. It is also the reason why we will move in the Central China region – there the workers may stay longer in our enterprise and the improvement of technology will be better (CA Electronics).

Is an innovation centre needed?

Qingxi has no innovation centre, and some enterprises would welcome the establishment of such a centre because it could help with professional certification; connections with other innovation sites in the Pearl River Delta; training; and the running of specialized fairs and meetings. Some enterprises, such as San Yang, believe that an innovation centre would enhance the services offered by the government:

> [The government] always offers us a foretaste of a service, how to attract buyers, how to attract enterprises...The government always helps, but it always gives us superficial services and never deep services. [The government should] participate in the production process...It would be perfect if some structure could gather all these services in one location, even if we, the enterprises, had to pay for these services (San Yang Company).

Finally, testing and certification processes could be handled by an innovation centre:

...when we want to test equipment, which happens very often, we have to send it to Guangzhou or Shenzhen, because in Dongguan there are no such facilities. It is very annoying. Another example is environmental norms. In Europe, North America, and Japan, they have these norms for products without toxicity and without lead and other metals. I do not know if the Government of Qingxi has already spread the news that every enterprise working for Sony has to respect a new Sony standard, called SS0009. It is a continuous testing process. If we can have such a structure in Dongguan, some sort of 'Department for Technical Tests, Dongguan City' and implement a subsidiary in Qingxi, this structure could help us to obtain the approval of companies like Sony, and we would not need to go to Shenzhen anymore (GQ Electronic Company).

Zhongshan University

Zhongshan University is the largest university in South China. It specializes in basic academic disciplines, as well as in humanities, social sciences, economics, and business management. The university is well respected and some of its laboratories are state-of-the-art in bioengineering, optoelectronics, chemistry, physics, and computer science. The relations of the university with the productive world are ample and diversified, but they are managed on a case-by-case basis, depending on the contacts, the nature of the involvement, or the amounts that are at stake. Many contacts are made through specific enterprises and academic personnel who act individually.

Like all universities in China, Zhongshan has undergone profound reforms. In September 2002, the university amended its internal legal statutes to give additional incentives to professors who linked their research activities with enterprises and R&D institutes. This change allows professors to obtain additional payments for their research activities outside the university. The new regulations are managed by the Office of Science and Technology. Compared with the former regulations, the new regulations include bonuses of up to 30% of the value of the project. Another prominent change is to strengthen patent protection for innovation products. Since being put into practice, the new regulations have greatly enhanced participation by teachers and researchers in activities linked with industry.

Table 3.3 summarizes data on links between the university and enterprises in 2000–2. The number of projects is quite low, and no additional details were available on the size and nature of the projects. This table only includes projects that were directly managed by the Office of Science and Technology. There is no technology transfer unit in the university to promote innovative projects, or to manage technology transfer to the productive sphere. In these projects, management is the responsibility of the Office of Science and Technology, which manages all projects that receive funding from public or international sources. Nonetheless, an effort is being made to promote innovation through research.

Environmental research provides an example of strong links between the university and specific enterprises. These efforts are undertaken to comply with environmental regulations. This is useful because it gives students some fieldwork experience, but it is not research. Many students take part in environmental research to gain experience and to help the enterprises solve technological difficulties. For example, Prof. He Jianguo, who is a professor working at the School of Life Sciences in Zhongshan University, undertook a project in collaboration with Hengxing Technology Development Co. Ltd. to study biochemical development. In his research, he conducted fieldwork with his students. As a result, the students improved their practical skills, while the project created innovation.

Many links are not technology innovation links but services to enterprises (mainly in training, where the demand is quite high). For example, the School of Management developed a curriculum in business management for students from management positions in various enterprises. The courses included business management skills and theories the students could use in their daily work. Almost 1,000 students have now graduated.

The services provided by the university can be quite elaborate, as is the case for studies and research projects done to respond to development issues. The university has set up a research institute (ZURIGuD) that responds to demands made by public or private entities to mobilize the intellectual capabilities of the university. ZURIGuD has undertaken a number of research projects since 1999. The institute integrates most of the major social sciences and has formed an internal network with numerous intellectual resources. When ZURIGuD undertakes projects, it mobilizes teachers with credentials that match customer needs. For example, to undertake a study of the Foshan Industrial Development Strategy, professors from economics, management, sociology, and urban planning with different intellectual and academic perspectives participated in the project. In addition, some enterprises have

Table 3.3 Research innovation projects that linked Zhongshan University to enterprises

Year	Total projects	Degree of novelty			
		Those with internal collaboration	Innovation at international level	Innovation for first time in China	Innovation that already exists in China
2000	12	5	5	0	7
2001	10	0	7	2	1
2002	9	0	5	2	2

Source: Various reports produced by the Office of Science and Technology, Zhongshan University (2000–2).

installed R&D laboratories on the premises of the university. For example, the Canadian company Nortel Networks installed R&D facilities in 1995 to adapt hardware and software products to local clients. This facility had 398 personnel at the end of 2003, of which more than 90% had higher education diplomas.

Apart from specialized services such as reports on development issues, the common opinion of many professors is that the main activity of the university should be education, not service. The very high prestige of the university is not 'on sale' for specific projects, and professors are very careful not to mix their research and education activities. The professors believe they should do useful things for society and help the development of the region and their country, but not at the cost of education. Moreover, the university has no mechanism to recognize the social activities, or services rendered to society, in the careers of the professors. Because most demands come from SMEs and for projects with a low level of technical expertise, the university is not seen as the appropriate entity to respond to these demands. Rather, it is seen as being best suited to provide support to large-scale projects in the basic sciences. The university does not appear to be oriented to the practical questions of SMEs or even large enterprises. Its role is to create a highly qualified workforce and an environment conductive to technological development.

Lessons and results

Neo-Marshallian industrial clusters

Industrial clusters are an important form of industrial organization. Because of the presence of SMEs in South China, most clusters resemble the *Marshallian* type of industrial cluster. Nonetheless, the empirical studies show that it is difficult to accept the notion of a 'Marshallian cluster' without some qualification. First, the links between industries are rare and rarely formal. It might be, as Alfred Marshall wrote, that the 'secrets of the industry are in the air', but the information travels through informal social relations rather than through specific collaboration between enterprises. Family ties and personal contacts certainly play an important role. Second, the suppliers are rarely part of the industrial cluster, and most of the technology is provided not by the providers of technology (like equipment providers) but by the clients, who introduce new designs and know-how in the productive processes. Suppliers of raw materials have little or no impact on the productive process. Equipment providers, because technologies are quite standardized and simple, are represented by traders within the cluster who are commercial agents with some technical personnel who provide maintenance in rare cases. Large process changes are introduced by the companies and the industrial clients, and new products are usually designed on behalf of a client or by copying designs from a client. These could be called neo-Marshallian clusters.

Xiqiao and Dachong represent this kind of neo-Marshallian industrial cluster in Guangdong. They specialize in one geographic area in the production of a single type of product. Mainly private enterprises have grown within these clusters, and the local government is involved in this process. The relations of the enterprises with local authorities are quite fluid, and there have been some strong complaints from the enterprises.

The Jiangmen cluster of companies around motorcycle production represents a 'hub-and-spoke' cluster, where a large company acts as a structural agent that organizes a network of supplier companies. As in Italy where Fiat has organized the whole industry around Turin, or Piaggio around Pisa, Dachangjian has organized most of the industry in the district of Pengjiang in Jiangmen. This company has not only developed a network of suppliers, but has become the largest company in the district. In addition, the link between Dachangjian and Suzuki has been instrumental in upgrading its provider network and bringing the experience of the Japanese corporation into the production in Jiangmen.

State-anchored clusters are best represented in China by the science and technology development zones. Clusters and high-technology zones are not the same because the dynamics are very different and the types of enterprises, and thus activities, are different. Technology zones are hubs open for investment; whereas, clusters are usually created by local entrepreneurs. This research did not study any science and technology development zones.

The imprecise role of innovation centres

Part of the difficulties of innovation centres lies in their objectives. For local SMEs, it is difficult to separate the technical and commercial aspects, and the commercial aspects are most important. Improvements to commercial aspects, and relations with the market, are essential. As well, as in practically all SMEs in Guangdong, funding is a difficult issue. So far, local governments have done little in this area because they believe financing should be undertaken by the enterprises themselves. However, there may be room for improvements in procedures for credit and loans.

In the Qingxi (Dongguan) industrial cluster enterprises are closely dependent on the value chains of foreign companies. The whole cluster depends on these value chains and it is not by chance that there is no innovation centre in this cluster. In another cluster we visited, which specializes in shoe making and where large companies are mainly Taiwanese producing for foreign markets, the local government wanted to create an innovation centre. Difficulties were encountered, and the government sold the centre to an entrepreneur, and then later bought it back from him.

Suzuki chose to locate its R&D centre in Jiangmen as a service centre for all China because of the driving force of the local Dachangjian Company. Of course, the dynamics of an R&D centre are different from an innovation centre that would serve SMEs in the region. Moreover, because Dachangjian is so strong, there is little room for an independent technical centre. The competitors, who are other motorcycle companies, are equally large, and the providers are equally dependent on them. In this case, the local government relies entirely on the private company, which has a strong pulling effect in the local economy.

The innovation centres have begun to create networks of enterprises, to improve innovation capacities, and to enhance communication with other bodies, such as universities and research centres. Their future development will depend on the homogeneity of policies, charges for their services, e-business, and relationships with other specialized industrial areas in China. Their survival is neither guaranteed nor impossible. In some districts, the policy of the government is to promote these innovation centres, as in the case of Nanhai. Many changes are occurring. The most prominent change has been in the management of innovation centres controlled by local governments. For example, the innovation centre in Xiqiao changed its management mechanism in May 2004. The network of the innovation centre is now managed by one of the largest private textile enterprises in Xiqiao. The Xiqiao district government does not interfere with the daily business of the centre and grants more development space to the innovation centre. Therefore, the dynamics of the innovation centre are dictated by private enterprises rather than by the government. This allows the centre to better meet the needs of the market and to develop independently.

The innovation centres are also facing new issues, such as intellectual property rights and action on competition. In Xiqiao, the innovation centre plays a central role in the structure of the industry. It is also aware that it modifies the conditions of competition (therefore, the rule 'sell a pattern only to one enterprise at a time'). From the beginning, Xiqiao authorities have taken a broad view of the industry and shown a willingness to structure the industry to ensure it ranks high in China. The main differences in Xiqiao and Dachong are differences in scale, not differences in nature, but the demands made by SMEs to innovation centres are the same.

Table 3.4 shows the main problems that innovation centres are facing. Local governments are now reconsidering their role in the process of technology innovation. Initial investment in innovation centres by local governments is necessary, but the ownership and management of innovation centres should be separate. Innovation centres should be made public platforms for technological innovation. Governments should be responsible for providing infrastructure and maintenance, but the innovation centres should remain a public resource. However, the management of the innovation centres should be transferred to private companies or trade associations.

We suggested to the government of Nanhai District that the local government should move one step forward and one step backward in terms of the technological innovation of the industrial cluster. 'One step forward' means that the local government should vigorously support the development of a trade association; whereas, 'one step backward' means that, when the

Table 3.4 Main problems reported by innovation centres

Centre	Priority problems		
	First	Second	Third
Guangao kou	Lower the activity (intervention) of the local government	Increase its position in the market, products innovation, and services	Enhance logistics (how to transfer logistic functions from government to enterprises)
Yanbu	The role and functions of the innovation centre and its position	Lack of funds	Lack of human resources
Pingzhou	Increase relationships with specialists in the sector; offer suitable services and information to SMEs	Intensify relationships and communication among enterprises; increase members of the cluster	Strengthen communication between members of the industrial association
Jinsha	Bring together the associations, the local government, and the enterprises; increase the services offered by the innovation centre	Increase the responsibilities of the employees inside the innovation centre; create a team	Improve the knowledge and capacities of this team
Xiqiao	Increase knowledge and know-how	Modernize the functioning of the centre	Open the centre to society and lower the financial expenses of the government
Heshun	Increase agricultural knowledge and funds in the centre	Increase technical capacities in the agricultural park and create leading products	Complete the tests on seeds and germination
Songguan	Support of government	Complete the installation of basic equipment	Wait for the support of the government to strengthen knowledge
Dali	Answer to the needs of enterprises, answer to their problems, and attract specialized service organizations	Attract in this area specialists in management, administration, and technology	Obtain agreement from the government to perform scientific and technological research

trade association becomes mature, the functions and management of the innovation centre should be gradually transferred to the trade association.

Links of enterprises and one large national university, Zhongshan University, were also examined. In the economic context of Guangdong, the links between Zhongshan University and the private economy seem quite loose. Usually, the innovation centres rely on universities that specialize in engineering or in some specific trade and technical specialty. Zhongshan University has few of these specialties, which explains why few contacts are made with the economic world. The relations are more often through some form of service (e.g. environmental reports and regulatory studies). Contacts with enterprises are not rare, but they are rarely technology based, and are usually in business management and training for managers. Zhongshan University is a higher educational institution where research is considered to be basic research. Only within the business school or the school of economics were regular contacts established with enterprises (e.g. service contacts provide training in business management).

The fact that the university has few 'official' contacts with enterprises, but many informal contacts through individual professors, does not mean the university could not establish more formal links. Moreover, no technology cluster has yet appeared around the university. The university, because of its importance in training and its cultural presence, has a role that goes beyond specific links between professors and enterprises. Its importance goes beyond practical, everyday, direct links with economic activities: professors participate in social and political activities; the university invites many foreigners as students or professors; respect for professors makes them social models of behaviour; engineers and managers from enterprises who come to the university become aware of modern up-to-date methods and theories; and the university attracts talented people to the city. All these factors make universities a stronghold of development, and explain why all special economic zones have tried to create a university. However, the experience of Zhongshan University, which has a campus in Zhuhai on the frontier of Macao, shows that direct links between the university and the economic world are difficult to establish.

Role of ZURIGuD

By integrating specialists and researchers in different subjects, such as economics, management, sociology, and economic geography, ZURIGuD played an important role in the study of cluster development in Guangdong. In the future, ZURIGuD could provide additional services such as: participate in the study of cluster development in Guangdong and draft research reports to the government of Guangdong Province; hold specific lectures and training on cluster development for local governments; evaluate the Guangdong Industry Upgrade Demonstration Zone, and draft a 'Blueprint for the Establishment of a Guangdong Industry Upgrade Demonstration Zone'; establish indicators to evaluate the Guangdong Industry Upgrade Demonstration Zone; and analyse cluster development in Guangdong with these indicators.

Conclusion: Toward a Regional Innovation System

This research was designed to help policy development by seeking to understand the technological development process in Guangdong. It has shown that the evolution of investments in the Pearl River Delta went through successive waves that produced different types of productive units. Local investors generally create SMEs that link to foreign clients not so much to encourage exports but to acquire technology and products. Learning in enterprises is quite rapid, but is linked to changes in markets and is based mainly on a short-term view of the environment.

It is, therefore, very surprising to see the surge in R&D that has occurred recently in China. The increase is mainly due to large collective firms and foreign-owned enterprises. High-tech zones and enterprises have a preference for Guangdong because it has a good business environment, something that is quite new and the product of public policy oriented toward infrastructure. Collective enterprises abound in Guangdong and they are the main investors (along with foreign firms and firms with strong links to foreign clients). It is these enterprises that invest in R&D.

The policy to promote innovation centres appeared during a period of more difficult development in economic terms, when a need for better quality and higher priced products made sense in China. The government promoted innovation centres as a way to fulfil these needs; and the innovation centres were mainly oriented to servicing the local industry, most SMEs. The structure of these centres is still quite uncertain; however, in some cases, they have achieved a quite impressive record in traditional industries.

'Technology poles' and incubators of scientifically based companies seem more difficult to create. In China, it is common to mention the famous Zhongguancun technological pole in Beijing. A careful examination of local situations and the experience of Zhongguancun shows that universities, although they have many links with the economic world, are not large producers of high-tech firms or firms created by academics. Rather, foreign firms, collective enterprises, and private SMEs (as well as some large private groups) are the main development actors in Guangdong. These enterprises have little in common with the university. However, all these firms face problems in training – mainly in overall management, engineering, and mid-level management. The university is one place where such training could be provided.

On the contrary, 'marketized' research centres seem to succeed much better, usually because they are able to sell products and can transform quite rapidly. These centres have a long history of creating and developing products and of maintaining links with productive units. Not all of these centres will succeed, but those engaged in the market will be able to survive as enterprises, not as research centres.

Finally, the policy for innovation could be powered by a regional structure. This structure does not yet exist. To create such a structure it would be necessary to have a network of research units, of innovation centres, and a group of professionals to analyse both S&T and industry using appropriate indicators. These possibilities have been discussed with Guangdong provincial authorities.

Endnotes

1. With the help of Eglantine Jastrabsky, Du Junrong, Anne-Sophie Boisard, and Qiu Cuiwei.
2. 'Marketization' (*shichanghua*) is the privatization of public organizations by selling shares, or by obliging the organization to provide for its own expenses by selling products.
3. In 2000, the French Institut de Recherche pour le Développement (IRD) authorized a prolonged stay for Rigas Arvanitis. This cooperation gave birth to the Chinese–French Centre of Industrial Sociology and Technology in Zhongshan University, a cooperative endeavour between Zhongshan University, IRD, and the Université Lyon III. In 2003, additional funding was secured to conduct fieldwork on the Qingxi (Dongguan) Electronic Industrial Cluster and the Nanzhuang (Nanhai) Ceramic Industrial Cluster. Additional research at the end of 2003 and January 2004 studied the Dali (Nanhai) Aluminium Industrial Cluster; the Jinsha Hardware Industrial Cluster; the Xiqiao Textile Industrial Cluster; the Guanyao Toy Industrial Cluster; the Songgang Electronic Industrial Cluster; the Pingzhou Shoemaking Industrial Cluster; the Yanbu Underwear Industrial Cluster; and the Heshun Vegetable Industrial Cluster.
4. Although there is a large body of literature on the development of Guangdong (Vogel, 1989; Sung et al., 1995; Douw and Post, 1996; Yeung and Chu, 1998; Sanjuan, 1999; Cheng, 2000, 2003; Segal, 2003; Yeung et al., 2004), we conducted an economic analysis that better fitted the needs of our research (Arvanitis et al., 2003).
5. US$1 = CNY7.86.
6. This phenomenon can also be observed in the border regions of Northern Mexico, where the *maquiladoras* developed from being simple low-cost assembly plants to more complex systems of production that participated in the international flows of capital and commodities: the latter are in turn the source of investment capital for the factories located in Mexico or other foreign countries. Not only have the *maquiladoras* changed in form and function, they have become part of a truly innovative economic and technological dynamism (Villavicencio, 2003).
7. Regional innovation systems and science and technology policies in emerging economies: experiences from China and the world, 19–21 April 2004, Guangzhou, China. Some examples were published in a special issue of *Science, Technology and Society*, 2006, 11(1).
8. The 863 Programme was created in March 1986 to promote mainly basic research. The later Super 863 Programme in 1996 was designed to follow up this initial effort.
9. The report is not explicit in its definitions of 'research structures' or 'research organizations'. Later, in the same report, the figures appear to be lower because a more strict definition of 'research centres' is used (but it is no more explicit).
10. See Guangdong Office of Science and Technology 2002, Annex Table 6, pp. 246–249; China Statistical Yearbook on Science and Technology 2003, p. 434.

11. Not to be confused with Zhongshan University, which is located in the city of Guangzhou (Canton).
12. The first session of the Chamber of Commerce was attended by more than 70 enterprises (mahogany furniture manufacturers, clothing manufacturers, and plastic factories).
13. In-depth interviews were conducted with two companies: Hong Xiqian, which was established in October 1997 as a manufacturer and commercial agent, whose main products are sofas, commodes, and bedrooms; and Hexin, which produces ancient-style furniture and lacquered furniture.
14. Since 1995, it has developed very quickly and well: in 1995, it had 600 employees with an annual production of no more than CNY 20 mn; in 2003, it had 300 employees, but an annual production of CNY 1.3 bn. His manager recognizes, however, that the economic situation is bad.
15. Before 1978, Pengjiang specialized in the construction of machines and hardware.
16. Details on contacts between providers and Dachangjiang can be obtained from the authors.
17. *San lai yi bu* is short for *Lai liao jiagong, lai yang jiagong, lai jian zhuanpei, he bu chang maoyi*, transformation of materials, plans, and parts, obligation to resell. They are the Chinese version of *maquiladoras* enterprises in Latin America.

References

Arvanitis, R. (2000) *Apprentissage technologique et efficience productive: des outils pour l'analyse du développement technologique. Pratique des transferts de technologie et efficience productive dans les pays émergents, Guangzhou (R.P. Chine)*, 18–22 janvier 2000. Institut International pour le Développement des Technologies (INIDET) and Institute of Research for the Development of Guangdong (ZURIGuD) (French and Chinese version).
Arvanitis, R. (2001) *La situation des PME chinoises dans le Delta de la Rivière des Perles*. Institute for Research for Development (IRD) and French-Chinese Centre of Sociology of Industry and Technology (CFCSIT) (présentation à la Mission Économique de Canton), Guangzhou, 15.
Arvanitis, R. (2004a) *L'émergence d'un bourg industriel du Delta de la Rivière des Perles. L'exemple de Shuikou*. Institute for Research for Development (IRD) and French-Chinese Centre of Sociology of Industry and Technology (CFCSIT), Canton, p. 12.
Arvanitis, R. (2004b) La politique d'innovation en Chine – un essai d'interprétation. *La Lettre de l'Antenne*, Antenne expérimentale franco-chinoise de sciences humaines et sociales à Pékin. (http://www.antenne-pekin.com)
Arvanitis, R., Miège, P., and Zhao, W. (2003) A fresh look at the development of a market economy in China. *China Perspectives*, 48, 50–62.
Arvanitis, R. and Villavicencio, D. (1998) Comparative perspectives on technological learning: Introduction. *Science, Technology and Society*, 3(1), 1–9.

Arvanitis, R. and Vonortas, N. (2000) Apprentissage et coopération à travers la Recherche-Développement. *Technologies, Idéologies, Pratiques*, 14(1), 225–246.

Arvanitis, R. and Zhao, W. (2003) The industrialization of the South of China: Learning and limits from a successful case, in *X Seminario Ibero-Americano de Gestión Tecnológica* (ALTEC), 22–24 October 2003, Mexico, ALTEC (CD-ROM).

Arvanitis, R., Zhao, W., Qiu, H., and Xu, J. (2006) Technological learning in six firms in South China: success and limits of an industrialization model. *International Journal of Technology Management*, 36(1/2/3), 108–125.

Cao, C. (2004) Challenges for China's industrial development: a technological assessment. *China Perspectives*, 54, 4–16.

Cheng, J.Y.S. (ed.) (2000) *Guangdong in the Twenty-first century: Stagnation or second take-off?* City University of Hong Kong, Hong Kong.

Cheng, J.Y.S. (ed.) (2003) *Guangdong: preparing for the WTO challenge*. The Chinese University Press, Hong Kong.

Dalla Pria, Y. (2004) Proximity, networks and collective organization of labor: the Sophia Antipolis (France) technological district case. *Regional Innovation Systems and Science and Technology Policies in Emerging Economies: Experiences from China and the World*, Zhongshan University, UNESCO, Institut de Recherche pour le Développement (IRD), ISESCO, 19–21 April 2004, Guangzhou.

Douw, L.M. and Post, P. (1996) *South China: State, culture and social change*. North-Holland Publishing Company, Netherlands.

Gu, S. (1999) *China's Industrial Technology: Market Reform and Organisational Change*. Routledge, London, in association with UNU Press, Tokyo.

Guangdong Office of Science and Technology (2002) *Report on scientific and technological research in Guangdong (in Chinese)* (Guangdong keji fazhan yanjiu baogao). Guangzhou, Guangdong gaodeng jiaoyu shubanshe (12/2002).

Guerrieri, P. and Pietrobelli, C. (2002) *Industrial districts' evolution and technological regimes: Italy and Taiwan*, Rome, 21.

Guiheux, G. (2002) The incomplete crystallization of the private sector. *China Perspectives*, 42, 24–35.

Hong, S.B.H., Yim, D.S.Y., and Kim, K.K.K. (2004) *Characteristics and types of Chinese innovation clusters in comparison with Korean cases*. Science and Technology Policy Institute (STEPI), Seoul.

Huang, C., Amorim, C., Spinoglio, M., Gouveia, B., and Medina, A. (2004) Organization, programme and structure: an analysis of the Chinese innovation policy framework. *R and D Management*, 34(4), 367–387.

Huchet, J.-F. (1999) Concentration and the emergence of corporate groups in Chinese industry. *Perspectives Chinoises/China Perspectives*, 23, 5–17.

IDRC (1997) *A decade of reform: science and technology policy*. International Development Research Centre (IDRC), Ottawa.

Jastrabsky, E. (2004) *Review of industrial clusters in Italy and France*. French-Chinese Centre for Industrial and Technology Sociology, Guangzhou, February, 30.

Kong, X. (2003) Corporate R&D in China: The role of research institutes. *Conference on China's new knowledge systems and their global interaction*,

29–30 September, Lund, Sweden. Swedish Agency for Innovation Studies, Stockholm School of Economics and Lund University.

Liu, X. and White, S. (2001) Comparing innovation systems: a framework and application to China's transitional context. *Research Policy*, 30, 1091–1114.

Mahmood, I.P. and Singh, J. (2003) Technological dynamism in Asia. *Research Policy*, 32, 1031–1054.

MOST. (2004) *Science and technology statistics on-line (in Chinese)*. Ministry of Science and Technology, China. Retrieved 19 June 2004.

Naughton, B. (1995) *Growing out of the plan: Chinese economic reform 1978–1993*. Cambridge University Press, Cambridge.

OECD. (1999) *Boosting innovation: the cluster approach*. Organisation for Economic Co-operation and Development (OECD), Paris.

Pirela, A., Rengifo, R., Arvanitis, R., and Mercado, A. (1993) Technological learning and entrepreneurial behaviour: A taxonomy of the chemical industry in Venezuela. *Research Policy*, 22, 431–454.

Qiu, H. (2001) *Establishing Nanhai as a technology model city*. Research Institute for Guangdong Development, Guangzhou, 234.

Richet, X. and Huchet, J.-F. (2000) Between bureaucracy and market: China's industrial groups in search of a new corporate governance system. *Post-Communist Economies*, 14, 169–201.

Richet, X., Wang, H., and Wang, W. (2001) Foreign direct investment in China's automotive industry. *China Perspectives*, 38, 36–42.

Ruffier, J. (1996) L'efficience productive. Comment marchent les usines? *Presses du Centre national de la recherche scientifique* (CNRS), Paris.

Ruffier, J. (2006) *Faut-il avoir peur des usines chinoises? Compétitivité et pérennité de l'atelier du monde*. L'Harmattan, Paris.

Sanjuan, T. (1999) *A l'ombre de Hong Kong. Le Delta de la Rivière des Perles*. L'Harmattan, Paris.

Segal, A. (2003) *Digital dragon. High-technology enterprises in China*. Cornell University Press, Ithaca and London.

Sigurdson, J. (2002) A new technological landscape in China. *China Perspectives*, 42, 37–54.

Sun, P. and Xu, J. (2002) *Research report on the enterprises of the special product zone of Shuikou*. Zhongshan University Institute for Research for Development of Guangdong, Guangzhou, 6.

Sung, Y.W., Liu, P.-W., Wong, R.Y.-C., and Lau, P.-K. (eds) (1995) *The fifth dragon: the emergence of the Pearl River delta*. Addison-Wesley, Singapore.

Suttmeier, R.P. and Cao, C. (1999) China faces the new industrial revolution: achievement and uncertainty in the search for research and innovation strategies. *Asian Perspective*, 23, 153–200.

Tang, Y. (2003) Review of the reform of research institutes. *Conference on China's new knowledge systems and their global interaction*, 29–30 September, Lund, Sweden, Swedish Agency for Innovation Studies, Stockholm School of Economics and Lund University.

Tidd, J., Bessant, J., and Pavitt, K. (1997) *Managing innovation. Integrating technology, market and organizational change*. Wiley, Chichester and New York.

Verillaud, M. (2001) Les investissements étrangers en Chine, Rapport de stage, *Mission Economique*, Guangzhou.

Villavicencio, D. (2003) The Maquiladoras of the northern border of Mexico: what attaches them to the geographical territory? *Regional Innovation Systems and Science and Technology Policies in Emerging Economies. Experiences from China and the World,* 19–21 April 2004, Guangzhou, China.

Vogel, E. (1989) *One step ahead. Guangdong under economic reform.* Cambridge University Press, Cambridge.

Yeung, Y.M. and Chu, D.K.Y. (1998) *Guangdong: a survey of a province undergoing rapid change.* The Chinese University Press, Hong Kong.

Yeung, Y.-M., Shen, J., and Zhang, L. (2004) *Hong Kong and the Western Pearl River Delta: cooperative development from a cross-boundary perspective.* The Hong Kong Institute of Asia-Pacific Studies and the Chinese University Press, Hong Kong.

Zhao, W. (2006) *Economie de l'innovation et développement des capacités technologiques en Chine: L'apprentissage technologique dans les industries automobiles et électroniques,* Paris. Doctoral Thesis. Université Sorbonne Nouvelle (Ecole doctorale EEC), Paris, p. 347.

CHAPTER 4
Partnerships for agroindustrial research and development in Costa Rica and El Salvador

Frank Hartwich, Olman Quirós, and Jorge Garza

Abstract

> This multi-country study examines partnerships within the agroindustrial research and development sector in Costa Rica and El Salvador. The study diagnoses current trends and challenges in funding and in public–private partnering, examines the social, environmental, and economic effects of these partnerships, and identifies and compares the driving factors and constraints to agroindustrial research in both countries. The research shows that the agroindustry sector provides an example of where private-sector involvement has led to success in the development of new products and their marketing in competitive local and export markets. The authors conclude that there is little local knowledge about how to create a public–private partnership that can respond to both public and private stakeholder needs. The teams also found that public interests do not feature in partnerships as prominently as they should because the government sector often does not specify clearly how public money should be spent.

This project was designed to provide insight on how to increase the impact of agroindustrial research and development (R&D) on agricultural and social development in Central America via public–private partnerships in agroindustrial research. To achieve this objective, the project sought to make information and tools available to local governments, donors, and private-sector representatives to help plan and support private-sector involvement in agroindustrial R&D.

The project unfolded in two nine-month phases plus an extension. During the first phase, efforts were made to achieve a broad understanding of the patterns of agroindustrial R&D in Costa Rica and El Salvador and to identify the 'problems' of partnerships in agroindustrial R&D. Based on these findings, the second phase focused on creating and promoting partnerships in agroindustrial R&D in two specific agricultural value chains and identifying success factors and constraints. Based on a comparison of these experiences, policy recommendations were developed on how best to institutionalize agroindustrial

R&D with active participation of the private sector. The extension focused on a case study in another value chain that followed the same procedures and explored opportunities to foster public–private partnerships in a third country, Honduras.

The objectives of the project were fully met and the results have been published (see appendices for abstracts of these papers). The main result of the project was the development of a procedure to support partnership building for agroindustrial innovation. During the second phase, proposals were made for innovation development within three agricultural value chains, and the actors in these chains are now in a position to further develop and use these proposals to establish partnerships.

Activities and achievements

Diagnostic phase

The first phase of the project screened the agroindustrial sectors in Costa Rica and El Salvador to identify existing initiatives in which public research and private-sector entities worked together in the generation of innovations. Activities included:
- Collecting information on the agroindustrial sector and the research sector in each country and identifying agrichains in which collaborative arrangements for innovation development existed;
- Conducting workshops to create awareness among stakeholders in agroindustrial innovation in the public and private sectors and to identify opportunities to study partnerships;
- Interviewing stakeholders involved in public–private partnerships and other relations between public and private organizations that aim at innovation development;
- Preparing two diagnostic reports that reviewed the agroindustries, the existing research capacity to support agroindustrial innovation, and the existing collaboration and partnership between public and private organizations for innovation development; and
- Holding two workshops in Costa Rica and El Salvador to disseminate the results (in the form of a report) of the first phase to stakeholders and to plan activities in the second phase to create and strengthen partnerships.

Through the interviews and diagnostics, a good picture of the potential of partnerships, and the constraints to such relationships, were identified. About 50 stakeholders in each country were interviewed. Some of the reasons partnerships for innovation development sometimes do not work include: lack of initiative from the private sector; researchers seek funding in areas of their own priority; lack of priorities and strategic planning in the public sector; no definition of common interests; differences in organizational culture between the public and private sectors; and lack of policies that enable and promote collaboration between the sectors (see Appendices 4.1 and 4.2).

Following the interviews with stakeholders in the agrichains, meetings (about 20 in each country) were held with key actors in government organizations, universities, and private-sector organizations to get a clearer picture of the context in which partnerships for agroindustrial R&D evolve. It became clear that public research institutes and universities eagerly search for means to collaborate with the private sector. However, private-sector companies, although eager to get access to R&D results, are not very willing to pay for this access. As a general rule, smaller companies, producers, and processors are less interested in R&D.

The resulting diagnostic reports are a valuable resource for those who seek information on agroindustry and research in the two countries. Two hundred hard copies were disseminated to stakeholders, and many more copies were distributed electronically. Overall, the project has had success in promoting the idea of public–private partnerships for agroindustrial R&D in Costa Rica and El Salvador.

The principal researchers also presented the results of their studies at an International Service for National Agricultural Research (ISNAR) workshop in Brasilia. During this meeting, the project team had the opportunity to learn from partnership experiences in other countries and to discuss theories and concepts of partnership building with a wider group of researchers involved in ISNAR's efforts to support public–private partnerships for agricultural research in Latin America.

Prospective phase

Initially, the second phase was designed to study financing and partnering arrangements for R&D in existing partnerships. However, during the first phase it was found that few partnerships existed that successfully responded to both public and private demands. Therefore, project activities were adjusted to focus on how to support the creation of successful partnerships. This phase involved actual support to partnership building and the study of this endeavour. On the basis of the diagnostics in the first phase, two agrichains were selected for the second phase – organic coffee in Costa Rica and loroco in El Salvador. In the extension phase, the potato agrichain was studied in Costa Rica. These agrichains were considered to provide fertile ground for the development of public–private partnerships based on the results of the first phase. In these chains, the two national teams supported the process of partnership building with a sequence of interventions:
- Participatory predefinition of potential topics for innovations during a national planning meeting with stakeholders in the three agrichains (researchers, producers, processors, representatives of government organizations, and development agencies);

- Mapping of the agrichains to define their actors, flows of products, value added, and margins in a study that drew on statistical data and information gathered from interviews and field visits;
- Development of an inventory of potential partners for innovation partnerships;
- Systematization of technological options during various roundtable meetings in Costa Rica and one in El Salvador in which experts discussed R&D topics that might lead to innovation-led growth in the agrichains;
- Further in-depth analysis of the technological options drawing on the information gathered in the roundtable meetings and from the literature; and
- Dissemination of the results at a workshop attended by potential partners in the agrichains. These actors crafted five proposals that are available now for further development and use as a blueprint for setting up partnerships.

These steps were followed in both countries, although there were some unique differences given the different contexts of the agrichains. In Costa Rica, the organic coffee chain is part of the larger coffee chain on which about 150,000 people depend (from producers to farm hands, input suppliers, processors, transporters, roasters, exporters, and supporting government agencies). Therefore, this sector is of paramount importance to the country. Organic coffee production accounts for less than 5% of the national production and has been ignored by the government institutions that provide support to the coffee sector through a 1.5% levy on all coffee sales. No investments in R&D on organic coffee production have been made except for some donor-funded support to farm management and the setting up of a cooperative through the Tropical Agricultural Research and Higher Education Centre (CATIE).

Legislation that obliges producers to process their coffee in large-scale processing plants deprives them of the advantage of direct marketing. However, organic coffee production has been increasing by 12% annually and continues to provide an attractive alternative to conventional coffee by guaranteeing higher prices and providing positive environmental effects. Because organic coffee production is still new to many producers, there is a desperate need for knowledge and information on issues of farm management, processing, and marketing, some of which have to be addressed through applied R&D. Given this background, partnerships between producers and processors and local research organizations and the university could focus critical resources on addressing the knowledge and innovation needs of the organic coffee chain.

In El Salvador, loroco is a traditional product. This greenish-colour flower is used to flavour traditional Salvadorian food, especially the maize tortilla called *pupusa*. The crop has traditionally been produced extensively by small-scale producer in mixed cropping systems. Recently, some larger producers have started to set up irrigated loroco plantations for export crops. Exports to the United States, where one third of all Salvadorians actually live, have high potential. Salvadorians abroad would like to have access to their traditional foods; however, criteria of quality and food sanitation must be met. These same criteria are also important for the local markets, where health problems from consumption can still occur. Small-scale farmers are less able to deal with these criteria and many also need to improve the cost efficiency of their loroco plots. Research organizations, because the levels of production and value are low, have not considered R&D on loroco, and no donor funds have been made available to address production, processing, and quality problems in the agrichain. Therefore, a partnership between local small-scale producers (providing work and their plantations as inputs) and research organizations has the potential to address knowledge and innovation problems in the agrichain.

The main difference between the approach in El Salvador and Costa Rica was that in El Salvador a territorial approach was adopted and only small farmers in one specific farming community in a prominent loroco production region were involved. The approach was successful in meeting the interests of many producers in the various meetings. Particularly interesting were the discussions between researchers from universities and government officials (both parties have not yet supported loroco farmers) and the farmers. For researchers and government officials it was healthy to listen directly to the farmers' problems and discuss with them activities that would actually help the farmers. However, poor organization among the farmers impeded the final proposal to carry out partnerships. Further efforts with regard to the loroco chain were developed by one of the project members, Partners in Rural Development (now Canadian Hunger Foundation). In Costa Rica, the aim was to include actors involved in organic coffee nationwide and find ways to build the organic coffee chain as a whole. Additional details on innovation development in these cases are presented in Appendices 4.4 and 4.5.

Additional activities

A six-month extension was granted by IDRC to examine the Costa Rican potato chain in an effort to determine its innovation needs, examine the potential for creating partnerships, and conduct a rapid appraisal of the Honduran agroindustry, agricultural R&D, and partnerships. The project held a final results dissemination workshop (in Honduras) to disseminate guidelines on partnership development to the policymakers in science and technology and agroindustry development from various Central American countries.

In El Salvador, two workshops were held to disseminate and discuss the results of the study on partnerships in the loroco chain. One focused on producers in San Lorenzo while the other focused on policymakers, research managers, and donors who could support partnerships for innovation development in general. Similar workshops were held in Costa Rica.

Six project reports have been prepared and distributed to policymakers and key actors in agrichain development and R&D management. These dissemination efforts were complemented by training and sensitization workshops, personal visits, and articles in journals and newspapers.

Potential impact

The project had many interactions with different actors on various levels. In the diagnostic study, at least 30 key actors in agroindustry development and R&D management were met for interviews. In addition, 70 key actors, especially from the coffee, loroco, and potato chains, attended information and planning workshops. In the second phase, 150 individuals in the coffee and loroco agrichains were contacted for interviews. Those actors are now better prepared to build partnerships for innovation development. An even larger group has been reached by the project's website and news service 'PPP News'. (Public–Private Partnerships).

To support the project activities, four students were hired. They helped to collect data, conduct interviews, prepare analytical reports, and organize workshops. Now, together with the principal researchers, they have the capacity to promote the ideas of the project and to conduct further chain analysis and partnership-building efforts using the methodology developed by the project.

Because both principal researchers also teach at local universities, the project theories and concepts have already filtered into course-work related to environmental project planning (University of Costa Rica) and agroindustry development (University of San Salvador). The project advisor has also provided various courses to audiences at the Faculty of Agriculture of the University of Costa Rica and the University of Peace.

In El Salvador, the Ministry of Finance was interested in having the project provide a training workshop on partnership building for agroindustry development, although the Ministry has not followed up on the idea. The project has also provided the National Council of Science and Technology with some attractive possibilities for institutional innovation in the science and technology sector. Elections were occurring when this report was written and this restricted activity. However, after the new government is in place, it will be important to further promote the project philosophy of building partnership for innovation development and to persuade officials in the Ministries of Finance, Science and Education, and Agriculture. The potential exists for partnership building to become a national policy in El Salvador.

In Costa Rica, activities are planned to provide the Instituto Nacional de Innovación y Transferencia de Tecnología Agropecuaria (INTA) with a methodology to negotiate partnerships with 12 private-sector organizations. Further interest exists in using the partnership-building approach in the new Ministry of Production in Costa Rica, which combines agricultural sector development with other parts of economic development.

The proposals developed for partnership building in the potato and organic coffee agrichain have a high potential of being further pursued by the actors involved and of receiving co-financing by third-party funding agencies. In El Salvador, the Canadian Hunger Foundation plans to follow up on the options identified and to fund development of the agroindustry cluster that includes loroco production and processing. In Costa Rica, participation in the last workshop to disseminate results of the organic coffee chain study was low; however, participation in the final potato chain meetings was more active. Public funds, which often are needed to supplement private contributions, will most likely be made available through competitive grant schemes for R&D and a World Bank project on Environmental Conservation in Costa Rica.

Constraints

During the first year of project activities, it was realized that interests in public–private partnerships are very diverse. The private sector is not homogeneous. It includes small producers aiming at artisan processing, large-scale entrepreneurs, and transnational companies. The expectations that these private actors have for research and innovation partnerships for agroindustry development are also different: small producers seek access to markets and improved product quality; processors seek cheaper primary products at constant quality and quantity to try to lower processing costs. Public interests, however, do not feature in partnerships as prominently as they should because the government sector often does not specify clearly how public money should be spent to bring about development and to what extent the private sector can receive subsidies for this purpose. In this scenario, sometimes self-interest within the research sector takes over and becomes the driving force in building research partnerships. This situation can result in an unjustified allocation of public funds to research.

There are many determinants in the building of partnerships that the project cannot control (e.g. changing market situations, funding opportunities, and difficult personal relationships between actors). However, the primary focus of this research project was to study how partnerships build and how partnership building can be supported. There is no guarantee, but a good chance, that the project's efforts in partnership building in the three agrichains will lead to successful partnerships and innovation.

Conclusions

This project entered an unexplored and challenging field, the building of partnerships in the context of innovation systems and agricultural value chains. The study of partnership building cannot be easily carried out with standard research methodology. Intense interaction with stakeholders was essential, and the products were not simple research findings but insights into the process needed to build and support partnerships.

The project has hit a thematic area that is at the top of the (agroindustrial) development agenda in Central America. Key actors in science and technology and agroindustry development, both from the public and private sectors, are eager to develop policies for innovation-led growth and to try to get public and private actors involved. Efforts to partner are the order of the day, and they feature in declarations made by both the government and private-sector associations. However, there is little knowledge on how to build public–private partnerships that respond successfully to both public and private needs.

The goal of the project, to come up with guidelines on how to build partnerships, was ambitious, but the objectives were practical and the activities were well defined. The guidelines and recommendations appear generic, but this is related to the fact that there is no blueprint for partnership building – everything depends on the process, which is influenced by the agricultural value chain, the actors, and the available capacity and resources. Further dissemination of the findings of the project will be crucial and indispensable for further impact. Dissemination will go beyond the traditional ways of disseminating research results to include an information campaign focused on policymakers and decision-makers in agrichain development and research management, and further efforts to coach concrete partnership-building efforts.

References

Quirós, O. and Hartwich, F. (2003) Alianzas público-privadas para la investigación y el desarrollo en cadenas agroindustriales: La situacion en Costa Rica. *ISNAR, Proyecto Alianzas Público-Privadas para la investigación Agroindustrial.* ISNAR/Canadian Hunger Foundation/IDRC, San José, Costa Rica.

Garza, J., Garza, S. and Hartwich, F. (2003) Alianzas público-privadas para la investigación y el desarrollo en cadenas agroindustriales: La situación en El Salvador. *ISNAR, Proyecto Alianzas Público-Privadas para la investigación Agroindustrial.* ISNAR/Canadian Hunger Foundation/IDRC, San José, Costa Rica.

Quirós, O., González, V., Hartwich, F. and Jiménez, A. (2004) Propuesta para la formación de alianzas público-privadas para innovación en agroindustria: Caso del café orgánico en Costa Rica. Informe de estudio. *ISNAR, Proyecto Alianzas Público-Privadas para la investigación Agroindustrial.* ISNAR/IDRC, San José, Costa Rica.

Garza, J., Villacorte, J.L., and Paniagua, M. (2003) Propuesta para la formación de alianzas público-privadas para innovación en agroindustria: Caso del loroco en El Salvador. *ISNAR, Proyecto Alianzas Público-Privadas para la investigación Agroindustrial.* ISNAR/IDRC, San José, Costa Rica.

Hartwich, F., Garza, J., and Quirós, O. (2003) Fortalecer Alianzas Público-Privadas para un Desarrollo Agroindustrial en Centro America: Una guía para colaboradores en innovación. *ISNAR, Proyecto Alianzas Público-Privadas para la investigación Agroindustrial.* ISNAR/IDRC, San José, Costa Rica.

Hartwich, F., Jiménez, A., Quirós, O., and Valladares, R. (2005) *Opciones de Formación de Alianzas de Innovación para mejorar la Competitividad en la Cadena de la Papa en Costa Rica.* ISNAR/IDRC, San José, Costa Rica.

Appendix 4.1: Public–private alliances for research and development of agroindustrial chains in Costa Rica

This paper discusses the costs and benefits of research and development partnerships and demonstrates that the intangible effects of partnerships, especially economic, social, and environmental effects, must be considered. Although a number of rules, regulations, and structures exist to enable partnerships between the public and private sectors, neither sector has the culture for developing and properly managing these partnerships.

Existing partnerships are mainly based on a service offered by public research institutes or universities that respond to specific needs of the agro-productive sector. In the existing partnerships, communication between the partners is complicated and becomes more complex as the number of actors in the partnership and agrichain increases. As the number of actors increases, the benefits also become more diluted, and the perception of benefits and their governance is not always clear to the partners.

Some partnerships have been initiated by farmers' organizations (e.g. in the potato sector). In other cases, agroindustry companies did not proactively seek partners, instead they chose to perform R&D by trial and error. In the case of potatoes, the Foro Nacional de la Papa and INTA partnered to produce improved seeds. In the case of the oil palm, the partnership addressed control of the 'red ring' disease. In the case of organic coffee, a partnership between six farmers' organizations aimed at marketing organic coffee as high-quality brands.

This study concluded that partnerships have not yet reached maturity. Misunderstandings still exist between the public and private sectors and between those funding and carrying out the research. There is also limited understanding of what constitutes a 'real' partnership. In real partnerships, partners should participate actively in both management and finance, there should be an equitable redistribution of the benefits generated, and the partnership should be evaluated periodically by both parties (public and private).

Appendix 4.2: Public–private alliances for research and development of agroindustrial chains in El Salvador

The characteristics of partnerships between public and private entities in this chapter are described on the basis of their: legal framework; financing; governance; results; technology transfer; and public and private benefits. Eight partnerships were identified that included private entities, such as cooperatives, farmers' associations, processing and exporting businesses, and government organizations such as the National Centre of Agricultural and Forestry Technology (CENTA), the National School of Agriculture (ENA), and the University of El Salvador (UES).

Most of the partnerships studied tended to favour private-sector interests – the private companies looked to take advantage of public technological, financial, and knowledge resources. Public-sector organizations (represented by government ministries, research centres, and universities) did not have well-defined priorities when they entered the partnerships. This poses significant risk because public interests are not clearly represented in the partnership.

The study also demonstrated that El Salvador lacks formal government policies for setting up public–private partnerships for R&D in the agriculture and agroindustry sectors. However, the productive sector and the research organizations have strong interests in partnering.

Appendix 4.3: Proposals for public–private R&D partnerships in the organic coffee industry in Costa Rica

This paper presents proposals for public–private partnerships for R&D to improve the competitiveness of the organic coffee sector in Costa Rica. Public–private partnerships are contractual agreements between public research institutes (research centres and universities) and the private sector (producers, processors, and exporters) to collaboratively conduct research to address innovation challenges. Partnership agreements usually address property rights, resource contributions, and risks in the development of innovations. Important prerequisites for partnerships are the identification of common objectives, active partners, interdependent and complementary contributions from the partners, equality among the partners, and agreed upon methods of operation. Public–private partnerships for innovation development in agriculture evolve within the framework of agrichains that which the economic agents that contribute directly to the production, processing, and distribution of an agricultural product until it reaches consumer markets.

The research included mapping of the agrichain to identify actors and product flows, and identification of technological options. Six steps were used to generate the proposals for partnerships in innovation development: (1) a participatory predefinition of potential topics for innovations; (2) mapping of the organic coffee chain; (3) an inventory of potential partners within the chain; (4) a listing of technological options; (5) analysis of the options; and (6) an awareness-creating workshop. Three outcomes were achieved.

Mapping of the organic coffee chain: The chain is still developing, and most producers are small-scale and organized in cooperatives. These producers make efforts to add value to their product, not only through processing but also through effective marketing. However, they need knowledge to make the processing and roasting of their coffee more efficient. It is not necessary to conduct research on all aspects of the agrichain. Rather it is important to review innovations in other countries and contexts and to complement this information with adaptive research and validation.

Analysis of technological options: After a review of existing knowledge, technological advances, private-sector demands, and validation and prioritization of technological options, three topics were identified for research partnerships between public and private entities: the structure of costs and gross margins to improve the management of organic coffee farms; improvement of soil fertility and microbiology; and biological pest control to improve cost effectiveness in production. These topics were analysed during round-table meetings. The analysis of costs and gross margins was identified as having the highest potential for partnerships. It was suggested that the focus on the other two topics should be on a systematization and diffusion of information already available from research.

Institutionalization of partnerships: Suggestions were made on how to institutionalize partnerships between research centres and private entities.

The research must be conducted at the research centres, but the private sector must assume direct control and provide not only financial but physical (use of land and equipment) contributions. Resources and knowledge are critical to the generation of innovations. Potential partners for different research topics, estimates of research costs, and a sample contract are also presented.

Appendix 4.4: Proposals for public–private R&D partnerships in the loroco industry in El Salvador

This paper presents proposals for public–private partnerships for R&D to improve the competitiveness of loroco production in El Salvador. Public–private partnerships are contractual agreements between public research institutes (research centres and universities) and the private sector (producers, processors, and exporters) to collaboratively conduct research to address innovation challenges. Partnership agreements usually address property rights, resource contributions, and risks in the development of innovations. Important prerequisites for partnerships are the identification of common objectives, active partners, interdependent and complementary contributions from the partners, equality among the partners, and agreed upon methods of operation. Public–private partnerships for innovation development in agriculture evolve within the framework of agrichains which include the economic agents that contribute directly to the production, processing, and distribution of an agricultural product until it reaches consumer markets.

Loroco is a traditional crop that is found in the wild and in home gardens. Although it has been reported from various Central American countries and the South of Mexico, it is only in El Salvador where it is consumed. Loroco production has recently been extended to meet the demands of both local and export markets. The private sector, especially owners of larger plantations, is seeking alternative technologies for production and processing. Development of the agrichain requires R&D on new and refined technologies in production, processing, and quality control.

Loroco production is scattered across the country in small plots. The knowledge and technology used to cultivate loroco has been developed by farmers through trial and error. CENTA has tried to systemize existing knowledge and technology, and larger producers and processors have developed a technology package for production that has identified promising varieties, developed good agricultural practices, and suggested proper postharvest technology.

To focus the study on real problems in an important production zone, San Lorenzo in Ahuachapan was identified because it is a disadvantaged area in terms of access to information, technology used on-farm, and distance to sales points. Interactions with local producers were used to identify and prioritize research topics. Proposals were developed by: (1) sensitizing the actors in the sector; (2) mapping the loroco chain (including a characterization and classification of actors involved, a flowchart of product quantities, and the values and margins of the different actors); (3) developing a vision for the future of the chain; (4) identifying technological constraints and problems (including a summary of existing knowledge and technological progress and options); (5) identifying potential partners; and (6) developing proposals for partnerships. By following these steps, four conclusions were reached:

- The overall value added by the agrichain is low in comparison with other crops in El Salvador; however, this can dramatically change if the sector embarks on exports to the United States;
- The potential of small-scale farmers to contribute to public–private partnerships, in both knowledge and resources, is very limited. The larger plantation owner may be much more inclined to contribute to collaborative innovation development but is less in need of innovation;
- To develop the chain, the main strategic goal was to position the product on the export market by adopting a rigorous orientation toward consumer preferences, which are usually related to taste, freshness, and proper product appearance; and
- Two most promising topics for innovation development are development of: technology and equipment to ensure the product meets quality criteria such as taste and texture; and integrated pest-management technology and soil-fertility improvement programmes that will lead to a manual of best practices in loroco production.

Appendix 4.5: A guide to strengthening public–private alliances for agroindustry development in Central America

This study was designed to determine how to build and strengthen public–private partnerships that contribute to innovations for the development of agrichains in Central America. Based on a review of existing approaches to building partnerships, a methodology was designed to support the building of partnerships for developing innovations in the loroco chain in El Salvador and the organic coffee chain in Costa Rica. Seven steps in building partnerships were distinguished: (1) exploring partnerships option; (2) identifying technological options; (3) identifying and selecting partners; (4) negotiating and designing partnerships; (5) implementing the partnerships according to the commitments made; (6) monitoring and evaluation; and (7) continuation or termination.

The study also analysed interventions that support the building of partnerships. These interventions are defined as the activity of a third party (that does not form part of the alliance) to support the creation and conduct of a partnership. The project identified, in a generic way, some tools that support the building of partnerships: (1) participatory predefinition of the subject of the partnership; (2) mapping of the agrichain for which the partnership seeks innovation; (3) identification of technological problems; (4) development of a strategic vision for the agrichain; (5) sorting of potential partners; (6) analysing technological options during roundtable meetings; (7) supporting negotiations; (8) developing the proposal; (9) formulating the partnership; and (10) developing evaluation tools.

In the two case studies (organic coffee in Costa Rica and loroco in El Salvador), an action research approach was adopted – the building of partnerships was studied while the project intervened in the building of these partnerships. These experiences in partnership building indicate that:
- Partnerships should be seen as a means for generating innovations, and not as an end in themselves. In the case of agricultural research, they are neither a means for privatizing government institutions, nor a way to transfer roles, responsibilities, and resources from the state to the private sector;
- Studies that identify bottlenecks and technological problems in agrichains (e.g. mapping agrichains, developing a vision for the agrichain, or identifying technological or market demands) are indispensable for setting up partnerships for the development of innovations that respond to problems in the agrichain;
- To identify the technological options that the partnerships will address and map the agrichain, participation of the actors in the agrichain is important. It is difficult to achieve representation and articulation of interests, and a mix of approaches (individual interviews, roundtable meetings, and consensus-building workshops) is needed to motivate

the different groups of actors, who often have different and opposing interests;
- Roundtable meetings are well adapted to discuss in-depth technological options, problem fields, research achievements, how technology can help solve problems, potential impacts, and necessary resources. The participation of four to seven specialists in the field is recommended;
- To identify technological options to be pursued by the partnership, a 'promoter', either an individual or organization that promotes and supports the partnership from the outside, but does not participate in it, is crucial;
- After the technological options have been identified, the presence of a 'partnership champion', an individual affiliated with one of the partners who usually has a broader vision of the development of the agrichain and the partnership, and who supports the partnership, motivates partners, and defends its partnership interests, is crucial;
- In the process of partnership building, actors are required who have the technical and intellectual capacity to contribute to the work of the partnerships. As well, leaders are required to take decisions and make the partnership evolve.

Appendix 4.6: Options for building innovation partnerships to improve the competitiveness of the Costa Rican potato chain

The potato sector in Costa Rica is currently facing the challenge of maintaining the efficiency, quality, and safety of its products, especially potatoes for the industrial fresh market. The growing frozen pre-fried potato market is completely dominated by imports. Market protection schemes with high import tariffs are one factor adversely affecting innovations. Higher prices at the farm and higher consumption rates will provide growers and processors with more incentives to reduce costs and thereby become more competitive internationally. In Costa Rica, however, potatoes continue to be a commodity that potentially could be exported to neighbouring countries with less suitable agronomic conditions, including Panama, Nicaragua, and the Caribbean countries.

With the recent opening of the agricultural markets (where potatoes continue to be among the most protected products), the actors involved in the agricultural chain are aware of the need to increase the competitiveness of Costa Rican potatoes. As a result, what prevails is a lack of innovations, which prevents the potato growers, processors, and marketers from increasing their competitiveness in Costa Rica. With the support of the potato programme put in place by the Ministry of Agriculture, some key actors of the chain, including researchers and agribusiness processors, as well as innovative farmers and seed potato growers, are seeking ways to respond to the low competitiveness.

In July 2004, the Public–Private Partnerships for Agroindustrial Research in Central America project sponsored by the ISNAR, a division of the International Food Policy Research Institute (IFPRI), began to work with actors in the chain to study innovation options within the chain through the creation of public–private partnerships.

This paper highlights the findings of the study and the coordinated actions taken by the actors involved in promoting innovation partnerships. The information is not addressed solely to actors in the agricultural chain (e.g. producers, processors, and researchers); it will also be useful as a case study for key actors in governments and donor agencies interested in promoting innovation partnerships. The methodology used stems from experiences gained in a previous PPP project implemented in Costa Rica and El Salvador. This approach can be summarized in a series of steps: development of a chain map; methodological arrangement of the proposed topics; chain analysis and prioritization of existing topics in workshops with actors in the chain; evaluation and simulation of costs and economic, social, and environmental benefits of the research options; review of the research options in a broad meeting with chain actors; development of a research proposal in partnership by means of a chain committee. After these stages were completed, two research topics were put forward to be developed in partnership:

- Assessment and selection of promising potato materials with potential for industrial use and fresh consumption in Costa Rica; and

- Research aimed at improving production cost-structure practices and profit margins in the potato business.

The findings of the cost–benefit analysis showed that, although the two proposed innovation options have a high development potential, the first one, designed for research on potato varieties, is the one with the most positive relation to costs and social benefits. This means that the society as a whole gains from the adoption of the technology. This calculation uses moderate assumptions on yield increases, resistance to pests, adoption rates, and positive effects in the processing procedures that result from the introduction of a new variety. The first option also has the highest potential for enhancing the competitiveness of the chain, given its possibilities for lowering costs and improving quality. It has also generated interest among actors in the public and the private sectors.

The public research sector, represented in this case by INTA and the Centro de Investigaciones Agronómicas (CIA) of the Universidad de Costa Rica (UCR), has the infrastructure and the trained staff necessary to respond to the concerns involved in the two proposed partnerships. However, the public sector also requires a better understanding of the challenges involved in working in partnerships and will, in addition, require funds to complement the efforts that these two organizations may carry out.

All the actors must work together to redefine their positions, using approaches that engage competitors, potential collaborators in research, and the public sector. This also includes a willingness to commit themselves not only for the action planning stages, but also for the implementation stage and its financing. Issues such as the low level of organization concerning interaction among the chain actors (e.g. sharing of information and product exchanges) are still preventing the emergence of a comprehensive vision. Both the producers and the industrialists require more guidance for creating partnerships by means of contractual schemes that allow for the identification and definition of responsibilities, structure, and follow-up in partnerships and in the planning of actions, commitment, and distribution of benefits and products.

The examination of the potato sector in relation to the research topics during the study prompted the creation of a partnership committee with representatives from the various sectors in the agricultural chain. What remains to be done now is the follow-up, to see whether the suggested ideas are well received and can be developed into partnerships, and whether these partnerships are going to promote research and speed up the transfer process at the level of the producers.

CHAPTER 5
Public–private research, development, and innovation in Peru

Juana Kuramoto and Máximo Torero

Abstract

> This study examines institutional policies for innovation and research and development in Peru by assessing their effect on the performance of firms. The main goal of this research proposal was to explore, from a developing-country standpoint, the ways in which knowledge is produced, communicated, and applied to development problems, to investigate the policy and institutional frameworks that govern this process and to identify if there is a bias toward research and development and innovation in Peru. The authors conclude that recognition of the importance of research and development and innovation is a recent phenomenon in Latin America (with the exception of Chile, Brazil, and Mexico), as reflected in low research and development expenditures in the region. The team recommends the strong need for investment policies that encourage externality generating activities, complementary policies that facilitate both the dissemination of knowledge and the entry and exit of multinational companies, free mobility of people and capital, links between firms and universities and between industry and local research, and the development of funds for research and development.

Latin American countries were affected by severe economic and political crises during the 1980s. As a result, mechanisms for resource allocation were truncated, which caused an imbalance between financial and physical investment. In addition, market demand was reduced due to market contraction, which had negative effects on the innovation activities of firms.

The crises also affected the public sector. Public institutions experienced budget cuts that undermined their performance. Science and technology (S&T) institutions, including universities, were most damaged. Human capital fled to the private sector or migrated to other countries. Furthermore, the scarce links between these institutions and the private sector disappeared as economic conditions hindered all demand for S&T services.

Peruvian economic reforms in the 1990s stabilized the economy and provided a good climate for private and foreign investment, which was enhanced by the government's commitment to privatization. These reforms encouraged modernization of industries such as mining, telecommunications,

106 FUELLING ECONOMIC GROWTH

and energy generation. No special incentives were provided for manufacturing, and traditional industrial branches remained depressed. Internal demand remained weak, and the diminished competitiveness of existing firms impeded their access to foreign markets.

The situation of S&T institutions did not change after the economic reforms. Foreign firms that did invest imported all capital equipment and knowledge-intensive services. As well, the limited growth of industry hampered demand for domestic science and technological services. This paper addresses important questions with respect to R&D strategies. It also examines experiences in several countries to better understand how poor countries like Peru can maximize the benefits of R&D.

Methodology

Three types of analyses were undertaken: a macro review of the initial conditions of innovation and R&D, and the institutional policies of innovation and R&D in Peru; an assessment of the impact of R&D and innovation on the performance of firms; and detailed case studies.

Macro review

In-depth interviews at universities, research institutes, firms, and government agencies and a detailed literature review of previous work on S&T in Peru and other developing countries were carried out to answer the following questions:
- What is the current institutional framework for R&D and innovation in Peru?
- What is the current knowledge supply to universities and technical institutes?
- What are the main sources of innovation and R&D?
- What kinds of complementarities exist between public- and private-sector research expenditures?
- What has been the experience to date with public–private research partnerships, both at the national and international level, and what lessons can be drawn?

This macro overview helped to understand the ways in which knowledge is produced, communicated, and applied to development problems, and to investigate the policy and institutional frameworks that govern this process.

Innovation and R&D impacts

A database developed in August 2000 by the Peruvian Consejo Nacional de Tecnología (CONCYTEC) was used for this analysis. This survey, which was representative country-wide, by economic sector,[1] and by size (small, medium, and large enterprises), collected information on S&T indicators for 8,976 firms.

This dataset allowed us to determine, from the perspectives of the firms, whether investments in R&D and access to innovations were desirable in terms of their performance. The Boubakri and Cosset approach (1998) was used to determine whether firms increased their performance (measured by their operating efficiency, output, and employment). In addition, we also examined whether the source of the expenditures on R&D (e.g. own, private firms, government, public and private universities, or foreign firms) had an impact on the performance of firms.

The empirical strategy included a statistical analysis to understand both the process of innovation in firms and the performance change among firms that invest and do not invest in R&D. A regression analysis was used to isolate the impact of R&D and to model whether firms invest, the intensity of investment, and the impact of investment on performance.

Case studies

Two case studies, one in the mining industry and the other in agriculture, complemented the cross-section study. They provided insights into: the process of innovation and adoption; the institutional, legal, and regulatory framework; and the types of incentives that encourage firms to invest more actively in R&D and therefore to innovate. The advantage of analysing these two sectors is that they have different sources of R&D, different strategies, and different institutional frameworks.

Results

Where do Peru and Latin America stand in innovation and R&D?

Latin America is a latecomer in recognizing the importance of research and development and innovation. Figure 5.1 presents R&D expenditures of three groups of countries: low-income Latin American countries; lower and middle-income Latin American countries; and high-income OECD countries. Latin America, and especially the poorer Latin American countries, expends a lot less on R&D than high-income countries.

The United States expends approximately 2.67% of its GNP on R&D, i.e. its investment is about US$247,000 m and Canada invests about 1.5% of GNP, i.e. $12,744 m. In comparison, levels of expenditure for larger Latin American countries (Argentina, Brazil, and Mexico) are less than 1% of their GNP. The level is less than 0.1% of GNP for the smaller countries. Specifically for Peru, expenditures in R&D only represent 0.08% of GNP.

Brazil, Mexico, and Argentina account for more than 85% of R&D expenditures in the region. Brazil has the highest share and Peru has the lowest.

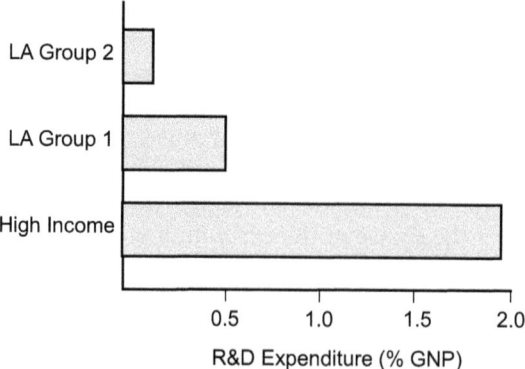

Figure 5.1 R&D expenditures (as a percentage of GNP in 1997) of three groups of countries. High Income includes Norway, Germany, Austria, United States, France, Finland, Canada, Italy and Spain; LA Group 1: Argentina, Brazil, Chile, Mexico, Costa Rica, Peru and Colombia; LA Group 2: El Salvador, Ecuador, Bolivia, and Nicaragua.
Source: RICyT, 1990–99; WDI, 2002.

Peru has spent $31 m in R&D, which is about 5% of Brazil's expenditure and 0.35% of the total expenditure in the region.

Figure 5.2 shows both R&D expenditure as a percentage of GNP and GNP per capita. There is a strong positive relationship between R&D expenditure and GNP per capita.

Figure 5.3 combines GNP growth with GNP per capita and R&D expenditures. The figure is divided in four quadrants to identify countries with high and low

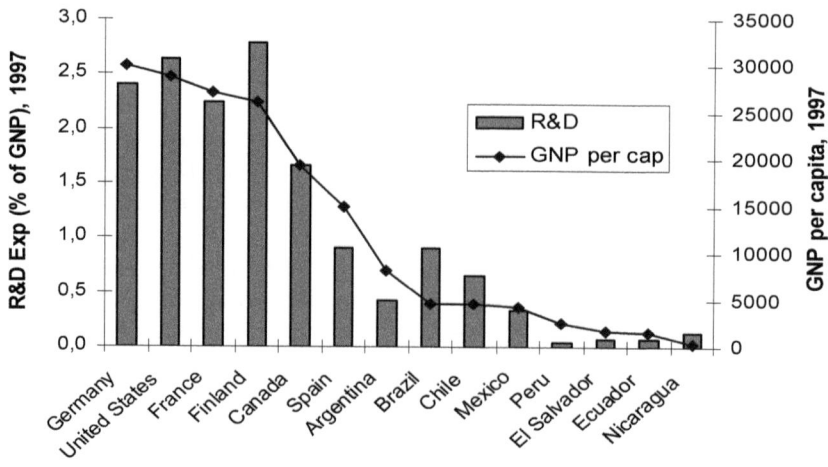

Figure 5.2 1997 R&D expenditures (% of GNP) and GNP per capita (constant 1995 US$)
Source: RICyT, 1990–99 and WDI, 2002

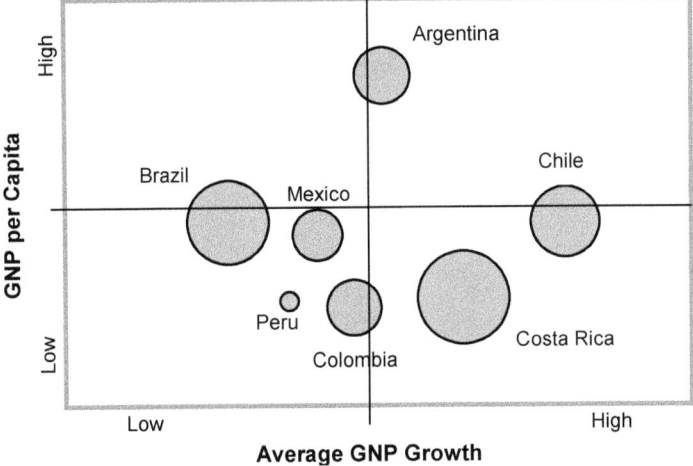

Figure 5.3 R&D expenditures (% GNP) and GNP per capita in 1997
Source: RICyT, 1990–99 and WDI, 2002

GNP per capita and show their corresponding GNP growth. Peru, Mexico, and Colombia have low GNP per capita and low GNP growth, whereas, Costa Rica has low GNP per capita but high GNP growth.

The circle reflects the amount of R&D expenditure as a percentage of GNP. Countries with very low expenditures on R&D, such as Peru, Colombia, and Mexico, have low GNP per capita and low growth; whereas, countries like Chile with high levels of expenditures in R&D are characterized by high GNP growth. The exception is Brazil, which has the highest R&D expenditures according to its high GNP per capita, but has low GNP growth. An analysis of the share of R&D expenditure by source shows that in industrialized countries (e.g. USA, Canada, and Spain), the highest share of R&D expenditure comes from the private sector (Table 5.1).

In Peru, the government has remained a dominant source of R&D expenditure, although, more recently, there has been a change in the composition of R&D expenditures. In 1980, firms only contributed 2.2% (Arregui and Torero, 1991); whereas, in 1999, firms contributed 42%, universities 30%, and research institutions 28% (CONCYTEC, 2001). It is important to note that firms contributed 20% of basic research budgets, 47% of applied research budgets, and 89% of development expenditures (CONCYTEC, 2001).[2]

Measuring innovative potential

Warner (2000) constructed an index, called the economic creativity index, to bring together several important aspects of innovation and technology

Table 5.1 Source of R&D expenditures (expressed as percentages)
Source: RICyT, 1990–99

	Government	Private sector	Universities	Not-for-profit	Foreign
Core group*					
Argentina, 1999	40.4	26.0	29.1	1.9	2.6
Brazil, 1996	57.2	40.0	2.8	0.0	0.0
Chile, 1999	64.3	21.5	7.3	0.0	6.8
Colombia, 1997	70.0	13.0	14.0	3.0	0.0
Costa Rica, 1996	53.4	17.4	14.8	4.5	9.9
Mexico, 1997	71.1	16.9	8.6	0.9	2.5
Peru, 1999	27.8	42.3	29.8		n.a
Venezuela, 1997	31.5	44.8	23.7	0.0	0.0
Developed countries					
Canada, 1999	24.4	49.2	9.8	2.8	13.8
Spain, 1998	42.7	49.8	0.0	0.8	6.7
Portugal, 1997	68.2	21.2	1.5	2.9	6.1
Other Latin American countries					
Bolivia, 1999	24.0	20.0	30.0	16.0	10.0
Ecuador, 1998	90.6	0.0	0.0	0.5	8.9
El Salvador, 1998	51.9	1.2	13.2	10.4	23.4
Uruguay, 1999	9.4	35.6	47.1	0.0	7.9

* For Argentina, Peru, and Venezuela, data are for S&T; for Peru, the first figure is for government and the not-for-profit sector together.

transfer and diffusion. This index is an average of two indices: the technology transfer index and the start-up index.

The technology transfer index is based on survey questions that capture pure innovation activity and international technology transfer. Because countries can obtain technology either by producing it or by importing it, Warner measured an overall technology index after scaling both components in similar units. The key idea is that countries get credit on the technology index for either innovation or technology transfer. What is important is that a country uses the newest technologies and innovations; it does not matter if it designs the innovation itself.

The ability to revive firms or start new enterprises is captured through an index of start-ups. The index is an average of two factors: whether financing is available, and whether it is easy to start a new business. The availability of financing is measured by averaging responses to two questions: whether venture capital is available for risk-taking entrepreneurs, and whether it is easy to get a loan with a good business plan but little collateral. The ease of starting a new business assesses the firm's capability to renovate technologies according to the institutional framework.

The economic creativity index ranges from –2 to +2. The average index of economic creativity for industrial countries is 0.92; whereas, the average index for developing economies is –0.19. The gap is observed in all subcategories involved in the economic creativity index, although it is more significant in the case of innovation (0.89 for industrial countries and –0.57 for developing countries). The economic creativity index for East Asia is 0.32; whereas, the creativity index for Latin America is –0.75.

Chong (2001) noted that most Latin American countries, with the exceptions of Chile, Brazil, and Mexico, rank low in terms of economic creativity. Innovation plays a major role in the economic creativity index of most developed economies. The top economies show high levels in innovation. In comparison, all countries in Latin America display negative scores (i.e. below the world average). Costa Rica and Chile are the Latin American leaders in this category; whereas, Bolivia, El Salvador, Peru,[3] and Ecuador are the poorest performers in terms of innovation. Unlike Latin America, not all the countries of East Asia register negative scores: Singapore and Taiwan are remarkably high (Figure 5.4).

Although innovation is the major force behind economic creativity in industrial countries, technological transfer plays a more important role in the developing world and in Latin America in particular (see Figure 5.4). Peru moves from position 54 out of 59 in the innovation index to position 40 in the technology transfer index. However, the overall scores for Latin America are negative for both innovation and technology transfer.

This implies that there is a lack of ability to adapt new technologies in the region, either by developing them or by assimilating those developed by others. Once again, Peru is ranked in position 54 of 59 countries for which the index was constructed. This is different to the situation in East Asia, where despite the innovation index being negative (although less than the one for Latin America) the technology transfer score is positive. This confirms that in East Asia, adaptations of existing technologies have played a key role

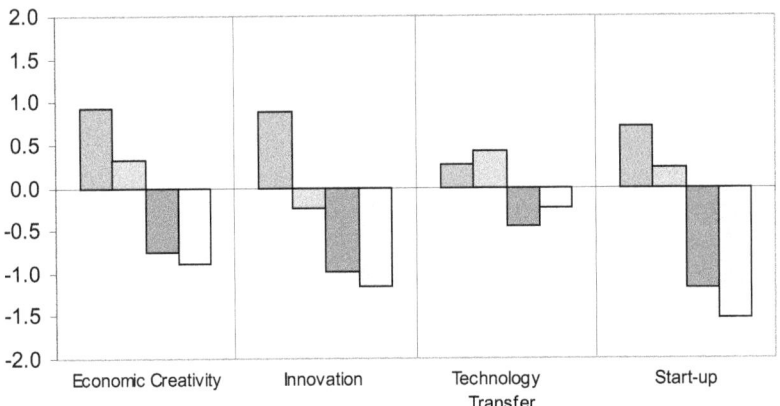

Figure 5.4 Economic creativity and its components
Source: Regional classification comes from World Bank, 2001

in economic creativity. This is an important experience from which Latin American countries can learn.

Economic creativity and innovation depend not only on the ability to adapt technologies, but also on the ability of firms to adapt them, which is captured by the ease of starting new enterprises (Warner's start-up index). This index shows that Latin American countries are even further behind developed countries than indicated by the innovation index. The reasons for this situation in Latin America include inappropriate and very expensive regulations to create firms, tight labour regulation codes, lack of credit, shallowness of capital markets, and lack of adequate infrastructure. Even more importantly, there is a lack of adequate institutional capital (adequate protection of property rights, independent judiciary system, and strong regulatory institutions), which negatively impacts the ability to start up new firms.[4]

Robustness of innovation indicators

These global measures of innovation and creativity are relevant, but they are based on subjective surveys that can be criticized for lack of comparability across countries and for having self-reporting biases. Nevertheless, different innovation indicators, such as Internet hosts, number of personal computers, telephones, and other information and communication technologies (ICTs), are highly correlated with this innovation and creativity index.

In fact, the correlation between information technologies and economic creativity is high, although it is higher for industrial than for developing countries. For the 49 countries[5] included by Warner (2000), significant correlations were formed between the economic creativity index and the density of telephone lines (0.77), cellular phones (0.76), Internet hosts (0.62), and personal computers (0.82). In Latin American countries the correlations were 0.62 for telephone lines, 0.54 for cellular phones, 0.48 for personal computers, and 0.84 for Internet hosts.

In general, the Internet is highly correlated with innovation, start-up of new business, and even technological transfer. The Internet is a useful proxy of economic creativity in the developing world, and in Latin America in particular. When evaluating the impact of innovation on firm performance, Internet access can be used as a proxy of innovation.

When analysing the availability of ICTs in Latin America, it is clear that Peru, similar to R&D expenditures, lags behind in terms of number of Internet hosts, personal computers, and telephones (Figure 5.5). After privatization in Peru, the number of telephones per hundred inhabitants increased from 2.7 to 6.6, and the number of Internet hosts increased from 1 per 1,000 inhabitants in 1994 to 39 per 1,000 inhabitants in 2000. The number of personal computers per 1,000 inhabitants increased from 1.49 in 1995 to 4.09 in 2000, and the number of personal computers per 100 white-collar workers increased from 5.48 in 1995 to 14.19 in 2000. However, similar to other ICT indicators, this represents one of the lowest scores in Latin America.

Because availability of ICTs complements scientific productivity, low levels of R&D allocations, coupled with the restricted availability of ICT infrastructure, have destined Peru to be less competitive than other countries in the region.

Technological innovation systems in Peru

The poor innovation performance of Peru is a direct result of a lack of understanding and interest in the role of S&T in economic development.[6] This is not a new situation. Peru has lagged behind other countries in the region in developing a scientific and technological institutional framework and designing promotion policies.

It was only in the late 1960s that the Consejo Nacional de Investigación (CONI) was funded. During the 1970s, various technology-related institutions were created: the Instituto de Investigación Tecnológica Industrial y de Normas Técnicas (ITINTEC); the Instituto Tecnológico Pesquero del Perú (ITP); and the Instituto Nacional de Investigación y Normalización de la Vivienda (ININVI). Later, CONI became the Consejo Nacional de Tecnología (CONCYTEC) to 'link the State with the scientific and technological community' (Flit and Barrio, 1994). However, like in many countries in Latin America, it was impossible to forge that link or to connect the scientific community with the productive sector. Neither was it possible to set a research agenda that corresponded to the needs of vast sections of the population nor to transmit knowledge within the scientific and technological community.

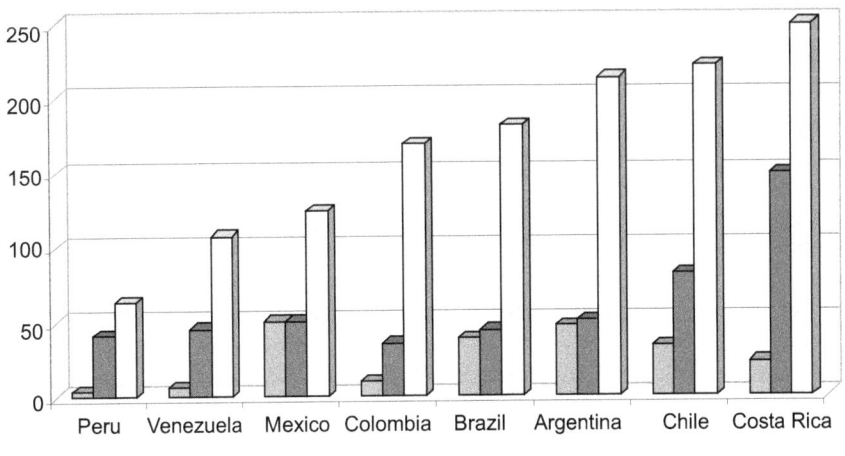

Figure 5.5 A regional comparison of the availability of ICTs in 2000
Source: WDI, 2002

The idea of TIS (Technological Innovation System) was recently adopted in the 2002 General Law of Promotion of Science and Technology for National Development. However, the belief appears to be that links among the different agents of the TIS can be created through a decree: 'The National System of Science, Technology and Innovation (SINACYT) is created as an open, non-exclusive, institutional space, whose components are all programmes, projects, and S&T activities developed by public, private, associative, or individual institutions or entities' (CONCYTEC, 2002).

CONCYTEC appears to have the mistaken view that a TIS is a mega institution that has a central unit for management support where different actors such as research or innovation centres, firms, NGOs, and funding agencies can take part. Accordingly, 'this participation will be ruled by a regime which includes qualification and register norms' (CONCYTEC, 2002).

In Peru, there is a series of institutions with scarce research and innovation capacities that have limited links among themselves or with other agents such as firms. There is also a complete lack of explicit policies to promote technological innovation or to support the formation of highly trained human resources. However, there have been some advances in the provision of technological services for firms, especially for small- and medium-size ones, and some financial mechanisms have been created for technical assistance.

Sagasti (2003) believes there is no such thing as a Peruvian TIS. However, there are institutions dedicated to S&T activities that may not be effective and that respond to misleading incentives. Mullin Consulting (2002) acknowledged the existence of a very fragmented TIS, whose parts do not interact in a constructive way but rather compete among themselves.

Firms

The 1980s economic crisis hindered private investment and severely damaged manufacturing firms, which responded by reducing the size of their productive units. Most Peruvian firms (96%) have 10 or less workers. These firms usually sell their products in the domestic black market,[7] thus they cannot access formal credit.

Small firms have scarce technological capabilities and seldom demand technological services. Robles et al. (2001) reported that on average 7 out of 10 microfirms in manufacturing, metalworking, and informatics services know of the existence of entrepreneurial development services,[8] but only 5 out of 10 have used them. However, this study noted that almost all microfirms in informatics services (i.e. internet coffee bars, computer assembly, and software creation) know about the existence of these entrepreneurial services (99%) and more than 80% have used them.

The openness of markets during the 1990s affected state-owned firms. Many firms that performed some research and development were privatized and acquired by foreign firms, which get their technological inputs from abroad. However, the vast majority of medium-size firms disappeared. This loss represents an important segment of firms with technological capabilities.

Of the remaining large- and medium-size firms, few see innovation as different from investment, which is associated with the expansion of productive capacity. Beside the firms that sell mainly to foreign markets, few understand that innovating new products and processes is necessary to gain new markets. For this reason, few firms will be able to take advantage of new trade agreements recently signed by Peru.[9]

The configuration of the Peruvian industrial sector makes relationships among firms, and the possibility of developing productive chains, difficult. Large firms operate with high technical standards; whereas, the small firms operate with obsolete technologies, lack management tools, and have poor quality standards. For example, the mining sector demands most of its inputs and services directly from foreign suppliers.[10]

According to CONCYTEC (2001), of 8,976 firms surveyed, only 9% invested in technology not embedded in capital. Of these, 61% acquired technological services, 20% technological licences, 10% trademarks, and 5% standardization and quality-control services. Despite these low figures, they do indicate an incipient demand and a willingness to pay for technological services.

Government

The government is an important component of a TIS because of its capacity to: formulate policies aimed at overcoming market failures that restricts technological innovation; assign resources for research and development programmes in government institutions; provide infrastructure; and establish systems to regulate the operation of firms. Edwards (2001) argues that the main factors that determine innovation and assimilation of technologies are education, a good institutional environment, access to credit, adequate infrastructure, and to some extent openness.

The Peruvian government has not formulated a coherent scientific and technological policy. Besides the legal framework that supported the creation of different scientific and technological organizations, policies have been designed to promote technological innovation in the productive sector. Even recently, the focus has been on formulating a National Plan of Science and Technology and on generating research programmes and projects that can be executed by public institutions. This scope implicitly disregarded the participation of the private sector. At the sectoral level, the few incentives to promote technological activities were incentives to import capital goods. The lack of policy instruments reflects the lack of technology-management capabilities in the public sector. The formulation of policies has been, and still is, in the hands of Peruvian scientists who are dedicated to basic research but have little knowledge of the interactions needed to transfer the results of basic research to the productive sector.

The government has not even formulated 'horizontal' policies, such as education policy, which is known to be important to increase productivity (Chong, 2001) and the capability for innovation. More educated workers are more able to devise more efficient ways to work. A skilled labour force plays a crucial role in taking advantage of the potential of new innovations, whether locally or externally developed.

Educational attainment in Latin America lags behind attainment in other regions (Barro and Lee, 2000). Duryea and Pages (2002a) note that average years of schooling attained by the population older than 25 in Latin America was approximately 6 years in 2000; whereas, the average was 11 years in the United States, Canada, and Sweden. However, when analysing the average years of education among the total population, Peru is ranked close to Taiwan, Chile, and Argentina.

The availability of skilled workers can be approximated by using the percentage of the population who has completed at least secondary schooling (Barro and Lee, 2000). Despite the percentage of skilled workers in South Korea, Taiwan, the United States, Canada, Japan and Sweden being at least twice that of Latin American countries, Peru, Argentina, Panama and Chile had rates over 30%, which are close to those of Taiwan and Japan. Therefore, Peru and other Latin American countries are above the average in terms of educational attainment and have a significant percentage of skilled labour. However, despite a significant improvement in enrolment in recent years, the quality of education shows a completely different picture.

There are scarce quality-assurance measures in Latin American schools, but all suggest that the quality of schooling in the region is very low. Only a few countries participate regularly in internationally comparable achievement tests, which makes comparisons across countries and regions very difficult (Duryea and Pages, 2002a). However, on the few occasions when Latin American countries have participated, students have performed below other countries, particularly those in East Asia. There is also wide inequality within the region.

Figure 5.6 shows the ranking of Peru and other Latin American countries in terms of the first regional comparable test in the subjects of Language and Mathematics for the third and fourth level of primary education. Peru's scores were among the worst of the countries included in the study, and Chile was among the best performers in the region.[11]

A large percentage of educated workers earn wages below poverty levels. Duryea and Pages (2002b) show that in Peru 46% of workers with some secondary education and 19% of workers with 4 years of university education earn very low wages. These percentages are similar in Nicaragua and Bolivia. However, in Chile these numbers are substantially smaller, 21% and 2%, respectively, and are similar in Argentina and Costa Rica. This result also explains why returns to primary and secondary education[12] are high in countries like Peru, given that they are measured in percentages (i.e. the final impact on absolute wages depends on the base to which that percentage applies, which in the case of Peru is very little).

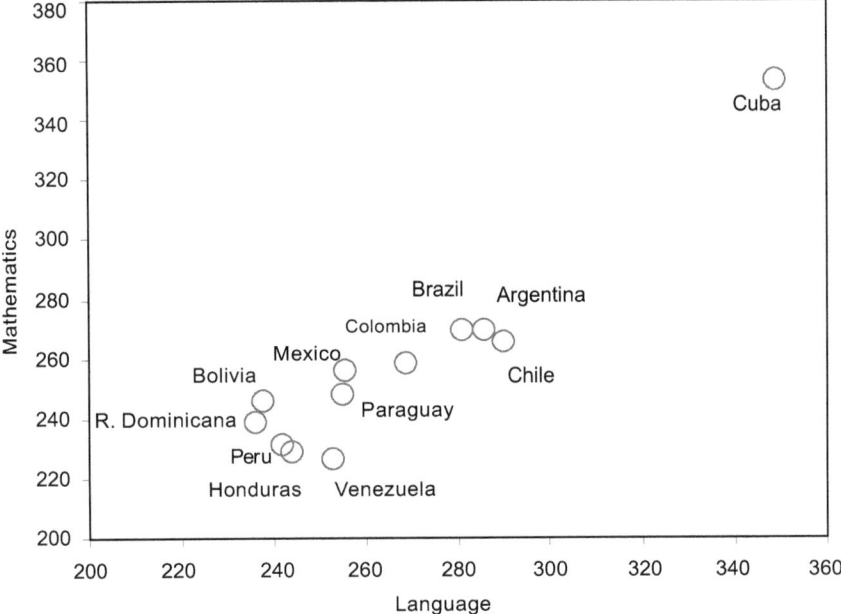

Figure 5.6 The relative quality of third and fourth levels of primary education
Source: UMC, Ministerio de Educación del Perú, Bulletin No. 9

Institutional environment

Improving educational attainment in Peru and other countries of the region would help to boost innovation, which in turn would foster more productivity (Acemoglu, 2002). However, workers will not be able to use their skills productively if the economic and institutional environment is not appropriate. This environment must include a good bureaucracy, clear property rights, and institutions and resources to enforce them, control of corruption, and good rule of law.

This institutional environment is clearly lacking in Peru and many other Latin American countries. Although the global index of public institutions registers Peru in position 45, several other indicators negatively affect the competitiveness of the country. For example, Peru is ranked in position 71 out of 75 countries in terms of the red tape required to open a firm; and in the indicator of trust of politicians, Peru is in position 74, just above Zimbabwe (Table 5.2).

In terms of property rights protection, Peru is ranked 56. These rights are essential to protect the significant costs of research and development required for new products or processes. If there are no clear property rights, then the incentive to develop knowledge is weakened. In Latin America, mainly Brazil, Mexico, and Argentina have realized this situation and taken actions to protect intellectual property rights.

Table 5.2 Competitiveness in the institutional environment (The Global Competitiveness Report 2001–2)

Institutional capital	
Judiciary independence	73
Corruption of public institutions	30
Trust of politicians	74
Competence of public servants	60
Organized crime	57
Property-rights protection	56
Institutional change costs	68
Informal sector	65
Governmental capital	
Government expenditures	18
Marginal tax rate to entrepreneural income	24
Not reported benefits and salaries	42
Fiscal evasion	53
Red tape requirements to register a new firm	71
Number of days needed to open a new firm	54

As a result, there has been a significant increase in the number of patents applied for by residents and nonresidents in these countries compared with other countries in the region (Figure 5.7).

Labour relations and regulations also affect productivity. By defining a set of rules that govern employment, labour relations can stimulate high motivation, high effort, and high productivity, or instead, can promote low morale and poor outcomes (Duryea and Pages, 2002a). The quality of labour relations and regulations is generally poor in Latin America. In terms of labour regulations, Heckman and Pages (2000) show that mandated benefits

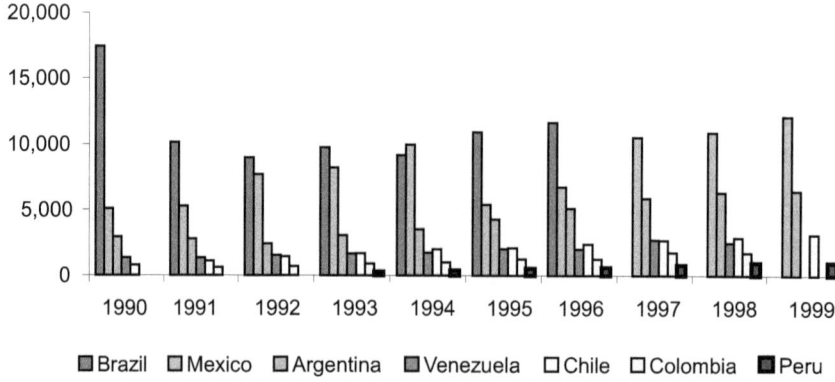

Figure 5.7 Patents applications by residents and nonresidents (1990–99)
Source: Indicadores RICyT, 1990–99

and job security regulations have a substantial impact on employment and turnover rates in Latin America. They also show that job security provisions are an inefficient way to provide income security to workers and that they can increase inequality.[13]

Contradictorily, Latin American countries, job security contributions constitute more than 85% of the total costs of labour regulations, Peru being one of the countries with the highest costs despite the reforms carried out during the 1990s.

In summary, there is a clear need for an institutional regime that assures information disclosure, transparency, accountability, and rule of law, and for government structures and functions that address issues of governance and the reduction of corruption.

Openness

Openness is another potentially important factor in innovation and technological absorption (Global Competitiveness Report, 2000). Open economies have access to the latest machinery and equipment and, therefore, to the latest technologies (Chong and Zanforlin, 2002). In a globalized economy, openness is essential to be able to access the latest technologies and to allow the free flow of ideas needed to develop a knowledge-based economy.

Access to credit and funding of S&T

A major bottleneck for productivity and growth in Latin America is the scarcity of credit. The supply of private credit as a proportion of GDP in the region is only a third of what is found in developed countries and Southeast Asia (IADB, 2001).

In developed countries, financial markets are well developed, access to credit is easy and fast, and creative financial instruments exist.[14] However, in Latin America financial development and access are quite limited, and there is a huge need for financial institutions to specialize in start-ups and venture capital.[15] In the index of access to external finance through banks and the bond market developed by Warner (2000), Peru ranks 41 of 59 countries; whereas, Chile and Brazil rank 21 and 34, respectively.

The reforms of the 1990s in countries like Peru increased access to credit, although the most severe institutional deficiencies remained – the lack of protection for financial creditors, various forms of interference by governments in financial markets, and uncertain legal frameworks. In addition, banks have significantly higher operational costs in relation to their gross margins: 80% in Peru, 60.8% in Chile, and 74.3% in Brazil.

Direct government funding for S&T is poor in Peru. According to the Ministry of Economics and Finance, the budget assigned to S&T institutions during 1994–98 was on average 0.25% of GDP, without including the budget assigned to universities. When universities are included, the budget averaged

0.80% of GDP, which is almost the same as the largest countries in Latin America (e.g. Argentina, Brazil, and Mexico). However, these figures are clearly overestimated because they include administrative costs and reflect the total appropriations given to these institutions. They do not reflect the actual execution of programmes and projects. The adjusted figure provided by the Inter American Network for Science and Technology (RICyT) is just 0.08% of GDP, which is far lower than average for a medium-income country like Peru.

Peru is still struggling to launch a Science and Competitiveness Fund (FONCYC) backed by a loan from the Inter American Development Bank. FONCYC will channel about US$35 million into: innovation projects presented by firms; S&T projects presented by universities and research institutions; the strengthening of S&T capacities; and the strengthening of the technological innovation system. These are competitive grants, and incentives have been designed to encourage projects that foster links among firms, universities, and other research institutions. Another fund, the Research and Development Fund for Competitiveness, will provide about $63 m to support the private sector. These two funds will complement isolated initiatives funded by cooperative agencies such as INCAGRO, which funds agricultural research in firms.

Provision of infrastructure

Peru, in common with most Latin American countries, has an inadequate and insufficient infrastructure that is concentrated in a few metropolitan areas. With the exception of Chile, Mexico, Brazil, and Argentina, there are few paved roads, inefficient ports,[16] and low penetration of telecommunications[17] in most countries (Table 5.3).

In addition, utility prices, particularly electricity and telephone services, remain high despite intense restructuring and privatization during the 1990s (Figure 5.8). Latin America has been a leader in the restructuring of the electricity sector, but these reforms have not been consolidated throughout the region. In many countries, competition remains limited and prices high. The regulatory systems have been criticized for their lack of transparency and their lack of legal and institutional framework within which regulatory systems must function. Much work remains to increase competition and improve infrastructure, given that this is an essential precondition for growth in productivity.

Regulatory function

The regulatory function of the Peruvian government is disperse, there is no coherent national system of standards and norms, and there is a lack of technical personnel. As a result, the country performs poorly in international meetings that discuss the use of standards as a way to regulate international trade. The country also has problems in applying international standards to domestic products, which is a constraint to penetrating international markets.

PUBLIC–PRIVATE RESEARCH, DEVELOPMENT, AND INNOVATION IN PERU 121

Table 5.3 Indicators of infrastructure in Latin America
Sources: for telecommunications ITU; for water and sanitation World Bank and OPS-OMS (Organización Panamericana – Organización Mundial de la Salud) (Evaluation 2000, and for roads World Bank).

Country	Telecommunications			Water and sanitation		Electricity		Roads	
	Fix lines per 100 people[1]	Cellular lines per 100 people[1]	Investment (million US$)[2]	Population with access to potable water (%)[2]	Population with access to sanitation (%)[2]	Electricity loss (% of output)[3]	Consumption (KW per capita)[3]	Roads, total network (km)[3]	Roads, paved (% of total roads)[3]
Chile	23.90	34.02	1101.0	94	97	5.48	2309	79353	18.9
Brazil	21.69	16.66	8852.5	87	77	17.29	1811	1726854	5.6
Argentina	21.63	18.61	1904.0	79	85	14.78	1938	215471	29.4
Colombia	17.05	7.38	1156.6	91	85	23.89	772	112988	14.4
Mexico	13.48	20.06	5082.2	86	73	14.36	1570	329532	32.8
Venezuela	11.20	26.35	293.5	84	74	23.35	2493	96155	33.6
Ecuador	10.37	6.67	44.5	71	59	22.79	620	43197	18.9
Peru	7.75	5.92	429.9	79	66	12.05	654	72900	12.8
Bolivia	6.04	8.74	109.6	77	76	17.85	390	53628	6.4

[1] Year 2001. [2] Year 2000. [3] Year 1999.

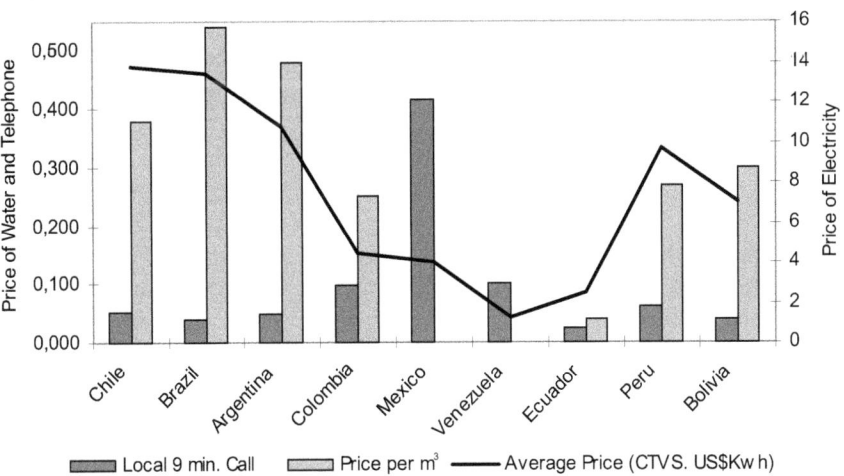

Figure 5.8 Costs of infrastructure
Note: Telephone costs are a weighted average of regular and reduced rates for a local 9-minute call within the same exchange area. Electricity costs are the residential average price between January 1994 and March 1998.
Source: Tarifica, World Bank, and OPS-OMS Evaluation 2000

As well, the system of national laboratories is not accredited at an international level, which is a major weakness (Mullin Consulting, 2002).

Research and technology institutions

Traditional

The vast majority of research and technology institutions are public entities created during the 1970s and 1980s to provide support for targeted industrial branches. These institutions were grouped under the National Centre for Research and Science, Technology and Innovation Services.[18]

Most of these institutions are funded by the central government, which means that they have limited financial resources to fund research and maintain an adequate infrastructure. However, a few have other sources of funding: INGEMMET, whose budget is covered entirely by 10% of the revenues coming from mining rights; IMARPE (Instituto del Mar del Perú), which has 30% of the budget covered by several payments such as fishing permits; and IIAP (Instituto Nacional de Investigaciones de la Amazonía Peruana), which receives 3% of oil taxes that represent 50% of its budget.

Research and technology institutions are not evaluated regularly to assess their contribution to the country, and only a few have internal systems to achieve quality standards. Administrative costs represent a high share of their budget (as much as 50%) and there are no performance indicators (Mullin Consulting, 2002). These observations suggest the need for a major restructuring of these institutions.

A sample of these institutions was evaluated to determine if they execute any of the four most common objectives these institutions must fulfil in developing countries: manage natural resources and environment; provide technical support for public utilities; provide technical support for regulatory functions; and promote technical change in the economy (Mullin Consulting, 2002). Most of these institutions were weak in the promotion of technical change, meaning basically transfer of technology, and some had abandoned this role (Table 5.4).

Several of the institutions have left behind their original missions or functions. Two (IPEN and INGEMMET) are far behind the technological frontier in their respective fields and have abandoned or modified the role they had when created.

Technological Innovation Centres

A system of Technological Innovation Centres (CITEs) was created under the Ministry of Production (formerly Ministry of Industry) to increase technology adoption and innovation by firms. The aim was to increase competitiveness and productivity. However, because the CITEs target mostly small and medium

Table 5.4 Achievement of specific roles by a sample of research and technology institutions (Mullin Consulting, 2002)

	Management of natural resources and environment	*Technical support for public utilities*	*Technical support for regulatory government functions*	*Promotion of technical change in the economy*
IGP Instituto Geofísico del Perú	Provides inputs for risk disasters assessment	Not a function	Can provide support for the planning of land use	This is not one of the institute's aims
IIAP	Main role	Not a function	Not a function	Performs some activities with marginal farmers
INGEMMET	Main role	Not a function	Can provide support for the planning of land use	Not a function since 1993
INIA	Moderate role	Not a function	Not a function	Main role but the feedback is weak
INICTEL Instituto Nacional de Investigación y Capacitación de Telecomunicaciones	Not a function	Its original role has disappeared. Now it is looking to help rural areas to fulfil its communication needs	Not a function in Peru but has assisted other countries in this goal	Weak performance in transfer of technology but a strong one in training
IMARPE	Important role	Not a function	Important role	Weak performance in transfer of technology
INS Instituto Nacional de Salud	Not a function	Produces biological agents and vaccines for the Health System	Has an important regulatory role	Weak performance in transfer of technology
IPEN Instituto Peruano de Energía Nuclear	Not a function	Its original role has disappeared. Now produces isotopes for the Health System	Has a regulatory function	Weak performance in transfer of technology. Looking for a redefinition of mission
ITP	Not a function	Not a function	Recently adopted mission but without resources	Main role but weak performance in transfer of technology. More successful in training

124 FUELLING ECONOMIC GROWTH

firms they generally do not help firms that already compete in international markets.

The main goals of CITEs are to: (a) promote Peruvian products for export and domestic consumption; (b) create a favourable technological environment for investments and collaboration among firms; (c) transfer technology for small and medium firms; (d) improve the quality and differentiation of products, and to promote design and the use of computer-assisted patterns; (e) perform research and development to improve the productivity and increase the value of natural resources; (f) train and upgrade human resources, and train trainers; (g) diffuse technological information about trends in markets and fashion; (h) monitor and assess prospects for technology; and (i) promote technical standards and norms in each industry branch (Carazo et al., 2000).

Table 5.5: Areas of specialization and locations of Technical Innovation Centres (PRODUCE, 2007)

	Specialization	*Location of clusters*
CITEccal	Leather, shoes and related industries	Caquetá – Lima Trujillo (Minka and PASE) Arequipa – (Habitat) Huancayo (INIDER)
CITEmadera	Wood and furniture	Villa El Salvador Pucallpa
CITEvid	Wine and grapes industry	Ica – Moquegua – Tacna Majes II – Cascas
CITEagroindustrial de Ayacucho	Horticulture (e.g. avocados, peppers, and paprika), Andean products, tara seeds, guinea pigs	Huanta
CITEagroindustrial de Piura	Mango, bananas, and carob tree jelly	Piura
CITEagroindustrial CEPRORUI – Arequipa	Aromatic organic herbs (oregano)	Arequipa
CITEagroindustrial MST – Tacna	Olives, oregano, and wine	Tacna
CITEfrutas Tropicales y plantas medicinales de Loreto	Tropical fruits (camu camu, passion fruit, araza) and medicinal plants (cat's claw, dragon's blood)	Loreto
CITEindustria textil Camélidos del Perú IPAC	Alpaca apparel Alpaca and other animal fibres, knitting and weaving	Arequipa
CITEconfecciones El Taller	Textile – cotton and mixed fibres apparel, Alpaca and other animal fibres, knitting and weaving	Arequipa
CITEmetalmecánico ATEM – Lima	Metal and machine industry	Los Olivos, Lima
CITElogístico	Logistic services	Lima

CITEs are created based on criteria such as: the generation of employment and incomes; the degree of linkage generation and synergies; the existence of a cluster of small and medium firms that will aid in the diffusion of technology; the level of value added, regional competitiveness, and national identity; markets; the availability of technologies with easy assimilation; and the existence of a critical mass of firms.

Table 5.5 shows the CITEs that are currently at work. At present, only three of them depend directly on the Ministry of Production. The other CITEs are administered by nongovernmental organizations or producers' associations.

CITEs have been very important in promoting technical change in small and medium firms. Although the coverage of the services they provide is small and limited to specific locations, they have helped introduce quality standards and increase productivity. However, to further boost overall productivity levels, it will be necessary to complement their work with other programmes aimed at creating links with large firms.

Universities

Peru has 27 state and 26 private universities. In addition, 7 more state universities and 17 private ones are being created. This high number is a response to the high demand for tertiary education in the country. The great majority of the universities have a mission to train professionals, despite the low quality of the education they impart.

State universities usually have performed some research but budget constraints have decreased the resources available to conduct research and maintain their scientific and technological infrastructure. In addition, institutional difficulties impede professors from managing their own research budgets and extensive teaching commitments constrain the training, recruitment, and retention of researchers. With a few exceptions, universities have tended to perform basic research and advances, if any, have had no impact in the productive sector due to a lack of technological demand from firms or government.

Budget constraints have also hindered the quality of education and training. Salaries in academia are extremely low; therefore, most universities have lost their best professors. Another concern is whether universities are producing skilled workers who can meet the demands of the productive sector. It appears that most skilled workers concentrate in education, the humanities, social sciences and less so in engineering and technologies (National Higher Education Census, Asamblea Nacional de Rectores e INEI, 1996).

A pseudo panel for Peru was developed to evaluate whether there was a mismatch between field of study and area of employment. Table 5.6 shows the results for 1996–98 for wage earners for metropolitan Lima with higher education, both from universities and from technical institutes. About 21% of workers trained in natural and basic sciences end up working in services, and 25% of workers trained in biological sciences end up working in public administration. Contrary to what might be expected, productive sectors employ less than 18% of skilled workers, and 16% of skilled workers in natural and basic sciences, technologies and engineering, and biological sciences. Overall, 18% of all workers end up working in commerce and restaurants, and 33% in other services.

In Peru, there is no clear correlation between economic performance and level of enrolment or number of students graduated, which are practically inelastic to growth in the economic sector. The exception is Chile, where a clear relationship was found with different economic sectors, although similar figures for number of graduated students were not available.

There is great diversity in the quality of private universities. Some are known for the excellent education they provide, but the great majority offer a mediocre education. Most of these universities do not perform scientific research; however, there are some remarkable exceptions such as the Universidad Cayetano Heredia, which has a solid research programme in medical and biological sciences. Another feature of Peruvian universities is the lack of postgraduate courses. Due to the lack of research, very few universities grant Masters or PhD degrees, which causes a shortage of research professionals. The great majority of researchers in Peru have been trained in foreign universities.[19]

Relationships among local actors

Weakness of different actors has contributed to the limited relationships among them. There is insufficient interaction between the government technology institutes and domestic firms. Large and medium firms see the technology institutions as entities whose research topics do not help solve their problems, and work on a different timeframe. In addition, small firms do not demand technological services because they do not know the existence of these resources or, even worse, because they believe they do not have any technical problems.

Relationships between universities and firms are also limited. Some universities do provide services to firms, especially in the area of management. As well, some entrepreneurial-support programmes have been launched recently to cover a variety of thematic areas such as environment, information systems, biological sciences, and industrial processes. One form of linkage that is seldom seen is theses aimed at solving the concrete problems of firms. Firms are reluctant to engage in such programmes, but they could become an effective way to forge ties between these two actors.

Relationships among firms themselves are also almost absent. Technological heterogeneity among firms and the lack of technical standards makes it very difficult to work together (e.g. by outsourcing) or to work in association (e.g. to satisfy large contracts). For the same reason, foreign firms cannot work with domestic ones because they have higher quality standards. As a result, opportunities to generate spillovers in the economy are lost. As well, cluster

Table 5.6 Supply and demand by field of skilled labour (Seudo Panel Encuestas de Empleo, 1996–98, Lima, Peru)

Field Studied	Fishing and agriculture	Mining	Consumption goods industry	Intermed. and capital goods	Water, electricity and gas	Construction	Commerce, restaurants and hotels	Transport and comm.	Finance, insurances, and services	Public admin. and defence	Other services
Professionals											
Natural and basic sciences	0.0	1.4	14.0	7.5	5.6	4.1	29.1	3.8	12.2	1.6	20.9
Technologies and engineering	0.4	2.5	13.2	16.0	2.7	6.6	13.2	11.0	10.5	11.0	12.8
Biological sciences	5.5	3.2	15.1	0.0	0.0	11.6	10.8	11.5	4.2	24.9	13.3
Health sciences	0.0	0.6	1.0	2.2	0.0	0.6	9.9	3.2	1.9	6.2	74.3
Education, humanities and administration	0.3	0.8	4.0	4.4	0.6	1.9	15.3	3.1	16.7	9.2	43.7
Social sciences	0.0	0.0	2.3	3.9	0.0	0.0	12.6	7.0	17.8	12.1	44.4
Other	1.0	0.0	2.1	1.1	0.0	0.0	4.0	9.2	5.5	73.2	3.8
Technical											
Natural and basic sciences	0.0	0.0	8.8	8.2	0.0	1.6	25.4	8.5	22.2	7.5	17.7
Technologies and engineering	0.5	0.0	11.8	14.6	1.4	8.1	26.1	14.1	11.4	1.1	10.9
Biological sciences	0.0	0.0	0.0	0.0	0.0	0.0	0.0	0.0	100.0	0.0	0.0
Health sciences	0.6	0.0	10.6	3.0	1.8	0.0	15.5	3.0	1.4	8.0	56.2
Education, humanities and administration	0.5	1.9	10.4	9.2	0.0	2.6	32.8	8.0	17.7	7.6	9.4
Social sciences	0.0	0.0	6.1	5.1	0.6	1.2	29.3	2.9	19.7	11.0	24.3
Other	0.0	0.0	0.0	25.1	12.3	12.8	37.7	0.0	0.0	12.2	0.0
Total	0.4	0.8	6.8	6.6	0.9	2.6	18.3	5.8	14.11	10.8	33.0

formation is limited because the locational and organizational factors are not present. Finally, because firms do not demand research and technical services, the supply of these services is limited.

Recently, a series of organizations and programmes aimed at providing technical support and advice have been created. Most of these have been created through the initiative of the productive sectors, both private and public, and have been supported by international technical cooperation funds. A salient feature of these organizations and programmes is that they are not linked to the established research and technological institutions. In addition, industrial training institutions such as TECSUP (Industrial Training Institution Peru) and SENATI (Servicio Nacional de Adiestramiento en Trabajo Industrial) offer technological support services in different areas. For example, TECSUP is offering mineralogical and hydrometallurgical testing, which covers a demand not satisfied by INGEMMET.

Relationships between local and foreign actors

Links between local and foreign actors have become one of the main knowledge sources in developing countries. These links are generally of three types: commercial, established between local firms and their suppliers; collaborative, between local and foreign institutions; and technical cooperation programmes.

Commercial relationships are typical between foreign or subsidiary firms and their foreign suppliers. Many of these firms sell their products in external markets and use state-of-the-art technologies that are created in industrialized countries. The lack of domestic capabilities and the strict standards that regulate these firms' products make them dependent on technological services supplied abroad. Firms from extractive industries, such as mining and oil, are good examples of this situation. Given that these relationships are forged through commercial transactions, spillovers are not generated and any diffusion of knowledge is made through equipment and technology suppliers.[20]

Collaborative relationships occur among universities and different types of research and development institutions. These relationships are forged by personal contacts among researchers working in both the local and foreign institutions. Their benefits include on-the-job improvement of local research capabilities, internships in foreign institutions, and scholarships to pursue graduate studies in the foreign institutions. These effects are enhanced when the local researchers are also engaged in teaching. In addition, these relationships make local researchers aware of different international sources of funding for S&T activities. However, local research agendas can sometimes be subordinated to those defined in industrialized countries. The effect of this subordination is not only reflected in research that does not solve local problems but in the frustration of local researchers who become over-qualified and do not have opportunities to apply the knowledge they have acquired (Kuramoto and Sagasti, 2002).

Technical cooperation programmes are aimed at transferring technical expertise to developing countries. However, they face a major restriction because donors are accountable to their constituencies at home. As a result, donors 'feel more comfortable...if they can point to visible activities which encourage a bias towards self-contained and pre-ordered packages (...) clos[ing] off options for creative learning or incremental discovery' (Fukuda-Parr et al., 2002). In addition, recipient governments may be reluctant to reject billions of dollars even if they do not agree with the donors' priorities, or because they lack the capabilities to define their own priorities.

The common feature in these three types of cooperation is that local agents have to invest in elevating their scientific and technological capabilities to take advantage of the transmitted knowledge. Local agents must pursue a more active role in the definition of their needs and negotiate the conditions of these relationships. This is the only way to take advantage of these types of cooperation and convert them into useful tools that can increase a country's capabilities.

R&D and firm performance in Peru

Starting with the work of economists such as Griliches (1980, 1990, 1994, 1998), and Mansfield (1983 and 1998), there have been numerous studies demonstrating the positive impact of R&D on productivity in the United States. Our analysis of the impact of R&D expenditures on the performance of the firms uses a new database developed in August 2000 (CONCYTEC).[21] This unique dataset is extremely valuable for understanding the innovation process of firms and its relationship with universities, research institutes, and public institutions within the existing institutional framework.

This survey, which was representative country-wide, by economic sector,[22] and by size (small, medium, and large enterprises), collected information on science and technology indicators for 8,976 firms. The relationship between firm performance measured in terms of output per worker and different indicators of R&D was plotted. For technology improvements in products and improvement in product design there was a clear positive relationship. For all other indicators the relationship is not clear. This could be because of the small amount of R&D in Peru and specifically in firms.

The statistical analysis, following Boubakri and Cosset (1998), analysed several science and technology indicators at the levels of firms, computed the means of performance variables for the companies that invest in R&D, and compared them with companies that do not invest in R&D.

After the means were calculated, the effect on performance of investment in R&D was expressed as:

$$\Delta \overline{P} = [\overline{P}^{investinR\&D} - P^{notinvestinR\&D}] \qquad [1]$$

The two-tailed Wilcoxon signed-rank test was used to test for significant changes in the variables. A proportion test was used to determine whether the proportion (*p*) of firms that experienced a change in a given direction was greater than what would be expected by chance (typically testing where *p*=0.5). The differences in means for each sector and for the different sources of R&D were also calculated.

The simplest possible model to capture the effect on performance (with no regressors) can be derived so that performance depends on the dummy of doing or not doing R&D:

$$P_{i,t} \alpha + \gamma R\&D_i + u_i \quad E(u_i/R\&D_i) = 0 \qquad [2]$$

Table 5.7 shows the impact of R&D, access to the Internet, and access to computers within the manufacturing sectors for which there was information on at least one firm using some of their resources in R&D. Although the amount spent on R&D was small, some sectors show a significant and positive difference with respect to firms that did not expend on R&D. This result is even stronger for the cases of IT technologies, where the link to productivity and R&D is significant for the sectors where there is some investment in innovation.

Case study: Technological innovation in copper hydrometallurgy

Mining is one of the most dynamic industries in Peru. Mining output has increased dramatically in the last 20 years. From 1980 to 1999, copper output increased by 55%, lead by 45%, zinc by 80%, silver by 60%, and gold by 1479%. These increases are the result of a boom in mining investment that resulted in the modernization of the industry and the adoption of state-of-the-art mining technologies that boosted productivity and output.

Among those technologies, hydrometallurgy was one of the most important. Hydrometallurgy made the exploitation of massive gold deposits possible. The result was a fourteen-fold increase in gold output that made Peru one of the eight largest gold producers in the world. The development of hydrometallurgy was tightly linked to the copper industry and Peru was one of the first countries to adopt and develop this technology.

Sales efficiency is total sales divided by total workers; production efficiency is the gross value of production (market value of total sales and inventories) over total workers; exports/production is the value of export over gross value of production; ROA is the rate of return over assets and ROS is the rate of return over sales.

Background

The commercial application of hydrometallurgy to produce copper is one of the major metallurgic innovations of the last half of the twentieth century. Conventional mineral processing (pyrometallurgy) involves several stages: prospecting and exploration of attractive deposits; mining or extraction of the valuable mineral; benefication to transform the mineral into a commercial

PUBLIC–PRIVATE RESEARCH, DEVELOPMENT, AND INNOVATION IN PERU 131

Table 5.7 Most important differences between innovative and non-innovative firms

T-test for difference in means between firms with R&D and firms without R&D

Description	Number of firms with R&D	Number of firms without R&D	Sales efficiency	Production efficiency	Exports/ production	RDA	ROS
Food and beverages	31	316	35,49**	34,99**	58,33	317,20*	113,37****
Textiles	7	160	6,01	6,01	6,29*	160,67	19,25
Garments	6	105	7,97	15,67	5,10	21,18	107,66**
Leather products	3	79	28,12*	28,26*	6,18	35,05	22,16
Production of paper and paper subproducts	2	44	43,01***	17,47***	1,22	1,39	1,99*
Printing and graphic reproduction	3	124	2,64	2,72	106,00*	11,10	5,22
Substances and chemical products	25	150	123,02	109,88	30,84	147,67	104,77*
Plastic production	7	102	8,95	8,92	6,14	17,52	13,81
Non-metallic mineral products	5	78	6,21	5,42	4,15	76,00	62,39**
Production of common metals	5	30	4,02	4,01	4,87	32,08	29,27
Metal-based products excluding machinery	12	127	13,33	13,81	46,73	76,93	132,40
Production of machinery and equipment	4	65	66,31	66,36	3,07	64,38*	66,99
Machinery and electric equipment	4	47	3,10	3,10	3,01	46,53**	3,74
Production of vehicles	2	27	1,02	1,06	1,24	12,32	1,29
Production of furniture	3	91	39,62**	39,83**	1,02	4,16	2,30

T-test for difference in means between firms with computers and firms without computers

Description	Number of firms with R&D	Number of firms without R&D	Sales efficiency	Production efficiency	Exports/ production	RDA	ROS
Food and beverages	167	124	287,65****	287,75****	123,70	124,00	287,59**
Textiles	96	47	139,03*	126,57	99,89**	44,94	53,43
Garments	44	35	43,99	43,91	61,37**	41,83	73,99
Leather products	42	27	50,51	49,71	65,82	28,61*	31,70*
Production of paper and paper subproducts	31	9	9,13	9,12	29,00	32,44	15,02
Printing and graphic reproduction	75	18	47,91**	47,13***	50,89	53,07**	18,41**
Substances and chemical products	122	32	32,01	32,04	57,78**	41,55	35,75

132 FUELLING ECONOMIC GROWTH

Description	Number of firms with R&D	Number of firms without R&D	Sales efficiency	Production efficiency	Exports/ production	RDA	ROS
Plastic production	89	20	19,97	19,90	87,00****	104,42	21,09
Non-metallic mineral products	49	21	67,93**	67,45**	48,00****	19,29	20,91
Production of common metals	21	7	20,01	20,01	20,00***	6,01	23,33
Metal-based products excluding machinery	83	26	41,58	38,33	89,27**	25,31	25,06
Production of machinery and equipment	46	22	45,01	45,01	47,00*	21,11	21,14
Machinery and electric equipment	38	9	44,55***	44,51***	32,00**	10,00	11,29
Production of vehicles	14	11	22,66	22,32	13,00	16,59	21,32
Production of furniture	44	20	44,45*	44,65*	48,67	19,28	20,27

T-test for difference in means between firms with Internet and firms without Internet

Description	Number of firms with R&D	Number of firms without R&D	Sales efficiency	Production efficiency	Exports/ production	RDA	ROS
Food and beverages	103	139	157,33****	158,19****	145,09	160,69****	230,32***
Textiles	64	60	79,83	69,74	93,55****	58,27	91,80****
Garments	22	45	21,13	21,12	22,67***	49,14	64,19****
Leather products	25	31	25,55	25,37	24,00	32,31	52,34
Production of paper and paper subproducts	23	15	22,23	22,19	21,00	22,07	35,25
Printing and graphic reproduction	40	43	62,59**	65,74**	34,14	59,34	79,70
Substances and chemical products	86	53	91,33***	93,84***	125,98****	83,25	77,81
Plastic production	64	38	93,71****	90,73****	66,20***	74,50	55,08
Non-metallic mineral products	36	28	46,26**	44,58**	51,50***	25,61	29,00
Production of common metals	19	7	18,01	18,01	18,00***	7,01	23,39
Metal-based products excluding machinery	59	38	94,80****	94,11****	55,30***	38,71	37,25
Production of machinery and equipment	29	32	28,01	28,01	48,99	31,64	31,80
Machinery and electric equipment	30	13	30,30*	28,35	34,37	32,42**	15,75**
Production of vehicles	10	9	11,04*	10,99*	12,56	12,37	9,35
Production of furniture	26	31	37,44	37,91	42,55	32,49	35,03

Note: **** significance at 0.001 level; *** significance at 0.01; ** significance at 0.05; * significance at 0.1.

product called concentrate; smelting to transform the concentrate into a higher content product called blister copper; and refining to purify the blister copper into 99.99% pure copper cathodes. Hydrometallurgy, which was developed mostly during the 1970s, made it possible to skip several operations within beneficiation, and all of the smelting and refining stages.[23]

Simplification of the conventional mining process had a great impact on operational costs. Hydrometallurgy was seen as a technology that could change the way copper and other metals were produced. First, it allowed the processing of marginal deposits with low copper content. Second, it facilitated the production of refined copper without the high investment costs required to set up smelting and refining facilities. Third, operations using this new technology did not rely on economies of scale to be profitable. Fourth, it facilitated vertical integration in the industry and reduced the cyclical volatility that affected mineral markets (Kuramoto, 2003).

Developing countries saw hydrometallurgy as the opportunity to catch up because they were dependent on mineral revenues and faced entry barriers in the mining business, given the huge investments required and the reliance on imported technology (Warhurst, 1985). In fact, the technology was not fully developed and required a lot of experimentation to deploy it in a mineral deposit. Specifically, the technical parameters of leaching were not fully optimized. Furthermore, a promising line of research, bioleaching, was being initiated because there was evidence that bacteria could help leach sulphur ores.[24]

In the context of nationalized mining industries that were eager to find a solid competitive advantage, the Andean Pact launched two technological projects: Acid or bacterial heap and dump leaching for marginal copper ores, and copper recovery from ion exchange in copper sulphate solutions. Both were aimed at developing hydrometallurgy (PADT-Cu) in Peru and Bolivia in the late 1970s.

The specific objectives of these projects were to: develop appropriate technology to exploit domestic mineral resources with biological sources available in the region; develop semi-industrial facilities to support the diffusion of this technology; implement bacterial leaching operations using complex mineral dumps or abandoned sulphur copper deposits; promote the increase of copper production via this new technology (Macha and Sotillo, 1975).

To conduct the activities of these projects, CENTROMIN[25] set up a laboratory in La Oroya and built pilot dumps in Toromocho (Morococha). In addition, MINERO PERU and INCITEMI (National Mining Research Institute)[26] set up research centres in Arequipa and Lima. A pilot solvent extraction and electrowinning (SX-EW) plant was built in Cerro Verde (Arequipa), which later became the fourth commercial plant in the world deploy to this new technology.[27]

Sectoral innovation system during the 1970s and 1980s

These two Andean Pact projects initiated a major research effort in Peru. Peru, and also Bolivia, had a large mining tradition and a series of institutions had been created to support this activity. Therefore, there was a technological infrastructure that could enhance the efforts of these recently launched hydrometallurgic projects.

Firms

During the early 1970s, the Peruvian government nationalized the large foreign firms. Two major enterprises were expropriated: Cerro de Pasco Corporation, a mining and metallurgical complex located in central Sierra; and Marcona Mining Corporation, an iron mine located in southern Ica. These two enterprises became the state-owned firms: CENTROMIN PERU and HIERRO PERU. In addition, another state-owned firm, MINERO PERU, was created to develop new mineral deposits. In fact, MINERO PERU developed the Cerro Verde mine in Arequipa and the Tintaya mine in Cusco.

Only one large foreign firm remained. Southern Peru Copper Corporation, the largest copper operation in Peru, was able to accelerate the development of a new mine. Unlike Cerro de Pasco and Marcona, Southern Peru showed that a foreign firm could contribute to the government's goal of turning mining into the driving sector of the Peruvian economy. With few exceptions, the government did not nationalize small and medium firms. Most of them were owned by long-established Peruvian mining groups.

The newly nationalized mining firms experienced an intense learning process because Peruvian engineers had to take charge of the operation of the facilities. This process was most welcome because under the foreign administration they had been relegated to subordinate positions. The largest learning opportunities appeared in Cerro Verde and Tintaya because the engineers had the opportunity to participate in the launching and operation of new, large copper mines.

The Cerro Verde project became a milestone for Peruvian mining. The Cerro Verde deposit had considerable copper oxide reserves that could be exploited using the new hydrometallurgic technology. Almost all studies for the development of Cerro Verde were performed by Peruvian engineers. The Andean Pact projects were instrumental because they provided the necessary data to optimize both the leaching and solvent extraction stages. These projects allowed tight collaboration among the different state-owned firms and efficient use of their testing facilities and laboratories. The small and medium mining firms were less active in research or in innovation.

Government

During the 1970s, the government relied on central economic planning, and the National Planning Institute was very active in defining priorities for the country. Despite this rigid framework, the government was able to set national priorities to spur economic development.

Mining had always been an important sector for Peru, but the government believed that it responded mainly to corporate interests and, therefore, its contribution to development was meagre. The new state-owned firms set their priorities on developing large deposits to increase mineral production, especially in copper, and on developing deposits far from the coastal region to promote decentralization (such as in Tintaya).

The government set the goal of adding value to mineral production. It promoted the construction of two refineries: the Ilo refinery to treat copper concentrates produced by Southern Peru and the Cajamarquilla refinery to treat zinc concentrates produced by firms located in the Sierra Central. The decision to deploy hydrometallurgy in Cerro Verde was also geared to achieve this goal. The government also established a policy to commercialize all mineral products. The objective was to increase the retained value from mining. This led to the creation of a state-owned mineral commercializing firm called Minero Peru Comercial (MINPECO).

Research and technological institutions

Mining is an industry that relies heavily on experimentation. Each deposit has unique characteristics and, even when the mining and metallurgical technology is standard, laboratory and pilot-plant tests must be performed to optimize each process. For this reason, various mining-related institutions were created years ago.

Most of these institutions were professional associations that linked engineers and helped exchange knowledge. As Peru became more interested in mining, geological information became more important. As a result, the Peruvian Geological Institute was created in 1940 and 20 years later the Geological Survey Commission was set up.

In 1973, the Scientific and Technological Mining Institute was created. This was the first attempt to diversify the focus from the geological research to other areas of mineral-related knowledge, such as metallurgy. This institute was merged in 1978 with the Institute of Geology and Mining to create the National Institute of Geology, Mining and Metallurgy (INGEMMET). Like many other technology research institutes, INGEMMET had limited links with firms and as a result its research was not successfully transferred. In the end, INGEMMET focused most of its research on completing the Peruvian geological map. The infrastructure of this institute is largely underutilized.

Universities

In the 1970s, the most important universities providing Geology, Mining, and Metallurgical Engineering were the Universidad Nacional de Ingeniería (UNI) and the Universidad San Marcos. Other universities, especially those located in mining areas, created mining-related faculties given the strategic importance the government placed on this sector.[28] Universities were mainly focused on professional training. They did have a limited role in generating mining knowledge, but had little interaction with firms.

Relationships among domestic agents

There were limited relationships among the different actors in this sectoral innovation system. However, the Andean Pact projects did contribute to collaboration between professionals from different divisions at CENTROMIN and MINERO PERU. Warhurst (1985) reported that the Peruvian team, as opposed to the Bolivian one, was able to create a collaborative environment and good transfer of knowledge.

Outside the boundaries of the Andean Pact projects, knowledge was mainly transmitted through informal means. The engineers working on the project shared their experiences with other engineers working at mining firms and presented their advances in conferences such as the Mining Convention. However, formal knowledge-transfer mechanisms were not designed. In fact, the advances made in bacterial leaching at Toromocho and Cerro Verde were not transferred to other research institutes or universities to continue further research. After the Andean Pact projects ended, the main depositaries of the knowledge were the people themselves.

Relationships between domestic and foreign agents

The Andean Pact projects allowed interactions between the Bolivian and Peruvian teams. Technical visits to experimental sites and workshops were part of the activities of these projects. These created personal links that were maintained.

The projects also fostered interactions with research groups from universities and laboratories in advanced countries and created opportunities for Peruvian engineers to pursue advanced training in foreign laboratories and universities.

The effect of legislative change

The reforms launched in the 1990s had important effects on the mining innovation system. The liberalization of markets and the incentives provided to the mining sector increased investment. For 1990–2007, investment in the sector was expected to reach $2 bn (Sánchez, 1998).

These new investments created new mining operations that used state-of-the-art, environmentally friendly technologies and led to the modernization of existing mining operations. The sector as a whole also benefited from the transfer of technology through imports of capital goods and equipment.

Several operations that used hydrometallurgical technologies were set up to exploit copper and gold. The Yanacocha gold project was launched in 1994[29] and became the first large-scale gold operation in Peru to use cyanide leaching and the Merrill Crowe method for gold recovery. In 1995, the Southern Peru Copper Corporation developed a leaching, solvent extraction, and electrowinning (LIX-SX-EW) operation in Toquepala with a capacity of 40,000 MT of copper cathodes. The plant was set up in Toquepala and was fed by the dumps that had been accumulated since the beginning of the operation in the 1960s. At Cerro Verde, capacity of the LIX-SX-EW operation was increased from 30,000 MT to 50,000 MT of copper. This operation was privatized and acquired by Cyprus Amax in 1993.[30] The Pierina gold operation was also launched in Ancash. This operation uses technology similar to that deployed in Yanacocha, belongs to Barrick, and has one of the lowest operating costs in the world.

More recently, Southern Peru has developed a new LIX-SX-EW plant in Cuajone with a capacity of 22,000 MT of copper cathodes. BHP Tintaya has developed a LIX-SX-EW plant to treat copper oxide ores, and several other smaller operations that use various hydrometallurgical methods have been developed.

The effects of increased mining investment in the sectoral innovation system have not been favourable. Most of the mining investment has been by foreign firms that developed large deposits under EPCM (engineering, procurement, and construction management) contracts. As a result, these projects have generated a limited demand for domestic goods and services. This has affected both Peruvian manufacturing firms and also research institutions and universities because services such as laboratory tests and environmental impact assessments are mostly performed abroad.

In the Peruvian mining sector, firms tend to be large or medium, in terms of both sales and employment. These firms do little research and development because the mining sector sells homogeneous products for external markets. Some research is done locally, but it tends to focus on optimization of operational processes. Research that could have major impact is done by foreign firms at other locations, whether in their home country or other places with better scientific and technological infrastructure.

Economic reforms have had an adverse effect on research institutions and universities. Their precarious situation during the 1980s, when budgets were decreased drastically, did not improve after the reforms. The prevailing idea in the government was that foreign direct investment and imports would become the main sources of technology transfer. Therefore, it was not considered necessary to strengthen research institutions.

This does not mean that no research is taking place. An industrial training institute began to provide laboratory analysis for small firms, given the high costs of accredited and recognized laboratories. However, the demand was very limited and this institute has decided to transfer the knowledge it accumulated in hydrometallurgical methods to the training of human resources.

The situation is similar in the universities. Their budgets have shrunk, they focus on educational tasks, and little research is done. A recent survey showed that only four universities with geology, mining, and metallurgical engineering faculties are apt to perform research (Arteaga, 2003).

Relationships among the different actors that form the mining innovation system are mostly informal and based on personal relationships. People who worked together in different mining projects tend to keep their contacts and discuss operational problems and ways to solve them. Consultants and suppliers are also important because they are a source of knowledge transfer. They offer state-of-the-art solutions and provide in-house training courses.

Mineral conventions are a more formal way to transfer knowledge. These meetings provide opportunities for exchanges among professionals working in different mining projects. They usually present papers related to operational problems or applied research performed in-house. These conventions also serve as a networking opportunity for professionals, entrepreneurs, suppliers, technical and financial consultants, and other people working in mining.

Links with domestic and foreign actors are mainly fostered and maintained at a personal level. Mining professionals retain links with their professors at the universities and with colleagues from companies with which they worked.

Roles of public and private sectors

Firms, whether state-owned or private, have been the most active in pursuing technological innovation. During the implementation of the Andean Pact projects, state-owned firms were crucial because they provided human capital and facilities. Their focus on problem-solving and consideration of economic viability were very important. In the case of Cerro Verde, learning was not restricted to technical aspects of hydrometallurgy. Skills were acquired in how to prepare feasibility studies and how to negotiate with representatives of financial and banking institutions and suppliers. In fact, some 'black boxes' may have been opened. For example, given the shortage of budgets[31] and the high costs of the anodes used for electrowinning, an anode plant was established with Japanese aid.

The links with research institutions, like INGEMMET, and universities were not very tight. These institutes tended to focus on scientific rather than applied research. In addition, their timeframes were different. State-owned firms wanted to accelerate the pace of projects, but research institutions and universities were less concerned with time than performing good research. As a result, the capabilities acquired by the mining professionals that participated in the Andean Pact projects generated limited spillovers in Peru.

In comparison, in Chile the spread of this technology, which was also spurred by new projects launched by the state-owned firm, CODELCO, was aided by the codification of knowledge via universities. In fact, during the 1980s, one of the most important researchers in this field, Esteban Domic,[32] set up courses in hydrometallurgy in the Universidad de Chile where he taught and was supervisor of several theses on the topic.

Lack of codification was responsible for feeble diffusion of this technology and shortages of specialized human capital. In fact, after the 1990s economic reforms, private firms that incorporated hydrometallurgical methods in their operations did not engage professionals who had worked on the Andean Pact projects.[33]

The LIX-SX-EW technology is now standardized, and there are suppliers for every stage of this process. Therefore, firms do not have to devote large amounts of time and effort to use this technology. All this is necessary to hire external engineering consultants to define the technical parameters of the project (e.g. size and equipment requirement). Some internal experimentation must be performed, but learning inside firms is limited because the technology has become dominated by the suppliers, especially engineering firms.

Even Cerro Verde, which was acquired by Cyprus Amax, has had setbacks since directors from Cyprus took over the operation. Fortunately, most of the technical staff (such as mine and plant superintendents) remained in their jobs but auxiliary facilities such as the anode plant were closed. Efficiency became imperative and Cerro Verde had to stick to its core competence: the production of copper cathodes.

An important feature of the spread of the LIX-SX-EW technology during the 1990s was that firms consulted each other on an informal basis. For example, Southern Peru consulted Cerro Verde and some Chilean mining firms about bacterial leaching. In addition, technical staff who assumed positions in other mining firms had previous experience in hydrometallurgy in Cerro Verde or Southern Peru.

There is some evidence of applied research inside firms. At the International Copper Conference in 2003, Cerro Verde and Tintaya presented the results of research aimed at improving their operational efficiency. Although the papers will be published in the conference proceedings, diffusion inside the country and to other actors in the Peruvian mining innovation system will be very limited.

Case study: Technological innovation to control the fruit fly in mango agriculture

During the last 40 years, Peruvian agriculture has faced major challenges to productivity growth. Agrarian Reform in 1969 focused on land ownership and resulted in increased state intervention in agriculture and the withdrawal of agriculture entrepreneurs and technicians. The 1980s were characterized by an unstable macroeconomic environment and a very severe El Niño phenomenon that contributed to deterioration in the sectors.

During the last decade, major economic reforms were launched in the agricultural sector: the elimination of price controls; the liquidation of the Agrarian Bank and the elimination of the preferential interest rates for agriculture; the elimination of state-owned firms for agricultural commercialization; and the elimination of nontariff mechanisms and imports quotas (Ministerio de Agricultura, 2002).

Output began to grow, and export-oriented agriculture became the fastest-growing segment. During the last 11 years, sales of agricultural products to external markets have increased 120%. In 2001, their value reached 9.3% of total Peruvian exports. The products responsible for this increase are the so-called nontraditional agricultural exports (e.g. mango, asparagus, avocado, paprika, marigold meal, and grapes).

Peru is becoming a major mango exporter.[34] In 1990–2002, accumulated exports reached 202 thousand metric tonnes, which represented $191 m and 74% of the total exports of fresh fruits. During the same period, the harvested area rose from 6,352 to 13,404 ha. Production is concentrated in 10 areas: Piura[35] (5,908 ha), Lambayeque (924 ha), Ucayali (720 ha), Ica (660 ha), Lima (643 ha), Cajamarca (590 ha), Ancash (390 ha), La Libertad (240 ha), Junín (169 ha), and San Martín (146 ha).

There are important constraints that must be overcome to fulfil Peru's potential as a major mango exporter. One of the most serious is the harmful effect of the fruit fly,[36] which not only affects mango but 200 other vegetable and fruit species. The fruit fly reduces productivity and causes losses of about $90 m per year and a decrease of about one third of all horticultural production. In addition, countries that import fruits (e.g. United States, Japan, and European countries) have very strict phytosanitary rules and procedures to avoid the entry of infected fruit.

Fruit fly and mango exports

The successful adoption of mango in Piura helped establish export-oriented agriculture. Mango became the fifth-most-exported agricultural product in Peru, and the quality of the fruit and its counter-season harvest provided competitive advantages to Peruvian exporters. Mangos are one of the host plants for fruit flies. According to a 2003 survey by SENASA (National Service of Agrarian Sanitation), mango is the fifth-most-infested crop in Piura, but the first among export crops. Given the sanitary measures in the United States, the main Peruvian mango importer, several measures have been adopted to eliminate the chance that infested mangos will enter the United States.

Before the 1990s, mangos were fumigated with methyl bromide. The 1991 Montreal Protocol defined this chemical as a contributor to ozone depletion. A phase-out programme was defined and by 2005 its use was to be discontinued in developed countries.

The US Department of Agriculture developed an alternative sanitary protocol to treat imported fruit. This hot water treatment immerses the mangos at a depth of no more than 4 inches of water at a temperature of 47°C, for 75–90 minutes. This immersion kills both the egg and larval stage, and also eliminates other infections such as the anthracnosis fungal infection.[37]

This treatment was introduced in Piura in 1988. Since then, the Animal, Plant and Health Inspection Service from the US Department of Agriculture has overseen the treatment, and the expenses are covered by Peruvian exporters. In addition, the treatment is only provided to fruit coming from farms that have been certified by SENASA.

Another available heat treatment uses steam. This treatment was developed and first applied in the United States in 1929. The fruit is exposed to steam at about 46°C for 8 hours. The disadvantages of this treatment are that it requires an expensive infrastructure and not all fruits resist the heat. This treatment is required by Japanese authorities.

Another, not so common, treatment is to use ionizing radiation. The radiation kills pathogenic microbes and insects in both their egg and larval phases. It also delays the ripening of some fruits and vegetables. The Food and Drug Administration approves ionizing radiation for fresh fruit as long as the dosage does not exceed 100 Gy (Tijero, 1992).

Sectoral innovation system

Although the agricultural innovation system is much larger,[38] only the innovation system related to the mango production chain and efforts to control the fruit fly are discussed. The mango production chain includes a large number of farmers, a reduced number of mango exporters, an even more reduced number of mango processors, and a series of institutions that support mango agriculture and exports. Most of the interactions in the production chain are found in agriculture because mangos are exported as fruit rather than processed.

Firms

A great number of farmers cultivate mango. Most of them are located in Piura, which accounts for more than half the area cultivated. Farmers belong to five major associations: PROMANGO (Asociación de Productores de Mango); ADEPROMANGO (Asociación de Productores de Mango de Piura); Asociación de Productores de Mango del Valle del Alto Piura; Asociación de Productores de Arroz – Centro del Valle de San Lorenzo; and APPEAP (Asociación de Productores Ecológicos del Alto Piura) (Table 5.8). PROMANGO includes farmers with the largest properties and the most extensive mango exports. This association is not part of APEM (Association of Mango Exporters), but is an important part of the industry. In fact, it manages CITE agroindustrial, a technological innovation centre in Piura. PROMANGO is looking for funding to increase mango production in Piura.

ADEPROMANGO is an important association of medium-size farmers that works directly with exporting firms to provide working capital and technical assistance. This is a regional association that has strong links to the regional government. The Asociación de Productores de Mango del Valle del Alto Piura is a regional association that includes smaller farms. This association is receiving technical assistance from PSI/PERAT (Special Programme for Irrigation and Technical Assistance). There are two other associations: one that includes farmers in San Lorenzo, a well-known valley that produces not only mangos but limes and rice; one that includes farmers dedicated to cultivating organic mangos. Finally, there are 4,000 independent farmers who do not belong to any association. The production of these farmers is used to complement export shipments, but they sell mostly in the domestic market.

Most of the non-organized producers also have lemon plantations. Mangos are harvested only once a year; whereas lemons can be harvested all year long, which provides farmers with a continuous positive income. However, the most important association of mango exporters is APEM, which includes 60% of all mango exporters. Among its members are the three largest mango exporters who control more than half of all mango exports: Bounty Fresh Peru (21.5%), Sunshine Export (17.4%), and Agrowest (13.7%).

At the end of the production chain are a series of service providers such as surveillance firms that certify production according to different protocols (e.g. ISO and HACCP, Hazard Analysis and Critical Control Point), customs agents, and logistic firms. The Chamber of Commerce in Piura provides a certificate for origin that is prepared to access tariff preferences in the United States and Europe. It also provides legal, foreign trade, accounting, and tax advice.

Although this study focused on fresh mango exports, there are agents that process mango and sell mango pulp and juice, mango slices, and preserves to external markets.

Government

The 1990 economic reforms severely hit agriculture by reducing the budgets for government institutions and programmes. The Ministry of Agriculture is responsible for defining policies to promote and develop this sector. The Planning Office surveys and evaluates foreign trade in agriculture, participates in international agreements, and evaluates the main government agricultural projects. The Ministry also seeks to strengthen farmers' organizations.

SENASA is the only government institution that works actively to control and eradicate the fruit fly. It runs a laboratory that produces 100–250 million sterile fruit flies, and monitors the presence of this plague in the 30 most important valleys in Piura, Lambayeque, Lima, Ica, Arequipa, Moquegua, and Tacna (about 75,000 ha). SENASA has also constructed an irradiation centre to treat fresh fruits for export.

Table 5.8 Mango farmer associations

Organization	No. of members	Cultivated area (ha)	Exports	Observations	Agreements and interaction
PROMANGO	26	1,500 ha and 50 ha of organic mango	10,000 metric tonnes	Is not part of APEM. Has its own greenhouses. Presides over the agroindustrial CITE	Has presented a project on the competitiveness of the Piura's mango production chain to INCAGRO
ADEPROMANGO (Asociación de productores de mango de Piura)	176	2,000		Exporter firms charge them 3% rebate for losses and 6 jabas per ha for technical assistance	Exporter firms finance the crops against the harvest. They are working with the regional government on a project for processing low-grade mangos
APEM	19		60% of total exports		Has signed an agreement with IADB, through the Multilateral Investment Fund, to train farmers in good agricultural practices
Asociación de productores de mango del valle del Alto Piura	63	200	8 containers	They are asking for the electrification of wells	They receive crop-management assistance from PSI/PERAT and the municipality of Chulucanas
Asociación de productores de arroz. Centro del Valle de Lorenzo	150	400			
APPEAP		200			Has a certification from Biolatina
Non-organized producers		4,485			

The PSI/PERAT helps farmers to reach reasonable profit margins. To attain this objective, the programme works with 300 demonstration farms and 150 learning circles to motivate farmers to incorporate technological innovations, such as technically sound irrigation.

INCAGRO is a special project aimed at funding technological innovation projects in agriculture. It promotes the participation of public and private actors to create interactions in the agricultural sector. INCAGRO has funded projects to provide technical and commercialization assistance to farmers in order to increase the supply of organic fruits and to increase the productivity of the mango production chain.

Other government offices dealing with mango production are the Ministry of Foreign Commerce and the Ministry of Production. The Ministry of Foreign Commerce, through its exports promotion office, PROMPEX (Exports Promotion Office, Ministry of Foreign Commerce), promotes mangos in external markets, manages a clearinghouse of demand and supply, and undertakes initiatives to promote improved quality. PROMPEX also helped create the two most important organizations in the mango production chain: APEM and ADEPROMANGO.

The Ministry of Production promotes the processing of mango through its technological innovation centres (CITEs). It created the CITEagroindustrial in Piura with the participation of six other institutions: University of Piura, University of Lambayeque, PROMANGO, ALGARROBO and CIPCA (Agricultural Institutions in Chile), and the Chamber of Commerce in Piura. This CITE is currently run privately and supports research, provides technical assistance in products like mango and algarrobina (carob tree jelly), and promotes interactions among the government, academia, and the private sector.

Local governments also play a role in the mango industry. The regional government of Piura has a division that promotes investments, projects, and exports. It organizes an International Mango Festival to promote this production chain. It provides a packing facility and seeks funding for the next agricultural season. The Municipality of Salitral supports initiatives by NGOs to promote organic agriculture.

Research and technological institutions

The most important agricultural research institution is INIA, Instituto Nacional de Investigaciones Agrarias, which generates and transfers technologies. Given the serious danger to the whole agricultural innovation system, INIA is trying to reconstruct the system and establish links among the different actors. Its main objectives for the mango industry are to: improve the quality and increase the variety of exported mangos; transfer agronomic best practices in nutrition, irrigation, pruning, and sanitary control; diminish seasonal productivity problems; and control the growth and vegetative development of new varieties of mango. INIA runs an experimental station in Hualtaco, Piura, which has the largest mango germplasm bank in the country.

Universities

The Universidad Agraria de La Molina is the main agricultural university in Peru. It has a major research programme in fruits to increase productivity and establish development nuclei for the main species and varieties of fruits. The focus is on fruits with high potential of commercialization; therefore, mango is not one of the targeted fruits for this programme. The Universidad de Piura has departments of Agriculture, Agribusiness Engineering, and Food Sciences. The university is currently working on the control and analysis of physical, biological, and physiological damage.

Relationships among domestic agents

Despite the diverse institutions and actors working in the mango production chain, there is little interaction among them. Because it is export-oriented, the main objectives of the different actors are to increase export supply and maintain adequate levels of quality. Although it is understood that to increase productivity it is necessary to improve technology and practices throughout the chain, current efforts are focused on harvesting, postharvest handling, and packing. There are tight links between the exporters and farmers, and some exporters provide technical assistance and working capital to farmers.

Initiatives to improve agricultural practices are provided by some government institutions such as INIA, SENASA, and the special irrigation programme. Some localized initiatives run by NGOs support mango exporters. For example, IDEAS (Initiatives in Development, Empowerment and Awareness Society) is providing technical assistance in Salitral to promote organic mango cultivation. This NGO has an agreement with a large exporting firm that purchases normal mangos at $81/tonne, but pays $100/tonne for organic mangos.

The Agroindustrial CITE promotes links among different actors, but because this institution is relatively new, its actions are limited. At the experimental level, an important interaction is between SENASA and IPEN, the National Institute for Nuclear Energy. IPEN is helping SENASA implement a radiation facility, which will provide an alternative treatment for fruit flies.

Relationships between domestic and foreign agents

The first Technical Agriculture School was created in 1901 with the help of a Belgian mission coming from the Faculté Universitaire des Sciences Agronomiques de Gembloux. The university maintains several agreements with different universities from Europe and the United States.

With regard to mangos, the first varieties were introduced from Florida in the late 1950s by the Ministry of Agriculture. Although there was an extended phase of experimentation at La Molina and Piura, some farmers have imported seeds from other countries, such as Puerto Rico and Venezuela. This reflects the difficulties that government institutions have in reaching the production sector.

One area of close interaction is sanitation. Because the United States is the main export destination and mangos require heat treatment to be admitted, the

APHIS (Animal and Plant Health Inspection Service, United States Department of Agriculture) supervises this process in conjunction with SENASA, which provides certification only for mangos that come from SENASA-certified farms.

There is some interaction between Peruvian authorities and Chilean institutions to control and eradicate the fruit fly. Chile, a major agricultural country that is free of the fruit fly, has a vested interest in Peru eradicating this plague to minimize the chance of cross-border infestation.

Roles of the public and private sectors

The public and private sectors have very specific roles in the mango production chain. Long-term issues such as the collection of mango germplasm, the training of farmers in farm management and the transfer of agricultural best practices are, not surprisingly, in the hands of public or not-for-profit institutions. These activities do not generate revenue for the providers of these services; therefore, private actors are not attracted to participate in these activities, even when the benefits are higher productivity.

However, postharvest activities and packing are of complete interest to exporters. They are likely to provide technical assistance to the farmers that supply them mangos, and with whom they have established long-term relationships. Exporters must meet the terms of their contracts with foreign clients. If they fail to do so, they will lose their contracts.

Given that these exports are profitable and do not require any sophisticated methods, exporters are not interested in looking for ways to add value within the production chain. Only a few of the major exporters are dealing in basic processed mango products like juices or pulp. Major investments would be required to increase production and compete with established exporters like India and Mexico.

Lessons learned

This paper addressed several questions related to innovation and previous R&D strategies and how they could be applied in countries like Peru. It is clear from the macro overview that Peru and most Latin American countries, with the exception of Chile, Brazil, and Mexico, are latecomers to recognizing the importance of innovation and R&D because they expend significantly less in these activities than high-income countries.

Latin American countries are characterized by several scarcities: scarcity of capital in general, and especially for technology-based start-ups, such as venture and seed capital, limits growth and diversification; scarcity of an ample knowledge base, such as a concentration of dynamic industries, high-level research programmes, and a critical mass of high-quality scientists, engineers and technical workers; and scarcity of links between universities and research institutes. With rare exceptions, universities are isolated from industries and have not developed links. As a result, they have lost the possibility of generating positive externalities and neglected the fact that commercially valuable science will be more highly compensated, attract more students to enter the field who would otherwise be lost to science, and encourage more work by those in the field.

Basic research, education, training and physical infrastructure in these countries are not only inadequate, but are concentrated in a few metropolitan regions, mostly the capital cities. This geographical concentration of technology sources and skilled labour, when combined with generally poor transport and communication links, means that few localities are viable options for technology-based industrial development.

In addition, costly labour regulations, high taxation, and a general lack of effective intellectual property rights constrain innovative activity and reduce the prospects of successful start-ups. Information networks are also poorly developed; however, access to ICTs is increasingly becoming less expensive.

All these scarcities and obstacles have influenced the way in which the TIS works. The Peruvian TIS, similar to others in developing countries, is fragmented, has few interactions among different agents, and responds to competing and contradictory incentives that reflect a lack of coherence in government policies. Moreover, there is no clear understanding of the TIS concept by policymakers, who believe this system can be created by law.

Some light has been shed on the performance of sectoral innovation systems and the adoption and diffusion of a particular technology. Two findings are worth highlighting. First, the lack of interaction between knowledge-generating institutions, such as universities and government research institutes, and firms is pervasively limited. Second, the role of firms, whether state-owned or private, is crucial to the improvement and adoption of technology. Both findings are independent of changes in economic and institutional conditions, such as those experienced after the 1990 economic reforms in Peru.

Finally, at the microeconomic level, the analysis has shown that in some industrial sectors, firms show a significant and positive difference in their performance indicators (sales efficiency, production efficiency and ratio of exports) with respect to those that do not invest in R&D and do not have computers or the Internet. In addition, there is a clear association between technology improvements in products and improvement in product design and production efficiency.

Policy recommendations

Scarcities found in countries like Peru, and the rest of Latin America, require investment policies that encourage externality generating activities (improvements in education) or introduce increasing returns (improvements in physical infrastructure). Also important are complementary policies that facilitate the spread of knowledge and that permit free entry and exit from firms – and free mobility of people, capital, and technology (World Bank Report, 1995: 35).

Three major factors have been identified that can summarize what countries in Latin America can do to increase their innovation capacity.

There is a clear need to develop links between firms and academia. Links with universities and research institutes play a pivotal role in the development of innovation and innovation clusters by: achieving scientific preeminence; creating, developing, and maintaining new technologies for emerging and traditional industries; educating and training the required workforce and professions for economic development through technology; attracting large technology companies; promoting the development of home-grown technologies; and contributing to improved quality of life and culture. Appropriate institutional frameworks are crucial to establish the right incentives to encourage university scientists to collaborate through adequate property rights in business ventures.

High-quality universities and research institutions are a necessary condition. For example, in the case of Intel in Costa Rica, the availability of a relatively high-quality local labour force was key. In addition, Costa Rica responded to the increased demand for skilled labour at different levels by improving the overall quality of universities and high schools.

Simultaneously, the presence of catalyst agencies to promote these links is crucial. The lack of these institutions, and therefore the lack of more links, explains the failures of most of the clusters. The loss of the Peruvian knowledge base in hydrometallurgy has much to do with the lack of linkages among firms, universities, and research institutions. However, as in the case of Silicon Valley, and many other clusters in developed countries and in Costa Rica and Chile, these types of institutions were of significant importance in their success and are a policy instrument that governments can use.

Externality generating activities are not exclusive to the public policy arena. Within the private sector these activities are referred to as the creation of a critical mass of productive and institutional agents that help diffuse and create technologies. These activities are related to cluster development.

Two dimensions are important proximity; and a long time frame. Tight linkages between industry and local research institutions are a must to ensure an adequate supply and demand for knowledge, as well as to promote spillovers. These tight relationships require a long incubation period and champions to foster them. Successful clusters, such as Silicon Valley, required more than 50 years to develop.

Consistent with one of the major restrictions in poor countries, there is a need to develop funds for R&D. Chile provides a good example of the use of public and private partnerships to provide access to funding and increase linkages between firms, research institutes, and universities. At the same time, these partnerships ensure that private-sector participation increases over time.

In addition to the scarcity of financial capital, most firms in countries like Peru are SMEs and therefore they will face the usual problems of lack of capital and marketing expertise. Experiences, such as those in Banglore, India, where the government, financial institutions, and industry are working together to address these issues by setting up venture capital funds, establishing marketing channels to target countries, and developing infrastructure needed for an IT cluster are essential.

Alternatively, as in the case of Malaysia, attracting foreign direct investment (FDI) could be the cornerstone of an economic development strategy. However, it is important to have an umbrella strategy to create links between the FDI and domestic investment to move toward higher value-added local production and technology development. As mentioned by Michael Porter (1990): 'A development strategy based solely on multinational firms may doom a nation to remaining a factor-driven economy. If reliance on foreign multinationals is too complete, the nation will not be the home base for any industry…Foreign multinationals should be only one component of a developing nation's economic strategy and an evolving one.'

Endnotes

1. The sectors included are: Commerce, Services, Fishing, Manufacturing, Hydrocarbons, Electricity, Transport, Communications, Construction, and Agroindustry.
2. Although these figures are official, they may not be accurate. The figures are from a survey that had several shortcomings, such as a poorly defined sample, and firms may have had different ideas of the concepts used in the survey.
3. Peru is ranked in position 54 of 59 countries for which the index was constructed.
4. In the start-up index, Peru is in position 46 of 49.
5. The countries included are: United States, Hong Kong, Iceland, Luxembourg, Finland, United Kingdom, Netherlands, Singapore, Sweden, Israel, Australia, Taiwan, Norway, Belgium, Denmark, Ireland, Canada, Switzerland, New Zealand, South Africa, Germany, Hungary, Turkey, Korea, Malaysia, Spain, Indonesia, Greece, Poland, Austria, Chile, Thailand, Egypt, Mauritius, France, Portugal, Jordan, Japan, India, Italy, Philippines, Slovak Republic, Brazil, Zimbabwe, Vietnam, Czech Republic, China, Argentina, El Salvador, Costa Rica, Mexico, Russia, Ukraine, Colombia, Venezuela, Peru, Bolivia, Bulgaria, and Ecuador.
6. The Advisory Committee for Technological Innovation at the National Competitiveness Council has declared that technological innovation does not have high priority among the different agents of the Peruvian TIS. This committee has stated that the TIS is fragmented and does not show links that facilitate knowledge transfer. It also stated that there is no market for technological services, that innovation capabilities are scarce, and that funding for innovation is limited. This committee has defined the following objectives: (a) to promote a culture that values innovation and quality improvement; (b) to increase the demand of firms for S&T; (c) to improve the generation, transfer, diffusion, and exchange of technology

systems; (d) to generate innovation capabilities; and (e) to increase the private investment and expenditures in innovation (Consejo Nacional de Competitividad, 2003).
7. Robles et al. (2001) estimate, based on a sample of microfirms in manufacturing, metalworking and informatics services, that they only contribute with 0.44% of the taxes paid in those sectors.
8. Entrepreneurial development services are offered by independent professionals who address topics such as law, taxes and accounting, and provide services in the areas of management, marketing, commercialization, and finances. In addition, these services can be classified by the intervention mode: (a) direct intervention services (i.e. training and capacity-building services, generation and transfer of technology, information, consulting and technical assistance, and commercial promotion and marketing); (b) intermediation services (i.e. entrepreneurial cooperation and assistance centres); and (c) context services (i.e. creation of infrastructure and regulation) (Robles et al., 2001).
9. Peru signed the Andean Trade Preferences and Drug Eradication Agreement (ATPDEA) in September 2002. By this agreement, the US government grants trade preferences to Colombia, Bolivia, and Peru for more than 5,600 products. In addition, Peru has been accepted as an associated member to MERCOSUR, the common market formed by Brazil, Argentina, Uruguay, and Paraguay.
10. The commercialization may be registered as a domestic transaction but the goods and services are not produced domestically.
11. Although it is not clear what is causing such failures in education, Duryea and Pages (2002a,b) point out three major reasons: reduced expenditure in education; low quality of teachers; and poor educational systems, which lack mechanisms of control and accountability at all levels.
12. To measure returns to education a standard Mincer equation is estimated of the following form: $\ln(y) = \alpha_0 + rS + \alpha_1 E_p + \alpha_2 E_o + \alpha_3 E_p^2 + \alpha_4 E_o^2 + \alpha_5 X + \mu$, where S is the number of years of schooling, r is the returns to education, E_p and E_o are potential and occupational experience respectively, and X represents sociodemographic characteristics.
13. They are inefficient because as shown by Heckman and Pages (2000) they reduce the demand for labour; they increase inequality because some workers benefit while many others are hurt. The impact on inequality is multifaceted. Job security increases inequality because it reduces the employment prospects of young and possibly female and unskilled workers. It also increases inequality because it segregates the labour market between workers with secure jobs and workers with very few prospects of becoming employed. Finally, job security provisions increase inequality if they increase the size of the informal sector.
14. In developed countries, a new firm can obtain a venture capital for perhaps 8 years, and then go public through an initial public offering (IPO) although no positive earnings are in prospect for many years until (and if) the products are successful.
15. Barajas and Steiner (2001) conducted a more detailed look at the evolution of credit and bank behaviour in Argentina, Mexico, Peru, and Colombia over the last 20 years and clearly showed the restrictions to credit in

Latin America. They also showed that in the 1990s there was a positive change, spurred in part by financial liberalization at the beginning of the decade. Unfortunately, later in the decade these measures were once again reduced.
16. Despite notable progress over the past decade, Latin American ports are still among the most inefficient in the world (IADB, 2001).
17. Although two thirds of Latin American countries have privatized their telecommunications, and are trying to bring competition to the sector, the penetration in developed countries is still five times greater. However, this gap is being reduced more rapidly in Latin America than in the rest of the developing world.
18. The 15 institutions are: Centro de Información e Interconexión Telemática (CENDECYT); Instituto Nacional de Becas y Crédito Educativo (INABEC); Instituto Nacional de Investigación y Capacitación de Telecomunicaciones (INICTEL); Instituto Nacional de Investigaciones de la Amazonía Peruana (IIAP); Servicio Nacional de Meteorología e Hidrografía (SENAMHI); Instituto Nacional de Recursos Naturales (INRENA); Instituto del Mar del Perú (IMARPE); Instituto Tecnológico Pesquero (ITP); Consejo Nacional de Camélidos Sudamericanos (CONACS); Instituto Nacional de Investigación Agraria (INIA); Instituto Geofísico del Perú (IGP); Comisión Nacional de Investigación y Desarrollo Aeroespacial (CONIDA); Instituto Geográfico Nacional (IGN); Instituto Peruano de Energía Nuclear (IPEN); and Instituto Geológico Minero y Metalúrgico (INGEMMET).
19. The Science and Competitiveness Fund (FONCYC) will provide funding to state universities to set up postgraduate courses.
20. Pavitt (1984) proposed different patterns of technical change for different industries. There are industries in which innovations are generated mainly by capital goods and inputs suppliers and, therefore, the transfer of technology is made via the purchase of equipment. In other cases, reverse engineering and licensing are the main means for technology transfer and imitation in industries that rely on economies of scale, whose products have incorporated high technology or depend on specialized suppliers. In any case, the transfer, diffusion, or imitation of technology requires investment aimed at elevating the capabilities of the recipient firms.
21. The research team had access to the database gathered by the Encuesta de Ciencia, Tecnología e Innovación Tecnológica 1999.
22. The sectors included are: Commerce, Services, Fishing, Manufacturing, Hydrocarbons, Electricity, Transport, Communications, Construction, and Agroindustry.
23. Using this technology, copper oxide ore is sprayed with an acid solution that percolates through the ground material and liberates the copper (leaching stage). This leachate is then pumped into tanks and mixed with organic reagents to extract the copper (solvent extraction stage). Sulphuric acid is used to strip the copper into an electrolytic solution. This rich electrolyte is then subjected to an electric current that causes the copper to settle on the cathodes (electrowinning stage).
24. Sulphur ores are the most abundant copper ores in the world.
25. CENTROMIN PERU was the state-owned mining firm that operated the previously owned facilities of Cerro de Pasco Corp.

26. MINERO PERU was the state-owned mining firm aimed at developing new mineral deposits, such as Cerro Verde, where part of the research activity was conducted. INCITEMI was the National Mining Research Institute, which later became the INGEMMET (Instituto Nacional de Geología, Minería y Metalurgia).
27. The first commercial SX-EW plant in the world was Blue Bird, which was constructed in the United States in 1968. It was followed by Baghdad (1970), also in the United States; Nchanga (1973) in Zambia; and Cerro Verde (1974) in Arequipa, Peru.
28. During the 1970s, the government launched media campaigns urging young people to study mining engineering.
29. Yanacocha is owned by the US firm Newmont (51%) and the Peruvian firm Minas Buenaventura (49%). This operation is located in Northern Sierra (Cajamarca), one of the poorest areas in Peru. By the end of 1998, proven and probable reserves were 20.1 million ounces. Yanacocha has become the largest gold operation in Latin America. In 2005, its annual production reached 3.3 million ounces.
30. In 1999, in one of the most important mergers to take place in the copper industry, Phelps Dodge acquired Cyprus Amax and thus, Cerro Verde is now property of the former.
31. Peruvian state-owned firms, like Cerro Verde, did not have control of their revenues, which were collected by the central government. The budget of Cerro Verde was prepared and justified, then the government approved the appropriation designated for the firm.
32. Esteban Domic was Director of Sociedad Minera Pudahuel, a company that devoted great efforts to optimize bacterial leaching. This company holds a patent on bacterial leaching.
33. For example, when Southern Peru representatives were asked if they had used information from the Andean Pact projects, they said they did not know of the existence of the projects.
34. Mango is a rounded fruit with a hard seed. This fruit is sweet and is high in calcium, magnesium, potassium, phosphorus, vitamin A, and various amino acids. The factors that contributed to this spread were: adequate soil and weather, with no rain, that produced sweet fruit with good colour; mango were harvested in Piura 'counter-season' therefore, prices are relatively high in international markets; there was good access to the export port at Paita; and there is a growing demand in the northern hemisphere for mangos compared with other tropical fruits such as bananas and pineapples.
35. Piura accounts for about 68% of total mango supply. Most of the harvested area is located in the San Lorenzo valley. This area recently had a major dispute with a mining firm that wanted to develop the Tambogrande gold deposit and required the farmers to be resettled in other areas. Through different actions, which included a plebiscite, the farmers faced the mining firm. In the end, the public rejection and the failure of the mining firm to meet certain financial requirements impeded the development of the mining project.
36. The two most dangerous species are *Ceratitis capitata* and *Anastrephia fraterculus*, which are both found in the coastal valleys in Peru. These flies

attack fruits and vegetables. The females deposit their eggs in the fruit, where the resulting larvae ruin the crop. Ceratitis capitata has a very broad global distribution, and in 1995 was reported in 82 countries. Different methods, such as biological and chemical control and sterile insect techniques, have been used to control and eradicate the fruit fly.
37. The anthracnosis fungi attack mango trees from the florescence stage until the fruit is partially developed. The tree loses its leaves and the fruits become soft and rotten. The unripe infested fruits present brown spots that grow after the harvest; therefore, the damage is only evident after the fruit has embarked.
38. For a complete definition of the agricultural innovation system, see INIA, 2003.

References

Acemoglu, Daron. (2002) Technical change, inequality, and the labor market. *Journal of Economic Literature*, XL, 7–72.

Arocena, Rodrigo and Sutz, Judith. (2000) *Interactive learning spaces and development policies in Latin America*. Universidad de la República, Montevideo, Uruguay.

Arregui, Patricia and Torero, Máximo. (1991) *Indicadores de ciencia y tecnología en América Latina: 1970–1990*. GRADE, Lima, Peru.

Arteaga, Douglas. (2003) *Investigación en ciencias geológicas y mineras – informe final*. Proyecto BID-CONCYTEC, Lima, Peru.

Barajas, Adolfo and Steiner, Roberto. (2001) Credit stagnation in Latin America. *International Monetary Fund, IMF Working Paper*, WP/02/53.

Barro, R. and Lee, J. (2000) International data on educational attainment: updates and implications. *Centre for International Development*, Cambridge, MA, Working Paper No. 42.

Boubakri, N. and Cosset, J. (1998) The financial and operating performance of newly privatized firms: Evidence from developing countries. *Journal of Finance*, 53, 1081–1110.

Blumenthal, David. (1992) Academic–industry relationships in the life sciences: extent, academic, consequences, and management. *JAMA (Journal of the American Medical Association)*, 268(23), 3344–3349.

Carazo, Mercedes Inés, Stern, Isaías Flit, and Erazo, Angel P. Hurtado. (2000) *Estrategia nacional de desarrollo de la innovación y la productividad en el Perú: Elementos para una propuesta*. Ministerio de Industria, Turismo, Integración y Negociaciones Comerciales Internacionales (MITINCI), Lima, Peru.

Carlsson, Bo, Jacobsson, Steffan, Holmén, Magnus, and Rickne, Annika. (2002) Innovation systems: Analytical and methodological issues. *Research Policy*, 31(2), 233–245.

Castells, M. and Hall, P. (1994). *Technopoles of the world*. Routledge, London, UK.

Chong, A. and Zanforlin, L. (2002) Technology and epidemics. International Monetary Fund *(IMF) Staff Papers* Vol 49(3), 1–33.

Chong, Alberto. (2001) *The Internet and the ability to adapt and innovate in Latin America*. Inter-American Development Bank (IADB), Washington, DC.

Consejo Nacional de Competitividad (2003) *Innovación y Competitividad – Documento Final*. Grupo Consultivo de Innovación Tecnológica, Lima, Peru.

CONCYTEC. (2001) Indicadores de ciencia, tecnología e innovación tecnológica: Década de los 90 – Perú. *Consejo Nacional de Ciencia y Tecnología*, Lima, Peru.

CONCYTEC. (2002) Anteproyecto de ley general de promoción de la ciencia y tecnología para el desarrollo nacional. *Consejo Nacional de Ciencia y Tecnología*, Lima, Peru.

Cooper, Charles. (1991) Are innovation studies on industrialized economies relevant to technology policy in developing countries? *Working Paper, UNU-INTECH* No. 3, Maastricht.

Cooper, Charles. (1999) National systems of innovation: The institutional framework for technological learning in developing countries. *Paper presented at: Creating a New Architecture for Learning and Development*, Organized by the Asian Development Bank, Tokyo, Japan.

David, Paul A., Mowery, David C., and Steinmuller, W. Edward. (1992) Analyzing the economic payoffs from basic research. *Economics of Innovation and New Technology*, 2(1), 73–90.

Davidovich, Monique and Polastri, Rossana. (1986) *Estructura de Mercado y comportamiento tecnológico: aplicación de un modelo teórico*. Batchelor's Thesis, Universidad del Pacífico, Lima, Peru.

Duryea, Suzanne and Pages, Carmen. (2002a). *Human capital policies: What they can and cannot do for productivity and poverty reduction in Latin America*. Inter-American Development Bank (IADB), Washington, DC (mimeo).

Duryea, Suzanne and Pages, Carmen. (2002b) *Achieving high labor productivity in Latin America: Is education enough?* Inter-American Development Bank (IADB), Washington, DC (mimeo).

Edwards, S. (2001) ¿Salvarán a Latinoamérica las tecnologías de la información? *Latinwatch*, BBVA. (http://serviciodeestudios.bbva.com)

Eisenberg, Rebecca S. (1987) Proprietary rights and the norms of science in biotechnology research. *Yale Law Journal*, 97, 177–231.

Erber, Fabio. (1999) Ajuste estructural y política científica y tecnológica. Taller de Innovación Tecnológica para el Desarrollo Económico de la Región, *Segunda Reunión de la Comisión Interamericana de Ciencia y Tecnología*, 30 October, Acapulco, Mexico.

Fagerberg, Jan. (1992) The home market hypothesis re-examined: The impact of domestic user-producer interaction on export specialization, in Lundvall, Bengt-Ake (ed.) *National systems of innovation: Towards a theory of innovation and interactive learning*, Pinter Publishers, London, UK.

Ferrati, David de, Perry, Guillermo, Lederman, Daniel, and Maloney, William. (2002) *From natural resources to the knowledge economy: trade and job quality*. The World Bank, Washington, DC.

Flit, Isaías, and Barrio, Sergio. (1994) *La nueva política científica y tecnológica*. CONCYTEC, Lima, Peru (mimeo).

Freeman, Christopher. (1982) *The economics of industrial innovation*. Pinter Publishers, London, UK.

Freeman, Christopher. (2002) Continental, national and sub-national innovation systems: Complementarity and economic growth. *Research Policy*, 31(2), 191–211.

Fukuda-Parr, Sasiko, Lopes, Carlos, and Malik, Khalid. (2002) Institutional innovations for capacity development, in Fukuda-Parr, S. et al. (eds). *Capacity for development: New solutions to old problems*. Earthscan and UNDP, London and New York.

Garland, Gonzalo and Kuramoto, Juana. (1988) *El rol de la ciencia y tecnología en el desarrollo de los recursos mineros*. GRADE, Lima, Peru (mimeo).

Griliches, Zvi. (1980) R&D and the productivity slowdown. *American Economic Review*, Papers and Proceedings of the 92nd Annual Meeting of the AEA, 70(2), 343–348.

Griliches, Zvi. (1986) Productivity, R&D, and basic research at the firm level in the 1970s. *American Economic Review*, 76(1), 141–154.

Griliches, Zvi. (1990) Patent statistics as economic indicators: A survey. *Journal of Economic Literature*, XXVIII, 1661–1707.

Grilliches, Zvi. (1992) The search for R&D spillovers. *Scandinavian Journal of Economics*, 94 (Supplement), S29–47.

Griliches, Zvi. (1994) Productivity, R&D and the data constraint. *American Economic Review*, 84(1), 1–23.

Griliches, Zvi. (1998) Productivity puzzles and R&D: Another nonexplanation. *The Journal of Economic Perspectives*, 2(4), 9–21.

Gu, Shulin. (1999) Implications of national innovation systems for developing countries: Managing change and complexity in economic development. *United Nations University, Institute for New Technologies*, Maastricht, Discussion Paper Series No. 9903.

Heckman, James and Pages, Carmen. (2000) The cost of job security regulation: Evidence from Latin American labor markets. *National Bureau of Economic Research*, Cambridge, Massachusetts, Working Paper No. 7773.

INIA. (2003) 'Plan Estratégico 2003–2007', Instituto Nacional de Investigación Agraria, Lima (mimeo).

Jaffe, Adam B. (1989) Characterizing the 'technological position' of firms, with application to qualifying technological opportunity and research spillovers. *Research Policy*, 18, 87–90.

Jaffe, Adam and Trajtenberg, Manuel. (1998) International knowledge flows: Evidence from patent citations. *National Bureau of Economic Research*, Cambridge, Massachusetts, NBER Working Paper No. 6507.

Jaffe, Adam B., Trajtenberg, Manuel. and Henderson, Rebecca M. (1993) Geographical localization of knowledge spillovers as evidenced by patent citation. *Quarterly Journal of Economics*, 63, 577–598.

IADB. (2001) *Competitiveness: The business of growth. Economic and social progress in Latin America, 2001 Report*. Inter-American Development Bank (IADB), Washington, DC.

Klevorick, Alvin, Levin, Richard, Nelson, Richard, and Winter, Sidney. (1995) On the sources and significance of interindustry differences in technological opportunities. *Research Policy*, 24(2), 185–205.

Kuramoto, Juana. (2003) 'The hydrometallurgical method and the techno-economic factors at play', in Lagos, Sahoo and Camus (eds) Plenary Lectures,

Economics and Applications of Copper, Proceedings of the 5th International Copper 2003 Conference, November 30–December 3, Santiago de Chile.

Kuramoto, Juana and Sagasti, Francisco. (2002) Integrating local and global knowledge, technology and production systems: challenges for technical cooperation, in Fukuda-Parr, S. et al. (eds) *Capacity for development: New solutions to old problems.* Earthscan and UNDP, London and New York.

Laboratorio Latinoamericano de Evaluación de la Calidad Educativa (LLECE). (2000) Primer estudio comparativo sobre lenguaje y matemática y factores asociados, para alumnos del tercer y cuarto grado de la educación básica. *Informe Técnico,* LLECE, Santiago, Chile.

Lall, Sanjaya and Teubal, Morris. (1998) Market stimulating technology policies in developing countries: A framework with examples from East Asia. *World Development,* 26(8), 1369–1385.

Lerner, Joshua (1993) Innovation and structure of high-technology industries. pp. 89–107, in Burgelman, Robert A. and Rosenbloom, Richard S. (eds) *Research on technological innovation, management and policy.* Volume 5. JAI Press, Greenwich, Connecticut and London, UK.

Lerner, Joshua. (1994) The importance of trade secrecy: Evidence from civil litigation. *Harvard Business School, Division of Research,* Working Paper No. 95-043, Cambridge, Massachusetts.

Lööf, Hans., Heshmati, Almas., Asplund, Rita. and Nååas, Svein-Olav. (2001) Innovation and performance in manufacturing industries: A comparison of the Nordic countries. Economic Research Institute, Stockholm School of Economics, Stockholm, SSE/EFI Working Paper Series in *Economics and Finance* No. 457.

Lundvall, Bengt-Ake., Johnson, Björn., Andersen, Esben Sloth., and Dalum, Bent. (2002) National systems of production, innovation and competence building. *Research Policy,* 31(2), 213–231.

Macha, William. and Sotillo, César. (1975) Potencial de la lixiviación bacteriana en el Perú. *Junta del Acuerdo de Cartagena,* Lima, Peru (mimeo).

Malerba, Franco. (2002) Sectoral systems of innovation and production. *Research Policy,* 31(2), 247–264.

Mansfield, Edwin. (1983) Technological change and market structure: An empirical study. *American Economic Review,* 73(2), 205–209.

Mansfield, Edwin. (1994) Academic research underlying industrial innovations: Sources, characteristics, and financing. *Review of Economic and Statistics,* 77(1), 55–65.

Mansfield, Edwin. (1998) Academic research and industrial innovation: An update of empirical findings. *Research Policy* 26(7–8), 773–776.

Meller, Patricio. (2001) *Chilean copper: Facts, role and issues.* Universidad de Chile, Facultad de Ciencias Físicas y Matemáticas, Departamento de Ingeniería Industrial, World Bank, Washington, DC (mimeo).

Ministerio de Agricultura. (2002) *Lineamientos de política agraria para el Perú.* Ministerio de Agricultura, Lima, Peru. (http://www.portalagrario.gob.pe/politica_1.shtml)

Mullin Consulting. (2002) Un análisis del sistema peruano de innovación. Proyecto *BID-CONCYTEC,* Lima, Peru.

Nadvi, Khalid. (1999) Collective efficiency and collective failure: The response of the Sialkot surgical instrument cluster to global quality pressures. *World Development*, 27(9), 1605–1626.
OECD. (1997) *Oslo manual: Proposed guidelines for collecting and interpreting technological innovation data*. Organisation for Economic Co-operation and Development, Paris. France.
Patel, Parimal and Pavitt, Keith. (1994) The nature and economic importance of national innovations systems. *STI Review*, 14, 9–32.
Pavitt, K. (1984) Sectoral patterns of technical change: towards a taxonomy and a theory, *Research Policy*, 13, 343–73.
Pisano, Gary. (1990) Using equity participation to support exchange: evidence from the biotechnology industry. *Journal of Law, Economics and Organization*, 5(1), 109–126.
Pianta, Mario and Sirilli, Giorgio. (1998) The use of innovation surveys for policy evaluation, IDEA Paper Series, STEP Group, *Studies in Technology, Innovation and Economic Policy*, Oslo, Norway.
Porter, Michael. (1990) *The competitive advantage of nations*. Free Press, New York, NY.
PRODUCE. (2007) Ministerio de la Producción, Lima, Peru, *PERU Innova*, Boletín No. 13.
Quandt, Carlos. (1998) *The concept of virtual technopoles and the feasibility of incubating technology-intensive clusters in Latin America and the Caribbean*. IDRC – IC² Institute, Curitiba.
Robles, Miguel, Saavedra, Jaime, Torero, Máximo, Valdivia, Néstor, and Chacaltana, Juan. (2001) *Estrategias y Racionalidad de la Pequeña Empresa*, Organización Internacional de Trabajo (OIT), Lima, Peru.
Rogers, E.M. and Larsen, J.K. (1984) *Silicon Valley Fever: Growth of High-Tech Culture*, Basic Books, New York, NY.
Romer, Paul. (1986) Increasing returns and long-run growth. *Journal of Political Economy*, 94(5), 1002–1037.
Romer, Paul. (1990) Endogenous technological change. *Journal of Political Economy*, 98 (Supplement), S71–S102.
Rule, James B. (1998) Biotechnology: Big money comes to the university. *Dissent*, Fall, 430–436.
RICyT, (1990–1999) *Red de Indicadores de Ciencia y Tecnología*. (http://www.ricyt.edu.ar)
Sagasti, Francisco. (2003) 'El sistema de innovación tecnológica en el Perú: antecedentes, situación y perspectivas', Programa de Ciencia y Tecnología BID – Perú, PE – 0203, Lima (mimeo). (http://www.concytec.gob.pe/ProgramaCyT/FONCYC)
Sánchez, Walter. (1998) Inversiones en minería y proyectos al 2007. *Informativo Mensual de la Sociedad de Minería, Petróleo y Energía*, 10(VIII), 14–21.
Schmitz, Hubert. (1999) *Does local cooperation matter? Evidence from industrial clusters in South Asia and Latin America*. Institute of Development Studies, Brighton, UK.
Teece, David and Pisano, Gary. (1994) The dynamic capabilities of firms: An introduction. *Industrial and Corporate Change*, 3, 537–556.
Tijero, Rafael. (1992) *El cultivo del mango en el Perú. Fundo para o Desenvolvimento do Agronegócio do Algodão* (FUNDEAGRO), Lima, Peru.

Torero, Máximo. (2001) Geographic association as an alternative for diffusion in the Peruvian traditional agriculture. *Quarterly Journal of International Agriculture* (forthcoming), 24.

Torero, Máximo. (1998) *Analyzing the spillover mechanism on the semiconductor industry in the Silicon Valley and Route 128*. Department of Economics, University of California at Los Angeles.

Vargas Alfaro, Leiner. (1999) Aprendizaje institucional y fomento a la innovación en Costa Rica. Taller de Innovación Tecnológica para el Desarrollo Económico de la Región, *Segunda Reunión de la Comisión Interamericana de Ciencia y Tecnología*, 30 October, Acapulco, Mexico.

Viotti, Eduardo. (2000) Passive and active learning systems. *Documento presentado en la IV Conferencia sobre Política Tecnológica e Innovación*. Networks de Conocimiento y Aprendizaje para el Desarrollo, 28–31 August, Curitiba, Brazil.

Voyer, Roger. (1997a) *Knowledge-based industrial clustering: International comparisions*. Nordicity Group, Ltd. (mimeo).

Voyer, Roger. (1997b) *Emerging high-technology industrial clusters in Brazil, India, Malaysia and South Africa*. International Development Research Centre, Ottawa, Canada.

Warhurst, Alyson. (1985) *The potential of biotechnology for mining in developing countries: The case of the Andean Pact copper project*. Doctoral Thesis, University of Sussex, Brighton, UK.

Warner, A. (2000) Economic creativity, in Porter, M.E., Sachs, J.D., Warner, A.M., Moore, C., Tudor, J.M., Vasquez, D., Schwab, K., Cornelius, P.K., Levinson, M., *The global competitiveness Report 2000*, Harvard University, Cambridge, Massachusetts. (http://www.amazon/Global-Competitiveness-Report-2000/dp/0195138201)

WDI, (2002) *World Development Indicators*. The World Bank, Washington, DC. (http//www.publications.worldbank.org/WDI/)

World Bank. (2001) *Global economic prospects and developing countries*. Washington, DC.

World Bank. (2005) World Development Report 2005: A Better Investment Climate For Everyone, Washington, DC.

Zucker, L.G., Darby, M.R., and Brewer, M.B. (1998) Intellectual human capital and the birth of U.S. biotechnology enterprises. *American Economic Review*, 88(1), 290–306.

Zucker, L.G., Darby, M.R., and Armstrong, Jeff. (1994) Intellectual capital and the firm: The technology of geographically localized knowledge spillovers. *National Bureau of Economic Research (NBER)*, Cambridge, Massachusetts, Working Paper No. 4946.

Zucker, L.G. and Darby, M.R. (1994) The organization of biotechnology science and its commercialization in Japan. *UCLA Institute for Social Science Research*, 6(1), 1–29.

Zucker, L.G., Darby, M.R., and Armstrong, J. (2001) Commercializing knowledge: University science, knowledge capture, and firm performance in biotechnology. *National Bureau of Economic Research (NBER)*, Cambridge, Massachusetts, Working Paper No. 8499.

CHAPTER 6

Trends in research and development in Tanzania: Funding sources, institutional arrangements, and relevance

Samuel Wangwe, Bitrina Diyamett, and Adalgot Komba

Abstract

This research explores trends in funding, institutional arrangements, and the relevance of research and development in Tanzania to better understand how policy is influencing both public and private support of research and development. The research focuses on agriculture, industry, and health, and the sample includes research and development institutes, industrial firms and managers, farmers, and health facilities and officials. The authors conclude that there has been a decrease in the share of public R&D funding; a shift toward more private funding, especially in terms of public–private partnerships; and a dominance of donor funding, which has raised concerns over ownership and undue influence on the development agenda. They recommend the need to increase public funding for research in agriculture and health; pay greater attention to the continuity and predictability of R&D funding; diversify funding sources; enhance domestic ownership of the research agenda to reflect national development priorities; and improve monitoring of research outputs and dissemination of results.

Founded in 1994, Economic and Social Research Foundation (ESRF) is an independent, not-for-profit institution for research and policy analysis. The focus is capacity building in the area of policy analysis and development management in the Tanzanian society: government, public and private sectors, and civil society.

Our participation in RoKS has provided us with unique experience of the functioning of research and development establishment in Tanzania. This is one area where much less is known despite the knowledge that science, technology and innovation are critical to sustainable development processes, including efforts towards poverty reduction.

The team members and their institutions are key stakeholders in science and technology policy research. Thus the experience gained will make a valuable contribution in follow-up research and in the long run help to inform policymaking processes in the country. As active members of African Technology Policy Studies (ATPS) network, the region also stands to benefit from the knowledge gained in the process.

Background

Tanzania, like any other developing country, faces the challenges of abject poverty, ignorance, poor health, low levels of productivity, and many more problems associated with underdevelopment. The past four decades have witnessed concerted efforts to address these problems, but the results have been mixed. The consensus is that development processes in developing countries are not linear; rather they are influenced by specific country conditions and by the existence of more developed countries.

More important, the driving forces of development have changed over time. Generation and use of scientific and technical knowledge has become an important determinant of development in an increasingly knowledge-intensive development process. This suggests that the development processes, and associated catching-up processes, can be better understood by analysing the role of technology and processes of technological learning.

Tanzania has over the past four decades taken many initiatives to provide a framework for the development of science and technology (S&T) and its integration into the mainstream of development strategies. However, the impact of these initiatives in changing the socioeconomic conditions of the country has been questioned in view of persistent poverty and underdevelopment. There is a need to revisit the role and relevance of science and technology in national development and to explore prospects for filling knowledge gaps in the generation and use of research results. This study examines trends in the flow of research funds and their sources; institutional arrangements and their influence on the use of research outputs; and the relevance and effectiveness of ongoing research programmes and projects.

Problem

In increasingly globalized, knowledge-intensive economies, science and technology constitute critical inputs to development processes. Investment in research and development (R&D) is key to the knowledge-generation needed to benefit from globalization. However, for countries like Tanzania, analyses of the effectiveness with which these investments have been translated into benefits to society have produced more questions than answers. Traditionally R&D has been conducted through public R&D institutions and been funded by the government and, to a large extent, the international donor community.

In Tanzania, restructuring initiatives introduced in the mid-1980s shifted the national economy from a largely public-sector led and administratively controlled economy in the 1970s and early 1980s to a private-sector led and market-oriented economy in the 1990s. Major changes have taken place in response to this new system of economic management. Institutional responses to changes in policy conditions have altered the functioning of the R&D system in Tanzania. Shifts in economic management and the approach to development have also had important implications on approaches to technology development and funding of R&D (Wangwe and Diyamett, 1998; Enos, 1995). Stakeholders other than the government now play new roles in development processes and in R&D activities in particular.

Objectives

This study sought to understand the motivation and impact of changing trends in R&D funding and to determine how relevant and effective the R&D system was in generating knowledge that would benefit key stakeholders. The main objective was to examine trends in R&D funding and the evolution of institutional arrangements over the past two decades and to assess the effectiveness and relevance of R&D programmes and projects to the intended beneficiaries.

Specific objectives of the study were:
- to document and explain trends in the funding of R&D activities in terms of volume and source for the past two decades;
- to determine and explain trends in the composition of various sources of funding;
- to determine the relevance and effectiveness of R&D programmes and projects;
- to identify and analyse institutional arrangements and factors that influence the relevance and effectiveness of R&D programmes and projects;
- to examine the role of policy in influencing public- and private-sector support to research and development with a view to enhancing its relevance to socioeconomic development; and
- to undertake a comparative analysis of research and development activities in different sectors of the economy.

Conceptual framework

This study adopted the National Systems of Innovation (NSI) as its conceptual framework. Within this framework, the R&D system is an important component. Traditionally, innovation was believed to result from research in basic science, and to flow from the automatic spread of new processes and products into the economic system. Science was believed to be an 'endless frontier' of new knowledge, products, and processes. The policy implication was to allocate sufficient resources to scientific research to generate knowledge that would percolate into the economy in the form of products and processes. However, it is now recognized that innovation is a collective endeavour that is facilitated by interactive learning between different actors – it is systemic.

According to Lundvall (1992), NSI is a system of elements and relationships (organizations, policies, rules, and regulations) in which the production, diffusion, and use of economically useful knowledge takes place. The national systems of innovation approach have been commonly used in the developed world. It has been shown that the more resources that enter the R&D system, the more innovative the national system (Nelson, 1993). In recent years, the NSI approach has been adopted in the developing world. Some initiatives have been taken to adopt this approach in the African context (Muchie et al., 2003; Wangwe, 2003).

This study recognizes that the essence of innovation is novelty. Innovation in this context refers to both the process of introducing something new and the new thing itself. In economic terms, innovation refers to the marketing of new or improved products, the successful application of new or improved techniques, or the introduction of new ways of working that improve the efficiency of an individual or organization (Archibugi et al., 1994). However, the crux of the matter has always been how can governments bring about innovative activities in the national economy? How can the process be best organized and nurtured? What incentives and other policy regimes can facilitate innovative activities? What is the role of the public and private sectors in supporting R&D systems?

An important difference among national innovation systems is the amount and sources of funding for R&D, which in turn determines the development and relevance of research outputs. According to past experience, especially in Europe, as more research is privately funded it becomes more socially and economically valuable. Private funding comes from the beneficiaries of the research outputs; therefore, relevance or appropriateness of the research output is assured. Because the private sector is still evolving in most developing countries (which were formerly public-sector dominated), it can be assumed that public funding (government and donor funding) is likely to continue to be the predominant source of funds for research in these countries. However, as private funding of research grows, there is a need to identify more innovative ways to use government and donor funding in research programmes and projects.

Methodological framework

Approach

The study examined broad trends through a literature survey; undertook research on some R&D institutions in selected sectors; made an in-depth study of selected programmes and projects; and examined selected case studies. This combination of surveys and case studies provided a broad coverage of sectors, institutions, and beneficiaries. The surveys generated information related to R&D activities: who is doing what, where, and with what resources. They gathered information on projects and programmes undertaken during the past 20 years, identified sources of funds, and assessed their success in realizing intended goals and objectives. The data generated were eventually used in the selection and design of case studies that have provided detailed accounts of select R&D institutions and programmes.

Sampling and sample size

The study sampled R&D institutes in the agricultural, industrial, and health sectors. The sample included: industrial firms, farmers engaged in production of both food and cash crops, and healthcare facilities.

Agricultural sector

Seven institutes were selected in the agricultural sector. Four were major public institutions that conduct research on cash and food crops, one was representing a public–private partnership (sisal research at Mlingano), and two were private research institutes [Tea Research Institute of Tanzania (TRIT); and Tanzania Coffee Research Institute (TaCRI)]. Beneficiaries were represented by farmers. A random sample of 30 farmers for each institution was selected, making a total of 210 farmers.

Industrial sector

For the industrial sector, four active R&D institutes were studied: Tanzania Industrial Research and Development Organization (TIRDO); Centre for Agricultural Mechanization and Rural Technology (CAMARTEC); Tanzania Engineering and Manufacturing Design Organization (TEMDO); and Tanzania Traditional Energy Development and Environment Organization (TaTEDO), which is a private, not-for-profit institution. Beneficiaries were represented by firms. A stratified sample of 30 large firms and 30 small and medium firms was randomly selected from various industrial subsectors (e.g. metalworking and engineering, textiles, and food processing).

Health sector

For the health sector, the study centred on the National Institute for Medical Research (NIMR), an umbrella R&D institution responsible for overseeing medical research in Tanzania. Four research centres under NIMR were studied. They cover a variety of diseases including two pandemics (malaria and HIV/AIDS), and relate to key beneficiaries such as healthcare providers (e.g. hospitals, health centres, and clinics), and medical personnel. Several hospitals (including administration and doctors) and health centres were picked for study.

Data collection

The study gathered data from primary and secondary sources. Secondary data were collected from: accounts maintained by R&D institutes, public agencies, industrial enterprises, and health facilities; research reports; and policy documents. The data sought included flow of funds and funding sources, and R&D programmes and projects that had been undertaken.

Primary data were gathered through semi-structured interviews and focus group discussions with key stakeholders in the R&D system. These include R&D personnel, farmers, industrial managers, and health officials. The data sought included: the nature and relevance of R&D activities; mobilization of both public and private resources; dissemination of results; future directions for the R&D system; and the role of public policies in ensuring efficient and cost-effective use of scientific and technological knowledge to achieve national development objectives.

Limitations of the study

The main limitation of the study was unavailability of data because of poor record keeping in most R&D institutions in Tanzania. None of the institutions had readily available data on funding; data were scattered in different files. In some instances, information was said to be available from the heads of personnel who had left the R&D institutes. Frequent changes in ownership and management made it difficult to obtain information. This situation led to two outcomes. First, study objectives one and two could only be partly achieved. Second, delays in the collection of the primary information meant that the study took longer to complete than had been planned.

R&D systems in Tanzania: An overview

Research and development activities started in Tanzania in 1892 during the German colonial administration, and by the late 1990s, the R&D system had expanded to include 62 research institutes and centres spread throughout the country. The organizations covered agriculture (28), including livestock and forestry, industry (10), medicine (11), wildlife and fisheries (4), and universities and higher learning institutions (9) where R&D was being undertaken.

The R&D institutes are organized by sector and each R&D institution receives policy guidance from the parent ministry. The NIMR reports to the Ministry of Health. The Tanzania Wildlife Research Institute (TAWIRI), Tanzania Forestry Research Institute (TAFORI), and the Tanzania Fisheries Research Institute (TAFIRI) are under the Ministry of Natural Resources and Tourism. The Ministry of Industries and Trade is parent to TIRDO, TEMDO, CAMARTEC, and the Tanzania Bureau of Standards (TBS).

R&D is conducted largely in the public sector, although the private sector has recently increased its participation in the management and funding of

R&D activities. The political and economic reforms undertaken during the 1980s and 1990s affected the R&D system in three important ways. First, liberalization of the political and economic system allowed various groups in society to explicitly articulate their interests and participate in development management. Various groups have organized outside the ruling political party, which has permitted stakeholders to play a more participatory role in the development of R&D activities. Second, the redefinition of the role of the state and the consequent decline of the public sector, coupled with growth in the private sector, has changed the pattern and sources of funding for R&D. Funding to the predominantly public R&D system has been on the decline. This situation has affected both the level of R&D activities and their direction (Wangwe, 2000). Third, a number of users of R&D products, especially those whose demand was derived from the domestic market under the import-substitution regime of the 1970s, were weakened by competition from imports under trade liberalization. To the extent that imports have replaced domestic production, the demand for import-substitution-based goods and services from the local R&D systems has gone down (Komba, 1999).

Agricultural R&D system

Agricultural research in Tanzania started in 1892 when the German colonial administration established the first agricultural institute at Amani in the Usambara Mountains. The main objective of agricultural research at that time was to support the development of the export crops (sisal, coffee, tobacco, and peanuts) grown either by foreign companies or individual settler farmers (Liwenga, 1988). This trend continued into the British colonial administration. A chain of crop-based agricultural experimental stations was established in the 1930s. The first research stations included: Lyamungu, near Moshi (for coffee); Mlingano, near Tanga (for sisal), and Ukiriguru, near Mwanza (for cotton). Research was expanded after the Second World War to include food crops, and later, livestock research.

Organization and institutional arrangements

Tanzania's National Agricultural Research System (NARS) is classified into three main categories: Public-sector institutions under the Ministry of Agriculture and Food Security (MAFS) and outside the agricultural sector (e.g. universities) – the dominant organizational form and institutional arrangement in agriculture until recently when other forms emerged; institutions managed on the basis of public–private partnerships; and private-sector research organizations (a recent innovation).

Public sector

This sector is governed by a public research policy. The state makes all planning and major decisions regarding research through the Directorate of Research and Development (DRD) in the Ministry of Agriculture and Food Security (MAFS). The directorate plans and executes public-sector agricultural research. It also disseminates research findings to those involved in agricultural production in Tanzania by providing extension services offered by another department within the ministry. DRD operates through a network of research institutions, centres, and substations that covers the main areas of crop research. There are seven zonal research and training centres located in seven agroecological zones, which are responsible for applied and location-specific adaptive research.

Public–private partnerships

Some groups of farmers, especially large-scale and commercial farmers, can induce a public-sector response to their demands. This group includes the associations for major commercial crops such as the Tanganyika Coffee Growers Association, cooperative unions in coffee-growing areas, and tea and sisal growers associations. These groups were able to negotiate with the government on specific policies (e.g. price policies, and credit) that served their interests and influenced the activities of the state from 'the bottom up'.

Private sector

Private initiatives are a very recent phenomenon. Although the initiatives involve all major cash crops, only two commodity associations have followed this path. Coffee and tea growers associations now own and manage coffee and tea research institutes. Because these are very recent innovations, little information has been documented.

Knowledge generation and dissemination

Extension services in Tanzania have generally been understood as the transfer of agricultural technologies from experts (including progressive farmers) to farmers and other stakeholders such as livestock keepers. These services are used by the DRD and its research institutions to transfer well-proven technologies from research institutions to farmers. The services have, however, been the object of much debate and criticism among stakeholders in the agricultural sector. The weak links between research institutions and their partners, namely extension services and farmers, have been widely recognized (Eponou, 1993; Expere and Idowu, 1990). It is also acknowledged that this is one of the main reasons why the agricultural technology systems in Tanzania, and many countries in Africa, are ineffective and inefficient.

Both 'top-down' and 'bottom-up' approaches are used to disseminate research findings from these centres. The 'top-down' approach has followed a familiar linear model of innovation where research is conducted on the basis of perceived farmers' needs. The development of new crop varieties by the public research institutions in Tanzania, largely for small-scale farmers in the food crops sector, has followed this path. This system was given a boost by collaboration with international research centres: International Maize and Wheat Improvement Centre (CIMMYT), International Rice Research Institute (IRRI), Centro Internacional de Agricultura Tropical (CIAT), International Institute of Tropical Agricutlure (IITA), and International Crops Research Institute for Semi-Arid Tropics (ICRISAT). As a result, research institutions were able to produce 'packages' of technologies by adapting available technologies to local conditions. These new technologies have largely contributed to increases in the use of fertilizers, herbicides, fungicides, and insecticides. On the other hand, the 'bottom-up' approach has permitted greater collaboration between stakeholders and actors in the public sector and has led to public–private partnerships.

Industrial R&D system

The industrial R&D system in Tanzania is a relatively young enterprise compared with agricultural and medical research. This is because industrial development is itself a recent undertaking and the colonial administration did little to promote meaningful manufacturing industries. The industries and industrial structures that existed during the colonial period did not create demand for industrial R&D beyond that which was undertaken in industrialized countries. The agro-processing industries used simple technologies and were labour-intensive. So were the food and beverage industries and the few metalworking and engineering workshops that served them. These activities attracted little demand for industrial research and development.

In the immediate post-independence period the East African High Commission was changed to the East African Common Services Organization (EACSO), and the East African Industrial Research Organization (EAIRO) and other research organizations and institutes provided industrial research services under EACSO. The formation of the East African Community (EAC) in 1966 left the set-up intact. After the EAC broke up in 1977, TIRDO was established in 1979 to promote technology development for manufacturing industries. In 1980, TEMDO was established to promote engineering services and provide technical training to enterprises.

Organization and structure

With the exception of university-based institutions and NGOs such as TaTEDO, all other industrial R&D institutions operate as parastatal organizations under the Ministry of Industry and Trade (MIT). These institutions are sponsored by the government through MIT, which is responsible for major activities and initiatives such as the development of infrastructure, administration and personnel, and appointments of Board members, chief executives, and other top-level appointments to managerial positions.

TIRDO promotes technology development for manufacturing industries. TEMDO promotes engineering services and provides technical training to enterprises. The Institute of Production Innovation was founded in 1981 at the University of Dar es Salaam to undertake product innovation, transfer to industry, and technical consultancy for enterprises. The TBS was established in 1976 under the Ministry of Industry and Trade to manage metrology standards, testing, and quality standards in Tanzania.

Knowledge flow and dissemination

When the R&D institutions were established two decades ago, the government became the main sponsor of R&D activities because the public sector owned and managed most large-scale industries. The R&D institutions were designed to feed these industries with technological innovations and other services. This situation established a substantial link between R&D institutions and industry because both were under public-sector ownership and management. In addition, the realities of import substitution forced industries to procure goods and services locally, especially during the economic crisis of the early 1980s.

Health R&D system

Medical research in Tanzania started during the colonial era when missionary doctors researched tropical parasitic diseases. After the First World War, Tanganyika, a German colony before the war, was placed under British rule together with Kenya and Uganda. What followed was the institutionalization of medical research in these three East African countries. The process involved the establishment of research centres, stations, and units specializing in various vector-borne diseases such as malaria, trypanosomiasis, tuberculosis, filariasis, and bilharziasis.

The institutionalization process culminated in the formation of the East African Medical Research Council in the 1950s to coordinate research on human diseases. Medical research in post-independence Tanzania continued to operate under the auspices of the East African Community. The sharing of resources and specializations made sense in resource-intensive medical research, in part because human and financial resources to support meaningful medical research programmes were in short supply to individual governments. However, with the break up of the East African Community in the mid-1970s, the Tanzanian government created the NIMR in 1979 to assume the duties and functions of the defunct Council under the Ministry of Health (MoH).

Organization and structure

NIMR is both a clearing house for medical research and a coordinating agency for resource mobilization for R&D activities in the health sector. In addition, it provides a link between research institutions and the government. With its headquarters in Dar es Salaam, NIMR oversees research activities in three centres and three research stations. These are: Amani Medical Research Centre (AMRC); Mwanza Medical Research Centre (MMRC); Ifakara Health Research and Development Centre (IHRDC); Tabora Medical Research Station; Tukuyu Medical Research Station; and Muhimbili Medical Research Station.

Knowledge flow and dissemination

The Tanzanian government is not only the main sponsor but also the major consumer of outputs from the medical R&D system. Considering the public investments that have been made over the past two decades, one would not expect as many problems in knowledge generation, dissemination, and utilization process. The main beneficiaries of medical R&D (medical service providers, which include publicly and privately owned hospitals and local authorities) experience significant problems in accessing information coming from medical research laboratories, and clinical and field trials. Decades of research on a wide range of diseases like malaria, filariasis, plague, schistosomiasis, and more recently on HIV/AIDS has been undertaken.

Research findings

Agricultural sector

A total of 150 farmers were interviewed, which included 100 small-scale farmers mainly growing food crops and 50 farmers growing cash crops (both smallholders and large-scale farmers). Four R&D institutions and their beneficiaries were also studied: the Tengeru Horticultural Research Institute (Horti-Tengeru); the Mikocheni Agricultural Research Institute (MARI); the Ukiriguru Agricultural Research Institute, Mwanza; Uyole Agricultural Research Institute, Mbeya; and the Kilombero Agricultural Training and Research Institute (KATRIN), Ifakara. The major crops involved were tomato, rice, coconut, maize, and banana. For each institution, two projects (one successful and one a failure) were selected for in-depth study.

Trends in R&D funding: Volume and shift in balance

The sources of funds for R&D in agriculture include the central government, foreign donors, local government authorities, cesses and levies, contract research, revenue retention, and cost recovery. Most R&D is being funded by external sources. Between 2000–1 and 2003–4, about 80% of expenditures made by R&D institutions came from donors. The government covers mostly salaries and other routine, nondevelopmental expenditures (Table 6.1).

Government funding has also been erratic, but since 1989, when the Tanzania Agricultural Research Organization (TARO) and the Tanzania Livestock Research Organization (TALIRO) were dissolved and research came directly under the parent Ministry, government funding to agricultural R&D has been reduced further. In recent years, there has also been a decline in donor funding of agricultural research and to the agricultural sector in general.

With donor support, the second phase of the Tanzania Agricultural Research Project (TARP II) was launched in 1998. This five-year project has a value of US$20.9 m, and $16.5 m had been spent as of December 2002. The programme covers institutional development, research programmes, and resource development and management.

The project objectives are: to increase agricultural productivity; support institutional development of the national agricultural research system; encourage privatization of agricultural research; strengthen links between farmers, extension officers, and researchers; and enhance the government's capacity to manage and coordinate agricultural research. The project has provided a major boost to agricultural R&D.

Agricultural research funds

In 1994, the government launched two sources of agricultural research funds: the National Agricultural Research Fund (NARF); and the Zonal Agricultural Research Fund (ZARF). They were started with aggregate seed money of $210,000, with the government meeting overhead costs of about TZ30 m ($23,000). The NARF has been used to finance research and links that cut across several agricultural zones. It has also been used to finance collaborative research that links government researchers and academic researchers. The fund has demanded high-quality research proposals from applicants.

Table 6.1 Trends in agricultural R&D expenditures, MAFS, Dar es Salaam (US$1 = TZS 1,252)

Source	2000–1(TZ m)	2001–2(TZ m)	2002–3(TZ m)	2003–4(TZ m)
Local sources OC[a]	89 (1.2%)	400 (4.3%)	410 (6.1%)	588 (12.9%)
(Government) DEV[a]	223 (3.1%)	250 (2.7%)	541 (8.1%)	340 (7.5%)[b]
Donors[c]	5,729 (80.3%)	7,268 (78.8%)	5,500 (82.2%)	3,600 (79.5%)
Private[d]	991 (13.9%)	1,120 (12.1%)	NA	NA
Other(specify) SHF[a]	105 (1.5%)	185 (2.0%)	238 (3.6%)	NA
Total (TZ m)	7,135	9,224	6,689	4,528

[a] OC = Other Charges; DEV = Development; and SHF (Self Help Fund).
[b] As of February 2004.
[c] Includes World Bank, Government of Netherlands, NORAD, and Irish Aid.
[d] Cess from cotton, sugarcane, tea, cashew, and tobacco.

As of June 2002, a total of $342,508 had been released ($148,326 from the World Bank), compared with the pledge of $350,000), ($62,000 from ADB (African Development Bank)/ADF (African Development Fund) compared with the pledge of $228,000), and ($132,182 from SIDA – Swedish International Development Agency – as pledged). The amount released is about 48% of the pledged amount ($710,182). The Tanzanian government contributed TZ30 m ($23,000) against a pledge of TZ43 m ($34,000). The NARF has not been built as fast as had been anticipated because there has been a failure to attract additional research funding from other sources. Lengthy review procedures for proposals have contributed to the delay.

Zonal Agricultural Research Funds (ZARFs) have been used to fund zone-specific research as part of decentralization, empowerment of local stakeholders to fund and influence research, and a move toward financial sustainability. District councils and local stakeholders are encouraged to contribute to this fund. Although ZARFs contributed by the local government authorities and the private sector are becoming an important source of research funds, the contributions are still small and some local councils have not honoured their pledges.

Cesses and levies

Local taxes are collected on the sale of crops and used to fund research (mostly on cash crops). The long-term goal is for these collections to be the main source of funds for crop research. For example, cashew research is largely financed by stakeholders. The cess is fixed at 3% of the export value: 1% goes to research; 1% to meeting the operating costs of the Board; and 1% to a development fund. Initially, 3% was allocated to the Board for reallocation to research and development funds. However, operational experience showed that sometimes the Board did not allocate funds in a fair and timely manner. Therefore, funds are now allocated directly to each use. Cesses are also levied on sugar and cotton to support research.

Contract research

In these arrangements between researchers and farmers, R&D institutes or organizations are contracted to undertake research on specific problems and the costs are paid by the farmer(s). Among NARS, only Sokoine University of Agriculture (SUA) has tapped into this source of funding. In the Northern Zone, contract research and levies contributed 30% to the research programmes.

Funding through networks

Major donors to the International Agricultural Research Centres (IARCs) provide funds for networking with NARS, and give preference to relevance of research to smallholders. In some cases, regional research organizations, such as the Southern African Centre for Co-operation in Agriculture and National Resources Research and Training (SACCAR), and the Association for Strengthening Agricultural Research in Eastern and Central Africa (ASARECA), coordinate these networks.

Revenue retention or cost recovery

Starting in 1994, the agricultural research institutes were allowed by the government to retain income generated from the sales of produce and services, user fees, rentals, and consultancy contracts. The amounts collected increased from TZS59 m in 1994–95, to TZS271 m in 1999–2000, and then declined somewhat to TZS185 m in 2001–2.

Problems of farmers and relevance of R&D

Three case studies were used to assess the relevance of research: first, public R&D – where major decisions on R&D are normally made by government-owned research institutions and research results are communicated by the government to farmers through extension services; second, public–private partnerships in R&D – where major decisions on R&D are made jointly by the government and farmers themselves (in this case, the farmers are normally large-scale commercial farmers who produce cash crops); and third, private research institutions owned by the farmers' associations – where decisions on R&D are almost exclusively made by the farmers themselves.

Government-funded (public) research

Farmers were asked to identify the main constraint facing them in crop production. About 75% mentioned three things: unreliable weather conditions; lack of inputs; and lack of markets. Lack of inputs was largely mentioned by farmers who could access improved crop varieties. They complained that improved varieties required many more inputs such as fertilizer, weed killers, and insecticides. Most of these farmers proposed that improved varieties should go hand in hand with credit schemes so they could buy the necessary inputs. It is of little use to provide farmers with improved seeds if they cannot afford to buy the required inputs. As one extension worker said, 'researchers are helpless in the absence of financial empowerment to enable farmers to buy the necessary inputs'.

However, the problem of low productivity, especially for smallholder farmers, goes beyond R&D. To promote the use of agricultural inputs, the government has established the National Agricultural Inputs Trust Fund to provide loans through local banks. To help solve problems with extension services, curricula have been revised to enable agricultural institutes to conduct refresher courses for extension officers, farmers, and agricultural technicians, and extension reference manuals have been produced.

Relevance of Research. Of the 100 farmers surveyed, about 50% knew of the existence of R&D organizations. Of these farmers, even fewer had actually ever come into contact with researchers or extension workers (30%), and about 15% felt that research outputs from R&D organizations were useful to them. Extension services were considered inadequate. Poor performance of extension services is explained by: the low ratio of extension staff to farmers (1:1,000–1,500 compared with the recommended ratio of 1:600–700); and the continued use of top-down extension methodology. The government has decided to adopt a Participatory Extension Approach (PEA) to replace this conventional top-down approach.

An attempt was made to relate the relevance of research to source of funding. The results showed no significant correlation between successful or unsuccessful projects and sources of funding. Furthermore, some projects that were termed very successful by the R&D organization were considered highly unsuccessful from the farmers' perspectives. According to 25 of the 30 farmers surveyed, the tomato variety Tengeru 1997 was not popular among farmers as tomato traders preferred the imported variety because of its marketability.

A similar situation arose in the KATRIN rice project, which led to productivity growth, but of an unpopular variety. Of the 20 farmers surveyed, all of whom were initially involved in the on-farm testing, only three were growing this variety. The reasons for the unpopularity of this variety were its deficiencies in terms of palatability, cooking qualities, and marketability. These examples suggest that researchers are merely concentrating on maximizing yields when evaluating the new varieties, regardless of other parameters such as palatability and marketability that are most valued by farmers.

Data from the Tengeru Horti-Culture Research Institute, where the major source of research funds is donors, showed that there were no significant differences between different funding sources in terms of the relevance of the research undertaken. According to the R&D organizations surveyed, use of research has increased in recent years because donors are starting to insist that research proposals clearly state how the results of the research will be disseminated. As a result, more R&D organizations have increased their effort to disseminate their research outputs through field visits and the production of leaflets and brochures.

What emerges from this study is the fact that leaflets are not very useful when it comes to smallholders and poor farmers, because farmers rarely mention them as ways in which research results reach them. As one farmer said: 'The printed materials are not reaching us. They are only found on the walls of the district headquarters.' Neither are workshops nor meetings appropriate means of communicating research results. The most appropriate and viable means of communication are face-to-face contact with researchers, extension services, and fellow farmers. There is, therefore, a need to strengthen extension services to reach this category of farmers.

Public–private partnership

Public–private partnerships are beginning to emerge in the landscape of R&D institutional arrangements in agriculture. For example, collaboration between ARI (Agricultural Research Institute) Mlingano (a public R&D organization) and Katani Ltd. (a private organization owning sisal estates and sisal processing factories) is a public–private partnership. The project, which was funded by donors, took an innovative approach. Instead of the research funds being managed by ARI Mlingano, they are being managed by Katani Ltd., the main beneficiary of the research outputs. The proposal for the research grant was jointly prepared by Katani Ltd. and ARI Mlingano. The evidence suggests that under such arrangements the R&D system is more responsive to the needs of the farmers compared with the situation in which government funds are managed by public research institutions.

These arrangements also allow farmers to be actively involved in setting research priorities. As a result, sisal farmers report that this arrangement has ensured generation of research that is relevant and appropriate to them as stakeholders. As soon as a research project is finalized, the results are immediately put into practice because the farmers have been eagerly waiting for the output. More importantly, they have a very good forum for dissemination. Every year at a 'Sisal Day', reports on completed research projects and progress reports on ongoing research are presented and discussed. At this time, all farmers are given the opportunity to air their views on the research results. In this way, the institute's researchers get feedback from the farmers on past and future research and can accommodate the interests of farmers as key stakeholders. The only problem that continues to face the sisal farmers and the R&D institute is inadequate funds for research.

Privately funded research

There are two private agricultural research institutions: TRIT and TaCRI. The major sources of research funds for these institutions are levies on the sales of commodities and donor funds. This study looked at TRIT and its systems in some depth. The coffee industry was reviewed to a lesser extent.

Tea research. Privatization started with tea research in 1996. Support was provided from the Department for International Development (DFID), presumably because most large-scale tea farmers are from the United Kingdom and the European Union. TRIT was established in 1996 as an autonomous organization representing the Government of Tanzania (GOT) and the tea industry. TRIT supports development of the tea industry (for both large- and small-scale producers) by realizing appropriate high-quality, cost-effective research and technology transfer.

TRIT is currently funded by a statutory cess and grants from donors (largely DFID and the European Union (EU)). It implements four main programmes: crop improvement; soil-fertility management; crop and water management;

and technology transfer. The crop-improvement programme develops or acquires clones that maximize productivity and economic benefits, and provide natural protection against pests and diseases and environmental stresses such as drought. The soil-fertility management programme optimizes the economic levels of fertilizer and irrigation in the main tea-growing areas. The technology transfer programme employs a farming systems approach (FSA) to involve stakeholders in the analysis and diagnosis of their problems.

The strategy to strengthen extension services included stakeholders' participation. TRIT organized a meeting that included all District Agriculture and Livestock Development Office staff working in the tea-growing areas in Rungwe district, TRIT staff, and representatives of tea growers. They discussed how an effective extension service could be organized and delivered, and how training could best be designed. Farmer training is a key activity of the technology-transfer programme. TRIT started with a baseline survey in 1998 to establish training needs and information gaps in tea-production techniques. The farmer training programme was designed to build capacity to meet the challenges of tea production, increase productivity levels, and improve the quality of green leaves delivered to the factory.

Therefore, TRIT has a very efficient system for identifying priority areas, conducting R&D, and disseminating information to end users. Of the 20 farmers, 19 said the research outputs were useful to them. However, smallholder farmers are less incorporated in the decision-making process as indicated by their relatively lower level of awareness. Although most smallholder farmers are members of Tea Farmers Associations, only 57% of these farmers were aware of their membership, for which they pay an annual subscription to the association. Only 32% indicated satisfaction with the services of their association, but most of the 68% who expressed dissatisfaction lacked information about their association and how it operates (TRIT, 2004).

The researchers seem highly motivated because they receive relatively good salaries and other incentives compared with those in public R&D institutions. Commitment of researchers and extension workers was one of the factors mentioned by R&D institutions as contributing to successful project outcomes. Of the 15 institutions in the sample, five mentioned this single factor. Other factors were: availability of funds; demand for the technology in question; participation of target beneficiaries in the project design; and reliable transport for extension workers to reach farmers in their places of work.

Since privatization of the Tea Research Institute in 1996, annual output has increased from 15,000 tons to 28,000 tons – an increase attributed to research work by TRIT. As a result, farmers are now willingly contributing research funds; whereas, earlier these contributions were more or less forced on them. What emerges from the study is that farmers, even the smallholder peasant farmers, are willing to contribute to research activities when they have been impressed by the outcomes of research. According to our survey, all farmers who have been using the improved variety (about 30 out of 150) said that they would be willing to contribute to research funds if they were asked to do so.

Coffee research. The successful privatization of tea research has been replicated for coffee and cashew nuts. TaCRI was established in 2000 and became operational in September 2001. Its privatization was modelled on TRIT with some improvements. TaCRI represents a major break from the model of its predecessor, the Lyamungo Agricultural Research Institute, which was government-led and financed. TaCRI conducts demand-driven research because it is owned and managed by its stakeholders. The stakeholders include small- and large-scale coffee producers, cooperative societies and unions dealing in coffee, coffee processors, coffee traders, NGOs, the private sector, and the Tanzanian government.

The Government of Tanzania has committed funds for some research expenses, the Stabex Fund is used for development, and operations costs are met through the cess. The policy is to increase the share of costs being met through the cess to enhance sustainability. As productivity improves through application of research results, it is expected that the cess will increase in absolute value as the value of output increases. For example, new coffee varieties have been introduced that do not need spraying but have higher yields. In addition, new varieties can now be planted while the current crop is in the same field.

TaCRI is organized around five main programmes: crop improvement; crop productivity and primary processing; crop nutrition; livelihood and income security; and technology transfer and training. So far it has identified 36 new varieties that show promise in terms of high yields, improved quality, and resistance to disease and environmental challenges. It was anticipated that by 2007, more than 5 million clones of the best new varieties would be produced and distributed. Discussions are under-way with CIRAD (French Agricultural Research Centre for International Development) to acquire their tissue-culture technology (somatic embryogenesis) for massive multiplication and distribution of the improved varieties. TaCRI has also begun to publish research findings in the form of relevant and practical technical packages.

Discussion

Generally, there has been a decreasing trend in R&D funding associated with the shift to more private funding, especially in terms of public–private partnerships and private funding by farmers who own and manage R&D institutions. The problems of funding agricultural research include the small size of the various funds and their fluctuation over time. Poor disbursement of funds together with inappropriate timing has adversely affected the effectiveness of funding of agricultural research activities. For example, during 2000–1 only $3.61 m out of the budgeted amount of $8.44 m (43%) was realized.

Research activities in agriculture have picked up in terms of generating new seed varieties; however, the overall impacts of R&D projects are still minimal. Very few farmers, especially in the smallholder sector, have adopted the technologies developed by the public R&D centres. There are three major reasons for this trend. First, as reported by the respondents, is the lack of inputs either because the institutional arrangements for input distribution are not functioning well, or access to inputs is hindered by limited access to credit. Second, some of the new varieties meet productivity criteria but do not meet consumer taste and preferences criteria because researchers paid too much concern to enhanced productivity and output and did not take into account consumer preferences. Interestingly, even some trial farmers have given up growing the varieties developed by the R&D institutions because the products were not marketable. Third, there is inadequate dissemination of research findings and weak extension services. Many respondents complained that they had never been visited by an extension worker, so very few varieties have moved beyond the farmers involved in the trials. One way to encourage researchers to formulate relevant research proposals and disseminate results may be to make availability of funds conditional on relevance, dissemination, and adoption of the results and possibly outcomes. This study suggests that private ownership of R&D and public–private partnership in research may be the best approach.

Partnerships are emerging in various forms. Partnerships work if each partner has something to offer and something to gain. However, substantial commitment to a partnership in terms of material and intellectual contributions will only arise when common interests, activities, and objectives prevail. Public–private partnerships are promising because they tie research to the needs of users, provide opportunities for improved efficiency and cost effectiveness, and augment investments by enhancing the impact of research results.

The implication for new arrangements is that the overall research programme must integrate the different objectives imposed by each funding source that represents the different stakeholder groups. This calls for administrative and intellectual flexibility, the capacity to communicate effectively and to work in teams, and the capacity to manage different interests and to enhance willingness to share risks. A governance structure that assembles representatives of different stakeholders to set research priorities through appropriate forms of consultations and negotiation is likely to have the best chance of success. The development framework in which these partnerships operate should promote participation, consultation, and development that is sustainable, equitable, and inclusive.

The diffusion of new varieties and other research results that are supposed to be adopted in the food-crop sector is rather poor. This is in contrast with the experience of privatized R&D activity for export crops, where the diffusion of new varieties is very good. This difference arises from the fact that researchers in the privatized export crops are highly motivated and facilitated to reach all the farmers. In addition, the varieties for the export crops were developed according to the farmers' requirements. Additional factors include a high level of literacy among farmers of large-scale cash crops, and the provision of training for smallholders, especially for tea growers.

Industrial sector

This analysis is based on data obtained through questionnaires, interviews, and discussions with stakeholders within Tanzania's industrial R&D establishment. Data were gathered from these institutions: TIRDO; TEMDO; CAMARTEC; and TaTEDO.

It is based on data from four R&D institutions (three government-owned and operated and one privately operated); 48 industrial establishments (public (18%); private (53%); and private–public joint ventures (23%) from an original sample of 60 establishments in five regions, namely Tanga, Dar es Salaam, Morogoro, Mbeya, and Mwanza); and interviews with 45 personnel (both managerial and technical).

Trends in funding R&D: Volume and shift in balance

Most of the R&D institutes that serve industries were established at a time when Tanzania was experiencing an economic downturn. The Tanzanian economy stagnated in the early 1980s when most R&D institutions in the industrial sector were established. The import-substitution manufacturing industries, the main beneficiaries of industrial research activities, were performing poorly and this was reflected in the declining share of manufacturing in the national economy (Table 6.2). These developments had dire consequences on the flow of resources to publicly funded R&D institutes.

In the late 1980s, the government stopped allocating funds for technology development, and in 1998, industrial R&D institutes were advised to restructure and commercialize their activities in line with ongoing liberalization and privatization (URT, 1998). The funding situation is illustrated by the flow of resources to TIRDO (Table 6.3). During the period, the government was a minor source of funding compared with donor funding. More importantly, donors were wholly responsible for funds given in foreign currencies.

The same trend was observed at two other research organizations where data were available. Table 6.4 shows the funding situation at the Arusha-based CAMARTEC, which is concerned with agricultural and rural technologies. Foreign donors were wholly responsible for supporting research and development work at the centre. More dramatic, however, is the fact that funding has stagnated since 1986. Of the total resources flowing into

Table 6.2 Trends in manufacturing GDP (1976 prices) (TZS 000)
Source: National Economic Surveys, various years

	1976	1977	1978	1979	1980	1981	1982	1983	1984	1985
Total GDP	21,652	21,739	22,202	22,849	23,419	23,301	23,439	22,882	23,656	24,278
Manufacturing GDP	2,811	2,641	2,730	2,821	2,683	2,382	2,304	2,103	2,159	2,075
Share of manufacturing (%)	13.0	12.2	12.3	12.4	11.5	10.2	9.8	9.2	9.1	8.6

CAMARTEC during 1986–95, more than 90% was received in 1986. After the initial investment was made, there was little subsequent funding for activities.

TEMDO, another Arusha-based R&D institute, has for over 10 years not received any funding from the government for technology development projects. In 1994, it received from UNIDO (United Nations Industrial Development Organization) a research grant of $1.5 m to support research on the development of a tractor-mounted seed-dressing applicator. Between 2001 and 2004, the government provided TZS15 m ($11,500) annually for technology development and commercialization. Accordingly, the funding situation is not likely to improve in the foreseeable future. When asked to suggest funding sources other than foreign donors, both research administrators and managers felt there was a need to lobby the government to increase allocations of research funds. Industries were never mentioned as alternative sources of R&D funds, other than for consulting services.

Relevance and effectiveness

Recent developments, including changes in ownership of industries and a more competitive environment, have not been translated into increased demand for outputs of industrial research and development. This analysis of the relevance and effectiveness of research projects was approached from two

Table 6.3 Funding for R&D at TIRDO
Source: Survey data, 2004

Year	Budget (US$)
1989	62,112
1990	2,563
1991	243,568
1992	58,885
1993	6,899
1995	167,523
1998	12,035
2001	144,742
2002	10,616

Table 6.4 Funding for R&D at CAMARTEC
Source: Survey data, 2004

Year	Budget (TZ 000)	Budget (US$)
1986	5,000	152,905
1987	500	7,776
1991	50,000	228,102
1992	70,000	235,136
1994	1,500	2,943
1995	45,000	78,288
Total	172,000	10,032,365

perspectives: the research institutes and people who perform research work; and the industries, which are the key stakeholders in industrial R&D.

Perspective of R&D institutes

The relevance and effectiveness of industrial research is a function of a number of related issues that must be considered when evaluating industrial R&D. Two main types of projects have been carried out by industrial R&D institutes in Tanzania.

First, there are those that address generic problems that are widely felt by the general population (e.g. excessive exploitation of wood fuel contributing to environmental degradation). Development of alternative technologies or products should attract the attention of R&D institutes. Similar examples can be found in agricultural and rural technologies, and in industrial products and processes. In these cases, R&D institutes will mobilize human and financial resources, and embark on research and development of products and processes, convinced that the outcomes will be useful to the beneficiaries (individuals, communities, or industrial groups). Relevance is not an issue.

Second, research institutes can undertake demand-driven research and development that is applicable to organized groups, especially manufacturing industries. During the period of financial constraints, R&D institutes were advised to commercialize. This meant that many of them were obliged to engage in commercial consultancies, which required more applied work rather than basic research based on public funding. This is the most common approach to industrial R&D in Tanzania. The demand side, however, was dampened during the trade liberalization regime because industry was free to import its inputs and other requirements. Faced with production bottlenecks of a technical nature, industries will approach research institutes to help find solutions. These activities include finding substitute raw materials, adapting production processes, and designing and producing replacement parts.

Appropriate communication channels are important for translating research results into something tangible. The three most commonly used communication channels are extension services, demonstrations, and participation in trade fairs and shows. It is not clear from the study whether these adopted communication channels are to blame for the observed ineffectiveness. However, when asked to identify obstacles and constraints that limit dissemination, these factors were mentioned: shortage of funds limits ability to reach beneficiaries; shortage of potential entrepreneurs to take up commercial production; lack of marketing outlets; low levels of technical skills; poor links between R&D institutes and manufacturers, and financial institutions; and lack of effective demand for developed prototypes.

Research institutes were asked to identify research projects that had been undertaken in the past and that had demonstrated high levels of effectiveness to the beneficiaries (Table 6.5). These research institutes are engaged in more or less similar projects. Most were undertaken during the 1980s when the

Table 6.5 Summary of effective R&D projects
Source: Survey data, 2004

TIRDO	CAMARTEC	TEMDO
Energy audit to industries	Community stoves	Oil-expelling technology
Glue for making chipboards	Biogas technology	Small-scale seed treatment technology
Fermentation of cassava	Oil expulsion	
	Rural transport	

economic conditions were characterized by an acute shortage of goods that called for local substitutes. In addition, increased demand for energy and its impact on the environment had necessitated research on energy-saving measures including the design of energy-efficient cookers.

Perspective of manufacturers

From the point of view of the manufacturers, the relevance and effectiveness of research projects is a function of the environment in which they are operating and the costs of procuring and using knowledge and information from R&D institutes. Most respondents agree they are operating in a competitive environment: 47% report very stiff to extremely stiff competition and 41% somewhat stiff competition. The rest are operating in a competitive environment, but they did not report any serious competition.

Except for those owned by multinational corporations with centralized R&D abroad, not a single company reported in-house research activities. Technical production problems are usually addressed through routine preventive maintenance. Asked how useful R&D institutions were in addressing their problems, 53% of respondents responded negatively. Those who responded positively were mainly large-scale and local, and they cited consultancies and commissioned research with R&D institutes.

More important, 71% of respondents had no contact with R&D institutes, and those who had contact had initiated it themselves. This confirms the weak links between R&D institutions and the productive sector, which has had a negative impact on the effectiveness of industrial research. It appears that consultancies may be a way to establish links between industry and R&D institutions. R&D institutes must aggressively advertise the kinds of industrial problems they can solve. This has two implications. First, investment in basic research will be reduced in favour of applied research activities that are currently in demand. Second, only those industries that can pay will be served by the R&D system.

Knowledge flow and dissemination

Tanzania's government-owned and operated industrial research institutes owe their existence to the government, which pays staff salaries and other administrative overhead costs. With the economic reforms of the 1990s, which included privatization of once public enterprises, more and more industries are falling into private hands. Donor funding is often focused on specific projects and on specific target groups. More often, projects are targeted at the poor and directed at poverty reduction. The financing of generic research and research directed at industries remains in the public realm.

Private support to R&D

With the exception of consultancies on specific problems, the knowledge and information generated from industrial research is not industry-specific. Products and processes can be easily copied at a fraction of original R&D investment by anyone with relevant technical knowledge. Small-scale engineering firms have been good at producing products based on designs from R&D institutes; therefore, they under-cut R&D institutes that want to commercialize the production of their own prototypes.

It is no wonder that private support to industrial research is lacking, there is overdependence on the government, and donor funding is much more targeted. TaTEDO is a modest attempt to privatize industrial research. However, even this is not a clear-cut case of privately funded industrial R&D.

Founded in 1990 as a not-for-profit NGO, TaTEDO 'is a coalition of individuals, professionals, farmers, community-based organizations and enterprises involved in the development and promotion of renewable energy systems for enhancing environment and socio-economic development of communities in Tanzania'. The only difference between TaTEDO and the other research institutes is that it does not receive government funding. However, like other research institutes, donor funds support the core of its activities, and its remaining funds come from consultancies and the marketing of its products to individuals, hospitals, schools, and church groups.

Discussion

The following issues emerge from this study of Tanzania's industrial R&D activities:
- Industrial R&D is resource-starved. Although the potential exists for R&D institutes to contribute to the national goal of competitive and sustainable industrial development, the decline in the flow of public resources makes it difficult to achieve this objective.
- Industrial R&D institutions in Tanzania continue to depend on support from foreign donors. This is not consistent with sustainability because this important source of research funds is unpredictable and prone to changing political dynamics.
- There is no evidence of privately funded industrial research in Tanzania, except for some occasional consultancies and other commissioned work. Problem solving in industries is accomplished through routine

maintenance and to some extent consultancies with R&D institutes, and science and engineering departments of universities and technical colleges. However, with import liberalization, some of the goods and services that would have been procured from the local R&D system are imported.
- There are weak links between research institutes and the productive sector. This can be explained by highly centralized research activities and the absence of systematic involvement of industries and other target groups in the design and implementation of the R&D activities undertaken by these institutions.

Health sector

This analysis is based on data obtained through questionnaires, interviews, and discussions with stakeholders within Tanzania's medical R&D establishment. The analysis includes data from four research centres and stations under the NIMR; one private medical research centre; 15 hospitals in four regions (Tanga, Dar es Salaam, Morogoro, and Mwanza); and interviews with 35 medical doctors and hospital administrators. Respondents included medical professionals working with public, private, and university-teaching hospitals as well as hospital administrators. At the policy level, officials with the Ministry of Health (MoH) were consulted. In addition, donors identified as the major sponsors of medical research were also contacted.

Trends in funding R&D: Volume and shifting balance

Although domestic sources account for most recurrent expenditures in health (more than 80%), the development budget is dominated by foreign financing (85%). The share of foreign funding in the total budget has been increasing since 2000, and reached 40% in 2003. Basket funding has grown from 2% of the total budget in 1999–2000 to 19% in 2001–2, and was estimated to reach 28% in 2002–3. Fears have been expressed that as donor funds shift away from earmarked basket funding to general budget support, there is risk of diverting resources to other sectors.

Domestic sources of funds outside the government budget include: the Health Service Fund (cost sharing); the Community Health Fund (World Bank supported community-based prepayment scheme); and the National Health Insurance expenditures (from the National Health Insurance Fund). These domestic sources are quite small and continue to be dwarfed by foreign sources. However, the Public Expenditure Review (PER) does not make specific reference to the budget for R&D in the health sector.

Although comprehensive data are hard to obtain, there are indications that medical R&D institutions have faced shortfalls in the resources needed for R&D activities. When asked about access to funds for medical research, 47% of medical doctors said it is extremely difficult and 27% said it is very difficult.

In other words, nearly three quarters of doctors have no easy access to research funds. Considering that about 60% of the respondents have participated in research activities as both full-time and part-time researchers, this is definitely a very serious problem.

Despite declining trends in public resource flows, the government remains the major supporter of medical R&D. However, most of the budgetary allocation is used to cover personnel and administrative costs (Table 6.6).

During the financial year 2000–1, 75% of government funding was used for personnel costs 14% for administration, and 11% for research expenditures. Of donor funds, 38% supported research activities. Therefore, of total R&D funds (TZ1,223,050 m) the government's share was only 14%; whereas, the donors' share was a whopping 86%. In total, 43% of funds were used for research activities. A large share of the funds has gone to support research on malaria (Table 6.7). Table 6.8 shows the overall flow of funds at NIMR between 1999 and 2004.

Tanzania's medical R&D establishment is currently experimenting with other arrangements to enhance resource mobilization, improve the relevance of its research programmes and projects, and exchange information among stakeholders.

Table 6.6 Allocation and use of funds at NIMR
Source: Survey data, 2004

Source of funds	2000–1 (TZ 000)	Share (%)	2001–2 (TZ 000)	Share (%)
Government grant	1,578,058	56	1,886,795	60
Personnel	1,184,174	(75)	1,433,964	(76)
R&D	168,992	(11)	207,072	(11)
Administration	224,892	(14)	245,759	(13)
Internal sources	174,554	6	147,751	5
Foreign donors	1,054,058	38	1,094,298	35
Total	2,806,670	100	3,128,844	100

Table 6.7 Distribution of research funds to various activities (1994)

Funds allocation	Total (US$)	(%)
Malaria research	2,622,727	61.2
Filariasis	17,159	0.4
Malaria and Filariasis	559,236	13.2
Onchocerciasis	306,267	7.2
Onchocerciasis and Filariasis	30,000	0.7
Lymphoedema and Adenolymphangitis	3,000	0.1
STD/AIDS	28,960	0.6
Malaria seminar	27,177	0.6
Training	148,831	3.5
Institutional building	366,392	8.7
Research capacity building	45,506	1.0
Health systems, policy and management	63,720	1.5

Table 6.8 Expenditures on health R&D by NIMR
Source: Survey data, 2004

Year	Local (TZ 000)	Percentage of total	Foreign (TZ 000)	Percentage of total	Total (TZ 000)
1999	19,904	8.7	208,101	91.3	228,005
2000	373,034	66.0	191,944	33.9	564,978
2001	477,374	46.6	547,113	53.4	1,024,487
2002	256,151	18.8	1,106,682	81.2	1,362,833
2003	173,000	20.4	674,843	79.6	847,843
2004[a]	450,000	43.3	589,851	56.7	1,038,851

[a] As of June 2004.

Health Research Users' Trust Fund (HRUTF)

The HRUTF was founded in 1996 by the NIMR to enhance demand-driven health research efforts to overcome problems associated with communicable diseases, pregnancy and delivery, malnutrition, chronic underfunding of the health sector, and management of the health system. HRUTF addresses health research problems identified by stakeholders. Established with seed money of $177,300 from the Swiss Development Cooperation, it is supported by an annual subvention of TZ50 m from the Ministry of Health.

Tanzania National Health Research Forum (TANHER-Forum)

This forum was established in 1999 as 'a consultative and advisory body to policy and decision makers as regarding health research coordination, undertaking, collaboration, dissemination of health research results, and enhancing utilization of research results for policy and decision-making'. The initial grant of $200,000 was provided by the Rockefeller Foundation.

Relevance and effectiveness

Tanzania faces numerous diseases that could be the subject of interesting research. However, the expertise of the NIMR focuses on a few endemic diseases using national and international resources. Hospital data show that malaria is the number one cause of hospital visits (70%) – followed by HIV/AIDS-related cases (40%) and diarrhoea (28%). Other causes are anaemia, acute respiratory infections (especially pneumonia), and a few cases of trauma.

More than 70% of the respondents are of the opinion that malaria and HIV/AIDS are priority areas for medical research in Tanzania that warrant additional resources. In addition, more than two thirds agree that research in these areas has been very effective in terms of both knowledge generation and utilization. For example, it was pointed out that malaria research had established that *P. falciparum*, the malaria parasite, had become resistant to chloroquine, the first line drug. Changes were therefore recommended to the antimalarial drug combination, which have now been adopted by the government.

Respondents were asked to assess the relevance and usefulness of medical R&D in Tanzania: 20% said it was extremely useful; 40% very useful; and 20% useful. Therefore, 80% of medical practitioners believe that the services provided by R&D institutions are relevant to their work. They believe that this research has: improved healthcare quality; led to better patient management; helped prioritize health problems; and helped to better understand local conditions.

Knowledge flow and dissemination

Medical R&D is centralized within a few research centres and stations under the NIMR. The exceptions include some teaching hospitals: Muhimbili Medical Centre in Dar es Salaam; Kilimanjaro Christian Medical Centre (KCMC), Moshi; Bugando Hospital, Mwanza; and Ifakara Health Research and Development Research Centre (IHRDC) at Ifakara. Such centralization makes it possible to develop the critical mass of staff and resources needed to sustain research in modern health sciences. For example, NIMR inherited 10 research scientists and 11 laboratory technicians from the defunct East African Medical Research Council in 1979. By 2002, NIMR had 53 research scientists (most with PhDs), 33 laboratory technicians, and 13 top-level administrators (NIMR, 2002).

There are some inherent limitations with such an arrangement. The most common complaint from the beneficiaries was the lack of involvement by medical professionals working with hospitals. About half of the respondents felt medical R&D was lacking an appropriate dissemination forum or feedback mechanism that could increase the usefulness and effectiveness of medical research. Refereed journals and books are the two most important sources of medical information or knowledge (53% consult journals and 40% rely on books). Workshops, seminars, and conferences were third in importance, followed by research reports.

It seems that research results are poorly communicated, which in turn reduces their use. Perhaps this is why the NIMR has embarked on several new approaches to disseminate its research results. In addition to a health research bulletin, annual reports, and annual joint scientific conferences, radio and television have been identified as effective communication channels. Regular media workshops are held to bring together both print and broadcast media to discuss the results of medical research. In this way, the mass media can be used to disseminate appropriate messages to the general public.

Privately funded health research

There is little evidence of private funding of medical R&D. Even pharmaceutical companies, the likely beneficiaries of such research, do not provide research funds. Perhaps this is because knowledge appropriation in medical research can be contentious. The government and donors remain critical to sustaining such research.

The IHRDC could be a good starting point for privately funded medical R&D. It operates under a trust and has been successful in mobilizing private funds for its activities. Over a five-year period, it almost tripled its research funds from TZ339 m in 1995–96 to TZ1,131 m during 2000–1. However, external collaboration and donor support have been indispensable.

Some of its research accomplishments include: evaluation of the SPf 66 vaccine for malaria control (proven protective in 31% of cases for children 1–4 years old); evaluation of the effectiveness of insecticide-treated nets (these results were fed to the National Malaria Control Programme); evaluation of Maloprim chemoprophylaxis and iron supplementation to prevent severe anaemia and malaria in infants; and evaluation of the efficacies of commonly used antimalarials (conducted as part of a national monitoring programme of resistance to antimalarial drugs).

Discussion

The following issues emerge:
- The government is the major source of support. Nearly all R&D institutions are government-owned and operated, the outcomes are public goods, and the main beneficiary is the government. The restructuring and reforms of the 1980s and 1990s had little impact, except for the reduced inflow of public resources.
- Donors provide up to 80% of funds for research. This is the most disturbing aspect of medical R&D in Tanzania. Only recently has the government started to provide more resources.
- Tanzania's medical research focuses on endemic diseases that affect rural areas, where up to 80% of the population earn their living. Malaria is the most prevalent and serious vector-borne disease. More work has been done on malaria than any other disease.
- Tanzania's medical R&D is relevant and timely as it addresses issues of national importance.
- The effectiveness of medical R&D is being reduced by poor communication. As a result, information is not reaching the beneficiaries in a way that is effective in solving problems. Additional effort is needed to involve stakeholders and better inform them of research results.

Comparative analysis

Trends in funding of R&D activities

Until recently, R&D was conducted almost entirely in the public sector. New modalities of financing have now been introduced. The patterns of funding in the different R&D systems have varied according to the restructuring of the specific sectors. The overall decline in public resources allocated to R&D activities has, since the mid-1980s, been associated with the standard policy packages suggested by the international financial institutions. These have included fiscal restraint to reduce the budget deficit, tight monetary policy, and privatization, all of which have a bearing on budgetary allocations to the public sector.

The decrease in the share of public R&D funding has been associated with a shift to more private funding, especially in terms of public–private partnerships and 100% private funding, as is the case in agriculture. Government funding for agricultural research was quite low, at 0.4% of the agricultural GDP in 1991 compared with the average within Eastern Africa (0.8%). By 2002, the share of R&D funding of total agricultural GDP had declined somewhat to 0.36%. During this period the composition of R&D funding changed. The private sector now participates in both funding and priority setting.

In industry, R&D activities have shifted to more immediate problem-solving activities, such as routine maintenance, and to some extent consultancies with R&D institutes, and science and engineering departments of universities and technical colleges. Health has remained largely in the public sector, and funding of R&D still comes largely from government and donors. The relatively greater amount of public R&D funding to smallholder agriculture and to health reflects the public-good characteristics of these sectors, a situation that makes it difficult to develop commercial markets for R&D output in these sectors.

The dominance of donor funding is quite explicit in R&D funding. Government funding has gone to maintenance and operational costs; whereas, donor funding and other forms of collaborative research have been channelled into actual R&D. However, donor funding can be unpredictable because of untimely disbursements, mainly due to conditions associated with the release of funds, change of donor policies, and limited domestic capacity to meet the accounting and reporting requirements of donors. Donor influence on priority setting has raised concerns about ownership and undue influence over the research agenda.

Relevance and effectiveness of R&D programmes and projects

R&D projects have had very minimal impacts on agriculture, which is dominated by many smallholder farmers, especially those producing food crops. Of the 100 farmers sampled, 85% did not find results of R&D institutes useful for their needs. In some cases, where new varieties had been adopted there was concern that these varieties did not satisfy consumer preferences. This was found to be the case with Tengeru tomatoes and KATRIN rice. Although productivity had increased, failure in the market led to discontinuation of these new varieties.

In the case of medical research, the government is the main owner and public resources are dominant. Tanzania's medical R&D is relevant and timely in addressing issues of national importance. Relevance is achieved because the main owner of R&D activity is also the formulator of health policy, and the major diseases are location specific. Thus, Tanzania's medical research has focused on endemic diseases that especially affect the rural areas where up to 80% of the population earn their living. Malaria, being the most prevalent and serious vector-borne disease, has attracted more resources than any other disease. However, the effectiveness of medical R&D is being blunted by poor communication channels.

The weakest link between research and users is in industry. More than half (53%) of the firms surveyed indicated that they had not benefited from R&D results, and most of those who had benefited were large firms that undertook consultancies and commissioned research for R&D institutes. The incidence of weak links was greatest for smaller firms because 71% had no contact with R&D institutes. Although the research activities and projects were relevant, their effectiveness in addressing issues is problematic. Little involvement of stakeholders in setting priorities, and poor communication of research results to intended beneficiaries, limit the usefulness of research activities. There are weak links between research institutes and the productive sector because research activities are over-centralized and industries and other target groups have little involvement in decision-making, especially in setting priorities for research.

Institutional arrangements and factors influencing relevance and effectiveness

Institutional arrangements have evolved according to the broad policies pursued by post-independence governments for sectoral development. These different paths are reflected in institutional arrangements, structures, and communication channels between researchers and beneficiaries or target groups. Institutional arrangements have been restructured toward public–private sector partnerships and privatization. This is especially true for the agricultural sector and cash crops. Privatization has proven to be relatively less complicated for single-crop research institutions. For multi-crop institutions, the problem of cross-subsidization arises.

The private sector is emerging as a source of expertise and financing to supplement public sources. However, private-sector participation had tended to be concentrated on a few export crops such as tea and coffee (presumably on those technologies that are proprietary). Overall, however, R&D capacity is still low after over two decades of poor funding and public support. Even privatized R&D activities are supplemented by public resources in two ways. First, they draw from human resources in the public sector, such as the research and extension system. Second, they benefit from public resources in the form of donor funding. These experiences suggest that successful private-sector R&D requires public support, including complementary, strong, publicly supported research.

Conclusion and policy recommendations

The pattern of funding different R&D systems has varied according to the path of restructuring of each sector. Generally there has been a decrease in the share of public R&D funding and a shift toward more private funding, especially in terms of public–private partnerships and also 100% private funding in the cases in agriculture.

The dominance of donor funding is quite explicit in R&D funding. Government funding has been dominant in maintenance and operational costs for R&D; whereas, donor funding and other forms of collaborative research have channelled their funds into R&D. However, donor funding has been associated with unpredictability, frequent changes in policies and priorities, and untimely disbursements. Donor influence on prioritization has raised concerns over ownership and undue influence on the development agenda.

The challenges of funding R&D activities include:
- The need to increase the allocation of public funding to research in priority sectors (agriculture and health) while recognizing the role of industry in enhancing value added in agriculture and increasing productivity in the economy. It is proposed that this sectoral prioritization be reflected in the allocation of public resources to R&D activities.
- The need to give greater attention to the continuity and predictability of funding R&D activities. Fluctuations in resource allocation from year to year are not consistent with continuity in research. There is a need to improve the predictability of resource allocation.
- The need to diversify funding sources to bring all stakeholders on board, consistent with sustainability and participation. Participation should be institutionalized both at the level of financing and the setting of research priorities. Most importantly, modalities should be put in place to make sure that smallholder and food-crop farmers are involved in setting priorities for research.
- The need to counterbalance donor domination in financing R&D activities and in influencing the research agenda by enhanced domestic ownership of the research agenda that reflects national development priorities. This imbalance should be corrected through concerted efforts to change aid relationships and to enhance Tanzania's leadership in setting priorities and ensuring that allocations of donor assistance meet national development priorities.
- The need to achieve efficiency and effectiveness in resource management and utilization through effective monitoring of research outputs and dissemination of results to achieve value for money invested in research. The steps that are being taken to improve public financial management and priority setting in budgeting are encouraging.

References

Archibugi, D., Evangelista, R., and Simonetti, R. (1994) On the definition and measurement of product and process innovation, in Shionoya, Y. and Perlman, M. (eds) *Innovation in Technology Industries and Institutions. Studies in Schumpetarian Perspectives*, University of Michigan, Ann Arbor, Michigan.

Enos, J.L, (ed.) (1995) *In Pursuit of Science and Technology in Sub-Saharan Africa: The Impact of Structural Adjustment Programmes*. Routledge/UNU Press, New York and Tokyo.

Eponou, T. (1993) Partnership in agricultural technology generation: linking research and technology transfer to serve farmers. *Research Report No. 1, International Service for National Agricultural Research (ISNAR)*, The Hague.

Expere, J. and Idowu, I. (1990) Managing the links between research and technology transfer: The case of agricultural extension research liaison services in Nigeria. ISNAR Linkages *Discussion Paper 6, International Service for National Agricultural Research (ISNAR)*, The Hague.

Komba, A. (1999) *Structural change and competitiveness in Tanzania's manufacturing industries*. PhD dissertation (unpublished), George Washington University, Washington, DC.

Kwanjai, N.N. (1999) Applying general systems of theory to put together NIS jig-saw puzzle pieces: A portrait of the Thai national innovation system. Prepared for UNU-INTECH Research Programme. 3.0.2. on *Characteristics of National Innovation Systems in Developing Countries*, United Nations University Institute for New Technologies.

Liwenga, J.M. (1988) History of agricultural research in Tanzania, in Ter, J.M. and Mattee, A.Z. (eds), *Proceedings of a workshop on science and farmers in Tanzania*, Sokoine University of Agriculture (SUA), Morogoro, Tanzania.

Lundvall, B.A. (ed.) (1992) *National systems of innovation: Towards a theory of innovation and interactive learning*. Pinter Publishers, London.

Muchie, M., Gammeltoft, P., and Lundvall, B.A. (eds) (2003) *Putting Africa first: The making of African innovation systems*. Aalborg University Press, Aalborg, Denmark.

Nelson, R. (ed.) (1993) *National innovation systems: A comparative analysis*. Oxford University Press, London.

NIMR. (2002) *Annual report*. National Institute for Medical Research, Dar es Salaam, Tanzania.

TRIT. (2004) *Annual report, 2002/03*. Tea Research Institute of Tanzania, Tanzania.

URT. (1998) *Budget speech by Minister for Industry and Trade*. United Republic of Tanzania, Dar es Salaam, Tanzania.

Wangwe, S.M. (2000) Economic reforms, industrialization and technological capabilities, in Szirmai, A. and Lapperre, P. (eds), *Africa's technology gap* UNCTAD Publication, United Nations Conference on Trade and Development, Geneva, Switzerland.

Wangwe, S.M. and Diyamett, B.D. (1998) Coooperation between R&D institutions and enterprises: The case of URT, in *Atlas XI Bulletin. Approaches to science and technology cooperation and capacity building*. United Nations, New York and Geneva.

Wangwe, S.M. (2003) African systems of innovation: Towards an interpretation of the development experience, in Muchie, M., Gammeltoft, P., and Lundvall, B.A. (eds) *Putting Africa first: The making of African innovation systems*. Aalborg University Press, Aalborg, Denmark.

CHAPTER 7
Public–private partnerships in fish genetics research: The Philippine experience[1]

Belen Acosta, World Fish Centre

Abstract

This research was undertaken to better understand the contributions of public–private partnerships in fish genetics research in the Philippines. It provides an in-depth look at the consequences of existing types of partnerships (public-funded, public- and private-funded, and private-funded institutions) on the sustainability and development of genetic research on fish. The authors explore how both public- and private-sector institutions have worked together to deliver improved tilapia breeds and technology to achieve maximum benefits from genetic research. They conclude by underscoring the importance of public- and private-sector collaboration through strategic partnerships that encourage cooperation among the major sectoral players. This cooperation has ensured that problems and visions are shared and that partners have been able to work together to identify and find solutions to mutual problems.

The tilapia industry is the fastest-growing enterprise for producing fish for food in the aquaculture sector of the Philippines. National tilapia production increased from 16,000 mt in 1976 to 122,000 mt in 2002, an increase of more than 700% over two and a half decades (Abella, 2004; Guerrero, 2004). The immense growth of the tilapia industry in the Philippines and elsewhere in the region is attributed to several factors that favour production of this species. Most important is the development of genetic-improvement technologies and improved tilapia strains – the main outputs of long-term genetic-improvement research undertaken by public-sector institutions (national institutions and international organizations based in the Philippines). As institutions moved to further development, widespread dissemination, and commercialization of improved tilapia strains, it became necessary for some of these institutions to establish partnerships with the private sector.

In the crop sector, public–private partnerships have been used increasingly to address global issues and deliver the potential benefits of agricultural research and biotechnology in developing countries (James, 1996; Pinstrup-Andersen et al., 1999). Private firms are the main source of plant biotechnology in many developing countries, accounting for at least 70% of the field trials of genetically modified and improved plant varieties (Huang et al., 2002). Agriculture has well-developed R&D programmes for public–private sector partnerships, and private R&D has been growing rapidly. However, in the case of fish, genetic-improvement technology is still in its infancy. Only recently have a few research institutions (public and international) established collaboration with the private sector to sustain the costs of genetic research and disseminate improved fish seed. Moreover, compared with crops where the implications of such partnerships have been well studied and established, information on the changes that have taken place with evolving partnerships in fish are unknown.

The main objective of this project was to understand the consequences of existing partnerships (i.e. public-funded, public- and private-funded, and private-funded institutions) on the sustainability and achievement of the development objectives of fish-genetics research. Specifically, the project aimed to: identify the effects of changes in partnerships and sources of funding on research and developmental activities in tilapia genetics; assess the delivery of research outputs (e.g. improved tilapia seed and GIFT technology) and results to seed producers and farmers; determine the effects of changes in partnerships on the levels of funding and spending, and their effectiveness; synthesize lessons from the study and formulate recommendations for better links between private and public sectors in fish-genetics research; and develop the Philippine experience as a case study for successful public–private partnership in genetics research.

Project implementation and management

The WorldFish Centre and Philippine institutions engaged in tilapia breeding programmes collaborated on this project. These Philippine institutions, which are all under the Tilapia Science Centre,[2] are the Freshwater Aquaculture Centre, Central Luzon State University (FAC-CLSU), National Freshwater Fisheries Technology Research Centre, Bureau of Fisheries and Aquatic Resources (NFFTC-BFAR), and the GIFT Foundation International Inc.

The WorldFish Centre provided overall coordination and management of project activities, technical input into the examination of trends in tilapia genetic research, and assessments of how well developmental objectives had been achieved. FAC-CLSU and NFFTC-BFAR led the research into the implications of private-sector involvement on the delivery of research outputs to end-users. The GIFT Foundation International provided technical expertise with regard to examining the effects of public–private partnerships on investments and spending on R&D.

A workshop of 16 participants representing the project's collaborating institutions was held to initiate project activities. The participants discussed and agreed on the objectives, the research issues that had to be addressed, the methodologies, and the implementation and reporting arrangements. The main outputs of the workshop were work plans for each project team.

Research methodology

The project objectives were addressed through field surveys, the gathering of secondary information from published sources, and the organization of stakeholder and final workshops. Analysis of three broad issues (effects on research and development activities; delivery of research outputs to end-users; and levels of research and development funding and spending and their effectiveness) was based on inputs received from major players in genetic research and the dissemination of research outputs. Finally, issues and constraints that emerged from changes in the partnerships were identified and recommendations were formulated.

Four genetically improved strains are disseminated by the public- and private-sector institutions in the Philippines under the Tilapia Science Centre: GIFT-GST (Genetically Improved Farmed Tilapia/GIFT Super Tilapia/GenoMar Supreme Tilapia); GET-EXCEL (Genetically Enhanced Tilapia); YY-GMT (Genetically Male Tilapia); and FAST (FAC Selected Tilapia).

Effects on research and development activities

To assess the issues that affect R&D in tilapia genetics in selected public- and private-sector institutions in the Philippines, the study examined trends in genetics research on tilapia. It also looked at how developmental objectives, research outputs, and major players had been affected by shifts in partnerships and the nature of funding.

To highlight public–private alliances, the study focused on the GIFT programme because it was the only one that had partnered with a for-profit private-sector company. Interviews were conducted with technical staff, and with accredited hatchery operators and farmers, to identify issues and concerns of the different agencies and individuals involved in the various alliances. Interview data were supplemented through secondary information from various reports.

Delivery of research outputs to end-users

The basic objective of this research was to determine the conditions and circumstances surrounding the adoption of genetics-based technologies. The focus was on: assessing how improved tilapia strains, technology, and results were disseminated by the public- and private-sector institutions to immediate end-users; identifying the product recipients or beneficiaries; determining the effects on local tilapia-seed producers in terms of their accessibility to research outputs and uptake of technology; and making recommendations for policy formulation. Data were gathered from questionnaires, a stakeholder workshop, existing project documents and reports, and other publications.

The field survey covered four regions of Luzon, the biggest island in the Philippines. These regions comprise 15 provinces and represent the major tilapia-producing areas in the country. In 2000, they combined to produce 78,491 tonnes, or 95% of national tilapia production. Respondents were hatchery and pond grow-out farmers who used the four genetically improved tilapias (GIFT-GST, GET-EXCEL, YY-GMT, and FAST). Primary data for production year 2002 were collected through personal interviews using separate questionnaires for institutional developers of the improved tilapia, grow-out farmers, and hatchery operators.

Representatives of various stakeholder groups in the tilapia industry participated in a workshop in Angeles City, Philippines, 25–27 June 2003. The participants identified, discussed, and analysed the issues and constraints and then formulated recommendations for effective partnerships for the delivery and uptake of genetics-based technology.

Levels of funding and effectiveness

This component of the project reviewed: the manner in which institutions involved in the Tilapia Science Centre obtained the resources they needed to conduct genetic improvement R&D; how partnerships with the private sector were used to generate resources; and the impact of partnerships on the resources available for genetic R&D. Secondary information, interviews, and levels of institutional investment in R&D were analysed to determine how they contributed to meeting project objectives. The institutions and organizations involved were those engaged in genetics research through the Tilapia Science Centre and the private-sector organization GenoMar Phils.

Formulation of recommendations

A workshop was held in Tagaytay City, Philippines, 21–23 January 2004, to present major findings, formulate recommendations on public–private research partnerships in tilapia genetics, and disseminate research outputs. Thirty-two participants representing the National Aquatic Research System (NARS), international and regional organizations, advanced scientific institutions, and the private sector attended the workshop. The participants reviewed the roles of public- and private-sector institutions; identified the issues and constraints that affected collaboration in genetics research on tilapia and the dissemination of genetic-research outputs to end-users; outlined the effects that changing partnerships were having on the accessibility of research outputs to tilapia-seed producers and farmers; and reviewed the levels of R&D investment by public- and private-sector institutions involved with genetic research on tilapia. Based on the issues and constraints that were identified, the participants formulated recommendations to improve the efficiency of partnerships and identified appropriate follow-up actions.

Research findings
Development of collaboration in genetics
Public-sector research programmes

Similar to agricultural research on crops, early research on genetic improvement of tilapia in the Philippines was instigated by the public sector. In 1979, public-sector institutions FAC-CLSU and the WorldFish Centre initiated genetics research on Nile tilapia to improve the genetic quality of broodstocks through hybridization. This research was undertaken in response to growing concerns in the tilapia industry and to problems faced by farmers: inadequate seed supply; and deteriorating growth of fish in many production systems. This was followed by genetic characterization studies that indicated that the genetic quality of farmed tilapia stocks in the Philippines and elsewhere was poor (Macaranas et al., 1986; Pullin, 1988; Pullin and Capili, 1988). In response, public-sector institutions (government institutions and agencies, and international organizations), with the financial support of both national and international donor organizations, undertook strategic research programmes to develop improved strains that would perform well in various culture environments (Table 7.1).[3]

A major example of such a programme is the collaborative research on Genetic Improvement of Farmed Tilapia (GIFT) that was undertaken in the Philippines from 1988 to 1997 with financial support from the United Nations Development Programme (UNDP) and the Asian Development Bank (ADB). The research partners included the WorldFish Centre and public-sector institutions in the Philippines (Freshwater Aquaculture Centre, Central Luzon State University; the National Freshwater Fisheries Technology Research Centre, Bureau of Fisheries and Aquatic Resources; and the Marine Science Institute, University of the Philippines and Norway's AKVAFORSK). This public-sector initiative developed both a strain of tilapia that performed better than existing farmed strains, and a selective breeding technology that could be applied for genetic improvement of tropical finfish (Eknath and Acosta, 1998).

In addition to GIFT, other genetic-improvement initiatives in the public sector included: the IDRC-funded Fish Genetics Project, which resulted in development of a faster-growing tilapia strain, formerly known as IDRC strain and renamed as FAST (FAC Selected Tilapia) strain; and the ODA-funded Genetic Manipulation for Improved Tilapia, a collaborative programme of FAC/CLSU and University of Wales, Swansea, that focused on YY male technology to produce genetically all male tilapia (YY-GMT).

Although the bulk of the research was performed by the public sector, the private sector played an important role in the adaptive research phase of performance-evaluation trials of genetically improved fish in different culture environments (Abella, 2004).

Table 7.1 Genetic-improvement programmes undertaken by public-sector institutions (modified from Abella, 2004; Rodriguez, 2004)

Research project	Years	Implementing institutions/donors	Significant results	Strain developed
Genetic improvement of Tilapia broodstock	1979–81	ICLARM; FAC-CLSU Donors: RF (Rockefeller Foundation)	Evaluated existing stocks of tilapia in Philippines	
Mass production of Tilapia fry	1980–82	ICLARM; FAC-CLSU Donors: RF; ARO (Agricultural Research Organization, Israel)	Showed differences in culture performance between different tilapia species and hybrids	
Genetic improvement of Tilapia in the Philippines	1983–85	FAC-CLSU Donors: PCARRD Philippine Council for Agricultural Resources and Research Development	Evaluated different strains of *Oreochromis niloticus*	
Genetic characteristics of food fishes	1983–84	UPMSI (University of the Philippines-Marine Science Institute) Donors: ICLARM	Showed poor status of Asian *Oreochromis niloticus* stocks; hybridization with *O. mossambicus*	
Evaluation of farmed Tilapia stock	1984–88	UPMSI; UHCL (University of Houston-Clear Lake); FAC-CLSU Donors: USAID; IDRC; PCARRD	Confirmed poor status of Philippine *O. niloticus* stocks and that breeders and farmers want quality fish; improved electrophoretic methods	
IDRC fish genetics project	1986–96	FAC-CLSU Donors: IDRC	Produced fast-growing strain of *O. niloticus*	FAST (also called 'IDRC' strain in the local market); produced by hatcheries who purchase broodstock from the FAC
Genetic manipulation for improved Tilapia	1988–97	UW Swansea; FAC-CLSU; NFFTC-BFAR Donors: ODA (Overseas Development Administration)	Produced genetically male tilapia for grow-out and YY breeders for fingerling production	YY-GMT (produced by FishGen Ltd. and Phil-FishGen and accredited hatcheries in the Philippines)

Genetic improvement of farmed Tilapia	1988–97	AKVAFORSK (Institute of Aquaculture Research, Norway), FAC-CLSU, ICLARM, NFFTC-BFAR, UPMSI Donors: ADB (Asian Development Bank); and UNDP (United Nations Development Programme)	Produced fast-growing strains of *O. niloticus* and demonstrated that *O. niloticus* respond positively to selection	GIFT strain of tilapia (formerly produced by GIFT Foundation and its licensed hatcheries (commercial distribution has been suspended in favour of GenoMar Supreme Tilapia-GST)
Development of saline-tolerant Tilapia	1998–present	FAC-CLSU, NFFTC-BFAR, UP Visayas Donors: DoA-BAR (Department of Agriculture, Bureau of Agricultural Research)	Formed a base population from four different *Oreochromis* species by combining best-performing purebreeds and crossbreeds after evaluation in different environments	
Development of genetically enhanced Tilapia		NFFTC-BFAR Donors: DoA-BAR	Developed fast-growing Nile Tilapia using GIFT strain as one of the base populations	GET-EXCEL (formerly GET, BFAR 2000) produced by NFFTC and its accredited hatcheries; BFAR lines for saline and cold tolerance
Genetic enhancement of Nile Tilapia	2001–present	WorldFish Centre, FAC-CLSU, FishGen Ltd. Donors: DFID		

Sustainability of public-sector research programmes

When donor support and three major genetic-research programmes (the IDRC Fish Genetics Project, and the GMIT (Genetically Modified and Improved Tilapia) and GIFT projects) were completed in 1996–97, public-sector institutions were faced with the challenge of finding ways to generate resources to sustain the genetic research and disseminate the products of their research. In response, public-sector institutions developed their own strategies that led to the emergence of new genetic-improvement programmes.

In the case of GIFT, a Philippine National Tilapia Breeding Programme (PNTBP) led by the Bureau of Fisheries and Aquatic Resources (BFAR) was initially envisioned to continue the programme after financial support ended. However, the plan to institutionalize the PNTBP did not materialize because of lack of financial commitment from the Philippine government (i.e. due to budget constraints, BFAR could not absorb the former GIFT staff and continue the selection work). Instead, a non-profit private foundation was created in 1997 to continue the GIFT breeding programme and disseminate the improved strain. The establishment of the GIFT Foundation International by the institutional partners of the GIFT project was an experiment in obtaining private-sector resources. To meet its objectives, the Foundation established alliances with private-sector hatcheries for seed production and distribution, technology transfer to farmers, and other industry-development activities. It entered into formal licensing arrangements with seven privately owned tilapia hatcheries in the Philippines (GIFT, 1997; Rodriguez, 2002).

The termination of the GIFT project also led BFAR to establish its own genetic-enhancement programme and develop, using the GIFT strain as parent material, a new improved tilapia strain called GET-EXCEL. Based on the New Philippine Fisheries Code (Republic Act 8550), BFAR has been mandated to enhance aquaculture production by providing improved tilapia strains to farmers nationwide.

Development of private-sector collaboration

Since the late 1990s, private-sector involvement in tilapia R&D has become increasingly evident. At the same time, the infrastructure and competencies that had been established by the GIFT project, and potential significant commercial gains that could be achieved, caught the attention of a foreign private commercial company and stimulated its interest in collaboration. The Foundation, with its existing collaboration with private-sector hatcheries, also recognized that a formal alliance with a private-sector company would enable it to advance its selective-breeding research, acquire a competitive edge in the commercial market (both locally and internationally), and improve its financial capability (Acosta and Gupta, 2004).

In 1999, the GIFT Foundation entered into a formal agreement with GenoMar, a private commercial firm in Norway that specializes in the application of bioinformatics tools to selective breeding. This marked the beginning of the entry of foreign commercial firms into the programme for genetic improvement and dissemination of improved tilapia in the Philippines. Rodriguez (personal communication) indicated that the agreement between GenoMar and the GIFT Foundation had the following major elements: (1) the Foundation was provided with shares in GenoMar in exchange for fish from the Foundation's tilapia-breeding nucleus, an assignment of the 'GIFT Super Tilapia' trademark, and other commercial assets; (2) GenoMar would contract the Foundation to maintain and breed GenoMar's tilapia germplasm collection; and (3) the Foundation would be involved in the distribution within the Philippines of seedstock produced from the GenoMar nucleus.

In this relationship, GenoMar, as a biotechnology company, bears technical responsibility for the R&D activities. GenoMar scientists in Norway finalize breeding models and plans, and instructions are provided to GIFT Foundation staff, who conduct the breeding work in the Philippines. With the establishment of GenoMar – GIFT Foundation and GenoMar-accredited hatcheries alliances – the Philippine tilapia industry entered a phase in which the traditional public-sector institutions and its partner farmers were no longer the only actors involved in the programme for tilapia breeding and the dissemination of improved seed.

Effects of changing partnerships on genetic R&D

Research focus and priorities

In agricultural research, there are differences in the nature of the plant-breeding research undertaken by the public and private sectors. For example, the research centres of the United States Department of Agriculture concentrate on long-term breeding activities; whereas, the private sector devotes most of its resources to short-term varietal development. The Agricultural Research Service has terminated most of its research on variety development, and increasingly concentrates on research areas not pursued by the private sector (Klotz-Ingram and Day-Rubenstein, 2003).

In the case of fish, early research by public-sector institutions on genetic improvement dealt initially with strain and species crosses (interspecific and intergeneric hybridization). However, in view of the growing needs of the tilapia industry, the focus of their genetic-improvement research shifted in the mid-1980s to long-term selective-breeding programmes and the application of other genetic-improvement technologies such as sex ratio and chromosomal manipulation and hybridization.

The GIFT programme provides an opportunity to examine whether increasing private-sector involvement has had any effect on the nature of genetic-improvement research. Genetic-improvement research by public-sector institutions during the GIFT phase, and the present private-sector collaboration (GenoMar – GIFT Foundation), have focused on selective breeding of Nile tilapia. However, the GIFT project focused on traditional selective breeding for growth and sexual maturation; whereas, private-sector collaboration altered the selective-breeding programme by adapting it to the use of DNA genotyping technology (Gjoen, 2001). With this technology, GenoMar claims it can generate genetic maps that can be used to select traits that are difficult to record using traditional schemes (e.g. feed-conversion ratio and disease resistance). By using DNA typing of broodstock and recording phenotypic traits, fish that carry the 'good' genes can be identified and used as breeders (Gjoen, 2001). Lee (2003) reported that private-sector genetic-improvement research using DNA tools has obtained genetic gains nearly twice as fast as selection using traditional breeding programmes.

Questions have been raised about whether increased private-sector efforts in agricultural research promote the development of technology that provides the most benefits to society. One concern is that increased private support of public research could unduly influence the research and development agenda. Klotz-Ingram and Day-Rubenstein (2003) suggest that public research programmes could be disproportionately leveraged toward the needs of private industry, rather than the broader interests of farmers or consumers. Our study indicates that differences in the goals and priorities of the public and private sectors could also lead to differences in the focus of clients. Because there are more opportunities for greater volume of sales and commercialization for medium- to large-scale farmers, the private sector, as exemplified by the present collaboration with GenoMar, has tended to focus on these groups of farmers rather than on small, subsistence and resource-poor farmers. As a consequence, the present collaboration with GenoMar is not only looking at selection for growth and sexual maturation, it is also considering the development of traits that are of economic importance and relevance to medium- and large-scale farmers (e.g. selection traits suited for high input, optimal environments).

Outputs of genetic research

Improved strains of tilapia are one of the main outputs of genetic-improvement programmes undertaken by both public- and private-sector institutions. These strains are: the GIFT-GST of the GIFT Foundation International, Inc. (GFII) and GenoMar; GET-EXCEL of the NFFTC-BFAR; YY-GMT of the PhilFishgen, FAC-CLSU; and FAST, also of the FAC-CLSU. Of the four strains, three (GIFT-GST, GET-EXCEL, and FAST) were developed using traditional selection procedures and the other (YY-GMT) was developed using the genetic sex-manipulation technique.

In the case of public-sector research on GIFT, the main research products were the improved Nile tilapia (GIFT strain) and genetic-improvement methods developed for adoption by member countries interested in establishing national fish-breeding programmes. At the end of the GIFT project in 1997, the WorldFish Centre, the project's implementing agency, and one of the national partner institutions in the Philippines (NFFTC-BFAR) were provided with family materials of the GIFT strain from the last selective-breeding experiment (Generation 9) conducted by the project. Because these outputs were developed using public funds, and given the mandates of the public-sector institutions that received the GIFT strain, these family materials have been used primarily for noncommercial purposes – for genetic-improvement research or public-sector breeding programmes. Through the international genetics research network that the WorldFish Centre is coordinating, the strain has been made freely available to developing countries for aquaculture and the development of their tilapia-breeding programmes (Gupta and Acosta, 2001a,b).

In the Philippines, as a result of an agreement among public-sector institutions that participated in the GIFT project, the GIFT Foundation received the remaining family materials of the GIFT strain in 1998 and obtained exclusive rights and the trade name of this strain for commercial dissemination in the country. In 1999, after its formal agreement with GenoMar to secure long-term continuation of the GIFT breeding initiative, the Foundation lost its commercial rights to disseminate the GIFT strain (Generation 10) in the Philippines. Consequently, commercial dissemination of this GIFT fish was completely discontinued to make way for commercial dissemination of a further improved GIFT strain – the GenoMar Supreme Tilapia (GST). However, to enable the Foundation to generate additional revenues to finance its independent activities, it is allowed to produce and sell the Generation 10 fingerlings on a noncommercial basis (for example, for research purposes). GenoMar obtained the trade name and exclusive commercial rights to all products emanating from its agreement with the GIFT Foundation, which included dissemination of the new strain GST developed from Generation 10. Therefore, the private sector (GenoMar) has obtained complete control of the commercial GST seed markets. In the Philippines, the GIFT Foundation and accredited hatcheries that have formal agreements with GenoMar disseminate GST to local grow-out farmers.

In addition to the selective-breeding technology and improved strains, the technical staff, who were trained and acquired skills and knowledge of GIFT protocols, were important outputs of GIFT project. Of these staff, six are presently working with the GIFT Foundation International. In view of the different focus of the private-sector collaboration, another aspect that was investigated was how the changes in the nature of the partnership and source of funding had affected these staff.

Similar to what has happened in the agricultural sector, the evolving alliances have influenced the activities of the GIFT-trained staff. To help defray costs, and given the differences in goals and priorities of the private sector, the former staff have increasingly become engaged in nonresearch activities and are now performing relatively different, although related, roles. Under the GIFT project, it was estimated that the majority of staff time was spent on research; whereas, their present work with the GIFT Foundation focuses on management and nonresearch functions in the areas of breeding, seed production and dissemination, marketing, training, and administration. Although a few of these staff are under contract to do breeding research, no typical research function is being performed. However, because of their new responsibilities and exposure, the former GIFT researchers have acquired new skills, for example in management and decision-making.

Effects of public–private partnerships on delivery of research outputs

The success of aquaculture operations depends heavily on the availability and effective delivery of quality fish seed to farmers. Farmers' access to quality fish seed can only be ensured if there is a viable and efficient dissemination system. In the crop sector, dissemination is facilitated through organized networks for seed distribution and a delivery system that generally consists of research institutions (mainly public), private seed production and marketing agencies, and seed quality-control organizations.

In the case of tilapia, the seed-distribution system often only consists of either the private sector or the public sector. Recently, because of the significant progress that has been made on genetic improvement (development of improved tilapia strains, advancements in farming technology, and increased domestic and global demand for tilapias), the private sector (local commercial tilapia hatcheries) has become increasingly involved in the production and dissemination of improved tilapia strains.

All breeding institutions in the Philippines involve the private sector to disseminate genetically improved seedstock. Under most partnership arrangements for distribution of improved seedstock, private-sector partners remain uninvolved in actual genetic-improvement R&D. The only example of collaboration where the private-sector partner is directly involved in the actual R&D activities is the collaboration between the GIFT Foundation and GenoMar.

Involvement of the private sector in dissemination helps provide the link that could facilitate the transfer of research products to end-users. However, there are also concerns that the efficiency and effectiveness of delivery, and accessibility to these products, might be changed by these partnerships. The products of concern are broodstock for hatchery operations and fry or fingerlings of the four improved tilapia strains (GIFT-GST, GET-EXCEL, YY-GMT, and FAST) for grow-out.

Dissemination pathways

Dissemination pathways are the routes or channels that the products (improved tilapia) go through from developer–producer to end-user. In general, the main actors in the dissemination process are primary multipliers (breeding nucleus), secondary multipliers (private or government-owned hatcheries), and grow-out farmers. The primary multipliers are the main source of the latest generation of improved strains and are responsible for maintaining the genetic integrity of the stocks. They produce the latest generation of breedstock and distribute these fish to private or government-owned hatcheries (secondary multipliers). These hatcheries mass-produce fish stocks and disseminate fingerlings to grow-out farmers (end-users). Their function is very critical to the dissemination process because they are an important link between the breeding nucleus and the end-users and ensure wider distribution of improved tilapia. Depending on collaboration arrangements, the breeding nucleus may also distribute improved fingerlings directly to the grow-out farmers.

Figure 7.1 illustrates the dissemination pathways for improved tilapia strains developed by public- and private-sector breeding institutions. Except for the GET-EXCEL strain that is being disseminated by the public sector, broodstocks of all the other improved tilapias can only be obtained from the primary multipliers (breeding nucleus). There are two types of multipliers for GET-EXCEL: central hatcheries located in each of the Regional Outreach Stations of the Department of Agriculture (DA), Bureau of Fisheries and Aquatic Resources (BFAR); and second-level multipliers, referred to as satellite stations, which consist of DA provincial hatcheries, local government unit hatcheries (LGU), state universities and colleges (SUC), and private hatcheries. These multipliers perform different functions. The central hatcheries mass-produce the GET-EXCEL broodstock, duplicating the function of the National Broodstock Centre (breeding nucleus); whereas, the secondary-level multipliers mass-produce fry and fingerlings for grow-out operations.

The GET-EXCEL, YY-GMT, and FAST strains are distributed through partnerships between public-sector institutions and the private sector (farmers). Only GIFT-GST is privately owned and distributed entirely through private-sector collaboration (Table 7.2). Improved strains can either be openly accessed or accessed through specific terms of agreement (e.g. licensing, accreditation, or certification). Among the different improved strains, only FAST can be obtained through open access.

The breeding centres for GIFT-GST, GET-EXCEL, and YY-GMT produce and distribute both broodstock for hatchery operations and fry and fingerlings for grow-out farming. Only FAST is distributed from the breeding nucleus as broodstock, which indicates that these product developers are the only ones to deal directly with the ultimate users of the improved fish because they distribute and market fish for grow-out operations.

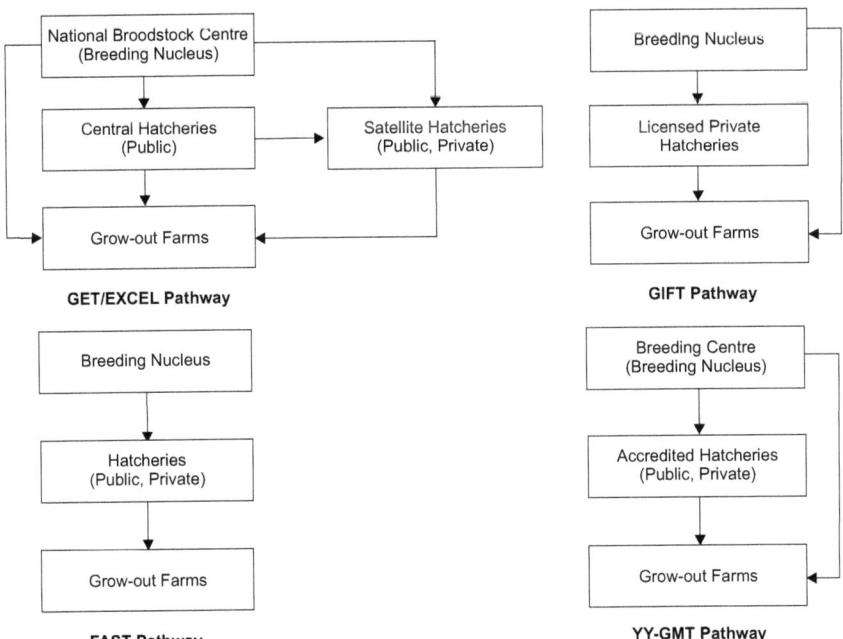

Figure 7.1 Distribution pathways for genetically improved tilapia

Table 7.2 Mode of access to tilapia genetics-based fish products being distributed by breeding institutions under the Tilapia Science Centre (modified from Sevilleja, 2004)

Improved Tilapia (commercial/ popular name)	Ownership of breeding nucleus	Year distributed	Distribution partnership	Mode of access	
				Broodstock	Fish for grow-out
GIFT-GST	Private	1998	Private	Licensing	Open
GET-EXCEL	Public	2000	Public–private	Certification	Open
YY male and XX broodstock and GMT	Public	1995	Public–private	Accreditation	Open
FAST[a]	Public	1993	Public–private	Open	Open

[a] This fish was initially distributed as IDRC selected Tilapia. It was renamed FAST in 1998 and is distributed only as broodstock.

Recipients of improved tilapia strains

Information about the users or recipients of the products of tilapia research can indicate whether one group of farmers is being favoured compared with others. Survey results indicate that there is little difference in the age and experience of users (hatchery and grow-out farmers) of improved strains owned and produced by the private and public sectors. The average age of tilapia farmers using genetically improved strains is 44 years, and respondents have been engaged in tilapia farming for up to 9 years. Hatchery farmers have been in the business longer than grow-out farmers. The educational attainment of the farmers is relatively high. The majority of the operators have some college education. In general, hatchery farmers have more education than grow-out farmers. Among different groups of users, farmers using the improved strain from private-sector collaboration (GIFT-GST) have the highest level of education.

Although tilapia farming in general is a male-dominated activity, 11% of respondents for both groups of farmers (hatchery operators and grow-out farmers) were women. Women's participation is more evident in operations that involve the production and multiplication (hatchery) of seed produced through private-sector collaboration. For example, 33% of respondents involved in hatchery operations of the GIFT-GST strain were women compared with only 6% of women involved in hatchery operations of the government-owned strain (GET-EXCEL) (Table 7.3).

Table 7.3 Distribution of users of genetically improved tilapia strain by gender.

Gender	Grow-out (% of farmers)					Hatchery (% of farmers)				
	GIFT	GET-EXCEL	YY-GMT	FAST	All strains	GIFT	GET-EXCEL	YY-GMT	FAST	All strains
Male	88	82	94	90	88.5	67	94	100	71	89
Female	12	18	6	10	11.5	33	6	0	29	11

Because production is highly correlated with ownership and landholding, the project team investigated the amount of land each respondent owned and his/her level of capital investment. Among respondents involved in hatchery operations, the users of the private-sector strain (GIFT-GST) had on average larger total landholdings (10.5 ha) than the users of the other strains. Among grow-out farmers, the users of the public-sector strain (FAST) had the largest landholdings (average 6.8 ha). In terms of capital investment, grow-out farmers who used the GIFT strain had relatively lower levels of investment (PHP166,369/ha)[4] compared with grow-out farmers using public-sector strains (e.g. PHP253,340/ha for GET-EXCEL users). However, among respondents involved in hatchery operations, those using GIFT-GST had higher levels of investment (PHP2,995,413/ha) than those using strains from the public sector.

Sevilleja (2004) reported that the majority of users of genetically improved tilapia strains are small landowners, suggesting that genetics-based technologies for tilapia are scale-neutral. However, a substantial investment is required to operate a tilapia farming business, and this may be beyond the reach of small farmers. The farmers who use these strains, although generally not owning large tracts of land, are financially capable because they have ready access to capital from their own sources. This suggests there is a need for a dissemination mechanism that specifically targets 'small and poor' tilapia farmers. The results also indicate that among farmers involved in hatchery operations, those with relatively higher levels of education, investment, and areas of land owned tend to be in a better position to receive the benefits of genetics-based technology from private-sector collaboration (i.e. GIFT-GST). In general, hatchery operations require higher levels of technical expertise and investment than grow-out farming.

Accessibility to genetic-improvement research products

Accessibility to products of genetic-improvement research (improved strains and technologies related to their production and farming) among users of improved tilapia strains was evaluated by analysing the sources of improved stocks (availability, price, and level of satisfaction of users), tilapia farming knowledge, and users' access to such information. The majority of respondents (grow-out farmers and hatchery operators) obtain their stocks from the same sources, and supplies are available whenever needed. This is most evident among farmers involved in hatchery operations using the GIFT-GST (100%) strain, when compared with farmers using any of the strains owned by the public sector. However, when the same group of farmers were asked whether they were satisfied with the price paid for their stocks, those using the strain produced from the public sector (GET-EXCEL) gave the most affirmative answers (90%). Among grow-out farmers, the highest and lowest levels of satisfaction in terms of fingerling price were expressed by users of the GET-EXCEL (98%) and the GIFT-GST (84%) strains.

In terms of how technologies relevant to farming of improved strains were accessed by the users, survey results showed that these were acquired through training programmes and seminars, self-study, and friends and fellow farmers. Among hatchery and grow-out farmers, the training programmes and seminars were the main sources of knowledge. There was little difference in the responses of hatchery farmers who were using either public- or private-sector strains (e.g. GIFT and GET-EXCEL). Sevilleja (2004) indicated that this was because technical services were provided regularly by the public-sector breeding nucleus (e.g. free weekly seminars of NFFTC-BFAR) and that training is required for hatchery farmers to become accredited and certified to use improved strains from both the public and private sectors.

Table 7.4 provides information on the effectiveness of existing delivery systems and the services provided by extension agents. The majority of farms (65–90%) received technical advice from suppliers of improved strains (private or public), but only 30–68% of the farmers were visited by external technicians or consultants. This indicates that extension workers have not been fully used by farmers as a source of knowledge.

In the case of GIFT-GST users involved in hatchery operations, all respondents indicated that technical advice is provided by resident technicians and only partly comes from external technicians and suppliers of the improved strains. However, grow-out farmers who used the GIFT-GST strain received most of their technical advice from suppliers of the improved strain (84%) and external technicians (30%). To determine whether there was any difference in accessibility to technical knowledge during the public-sector phase of collaboration on GIFT and the present private-sector phase involving GenoMar, six accredited hatchery farmers were interviewed who had previously used the GIFT strain and were now using the GIFT-GST strain. The majority of respondents (83%) indicated that, in the past, accredited hatcheries in alliance

Table 7.4 Access to technical advice[a]

	Grow-Out (% of farms)					Hatchery (% of farms)				
	GIFT-GST	GET-EXCEL	YY-GMT	FAST	All strains	GIFT-GST	GET-EXCEL	YY-GMT	FAST	All strains
Farms with resident technicians	8	8	4	12	8	100	18	31	29	27
Farms visited by external technicians or consultants	30	32	32	68	41	67	51	44	35	43
Farms receiving technical advice from fish suppliers	84	78	76	90	82	67	88	87	65	82

[a] Percentages exceed 100% because multiple responses were given.

with the GIFT Foundation and their grow-out farmer clients enjoyed relatively greater access to technical services provided by the Foundation's staff. Under the present arrangements, less emphasis is placed on providing services that will help them (accredited hatcheries and their grow-out farmer clients) to address their technical needs. They claimed that more focus is now given to monitoring the production and sales of accredited hatcheries (Acosta and Gupta, 2004).

The degree of awareness of tilapia-genetics technology was also examined among users of improved strains. Table 7.5 indicates that 83% of hatchery farmers are aware of the technology, compared with only 40% of grow-out farmers. Among hatchery farmers, the percentage of GIFT-GST users who are aware of the technology was not different from those who use strains produced by the public sector. However, among grow-out farmers using the GIFT-GST strain, only 42% claimed awareness of the technology. Their main source of information is technicians from suppliers of the improved strain. The level of awareness is even lower among recipients of the public-sector strain (GET-EXCEL). Only 28% are aware of the technology, and most information is obtained from government extension workers.

These findings confirmed earlier reports that indicated that tilapia farmers were adversely affected by the devolution of agricultural extension services from the Department of Agriculture to the local government units in 1993. The lack of technical support is a major need voiced by tilapia farmers throughout the country (Philippine Department of Agriculture, 2002). Rodriguez (2002) reported that tilapia farmers, especially the grow-out farmers and smaller producers, need more technical support and training (larger producers seem to have more access to technology and have taken the initiative to conduct their own inquiries). Our study indicates that fish breeding, nutrition, fish health, and water quality are the broad areas where farmers need technical assistance.

It is apparent that poor delivery of technical information, especially among farmers involved in grow-out operations, is the result of a lack of coordination among the private and government sectors that are overseeing the tilapia industry. The Philippine Department of Agriculture (2002) confirmed that links between research institutions, local government units, and fishfarmers were generally weak. Sevilleja (2004) emphasized the important role that farmers and private-sector producers can play in the delivery of technical information. In view of their direct participation in the distribution of improved tilapia strains, they could be harnessed as strategic partners in the dissemination process.

Technology diffusion and use

The project also examined the uptake of genetics-based technologies in tilapia in terms of their diffusion and extent of use among hatchery farmers who have direct interaction with breeding centres and other broodstock sources.

Table 7.5 Awareness and main sources of information on tilapia-genetics technology

	Grow-Out					Hatchery				
	GIFT-GST	GET-EXCEL	YY-GMT	FAST	All strains	GIFT-GST	GET-EXCEL	YY-GMT	FAST	All strains
Degree of awareness (% of farmers)										
Aware	42	28	46	42	40	83	82	88	82	83
Unaware	58	72	54	58	60	17	18	12	18	17
Sources of information	(% of responses)					(% of responses)				
Fellow producers and farmers	28	20	20	58	34	–	33	14	31	28
Government extension workers	12	32	26	6	16	40	56	19	24	38
Technicians from source	31	26	30	16	26	20	7	33	31	20
Technicians and sales people of feed companies	12	18	8	6	10	–	–	–	–	–
Media (radio, TV, and print)	5	–	8	2	4	40	4	10	–	6
Others (e.g. friends and researchers)	12	4	8	12	10	–	–	24	14	8

Overall, 92% of the recipients follow the set of broodstock management and production practices recommended by suppliers of broodstock (Table 7.6). All users of GIFT-GST follow the recommended management and production practices perhaps because collaboration arrangements with the breeding nucleus (supplier of the improved broodstocks) include terms of agreement that hatchery farmers must abide by when receiving the improved fish. The results also showed that hatchery farmers who are not bound by any hatchery agreement (i.e. users of the publicly owned strain FAST) were most likely not to follow the recommendations.

Table 7.6 Adoption and use of tilapia-genetics technology by hatchery farmers

	GIFT-GST	GET/EXCEL	YY-GMT	FAST	All strains
Does your source of broodstock recommend a set of management and production practices?					
YES	83	93	100	76	91
NO	17	7	0	24	9
Do you follow them?					
YES	100	93	94	85	92
NO	0	7	6	15	8
Do you use your own fingerlings as broodstock?					
YES	17	10	0	6	8
NO	83	90	100	94	92

Funding of tilapia R&D by public- and private-sector institutions

Generating resources for genetic-improvement research

Institutions involved in tilapia genetic research in the Philippines obtain resources for tilapia R&D through grants or allocations from government operating budgets, commercial activities (i.e. selling seedstock), and partnership arrangements with the private sector through new entities organized for this purpose (Rodriguez, 2004). Unlike public-sector institutions where funding is mainly through their institutional budget allocations, private-sector breeding programmes (i.e. GIFT Foundation International, Inc. and GenoMar ASA) largely depend on sales and other related revenues to fund R&D activities (Table 7.7). The GIFT Foundation, because it is a legal entity distinct from public-sector institutions, can enter into arrangements, agreements, and contracts with private entities to generate resources for R&D through business activities. Through its agreement with GenoMar for contracted research, the Foundation receives funds to cover the costs of breeding activities in the Philippines, which includes planning and analysis in Norway. Rodriguez (2004) reported that although the GIFT Foundation has this relationship with GenoMar, it also maintains its own independent breeding nucleus and conducts R&D using the resources that the Foundation generates from its other activities.

Impact of partnerships on R&D funding

Partnerships between the breeding institutions and the private sector to disseminate genetically improved seedstock provide business opportunities for the institutes to generate resources for R&D. These partnerships between the private and public sectors use models that include simple broodstock sales, accreditation programmes, and licensing agreements and are based on the use of broodstock by private hatchery operators to produce seedstock for sale.

Table 7.7 Operating revenues and R&D expenditures of non-profit private sector (GIFT Foundation) (Modified from Rodriguez, 2004)

Year	Revenues[a] (PHP m)	Expenditures[b] (PHP m)	Expenditures as percentage of revenue
1998	9.92	11.28	114
1999	9.95	9.43	95
2000	12.55	3.06	104
2001	15.04	12.72	85
2002	16.91	16.52	98

[a] Primarily from fingerling sales and fees earned from hatchery licensing programme (PHP53 = US$1).
[b] Represents expenses incurred by the Foundation for such items as personnel, supplies and services, travel, and depreciation.

The levels of funding and expenditure by public-sector institutions are largely influenced by grants and institutional budget allocations; whereas, the private-sector breeding programmes are influenced by revenues generated from commercial activities. The revenues generated and the genetic-research expenditures during 1998–2002 for the private non-profit GIFT Foundation ranged from PHP9.92 m to PHP16.91 m and from PHP9.43 m to PHP16.52 m, respectively. Annual expenditures on genetic research by public-sector institutions ranged from PHP0.07 m to PHP10.96 m, depending on annual operational budgets.

All of the breeding institutions under the Tilapia Science Centre, with the exception of the GIFT Foundation, do not have systems to track and monitor investments in genetic-improvement research. The absence of financial information and values may contribute to difficulties they face in negotiating public–private partnerships in R&D and commercializing research outputs.

Issues and recommendations

The stakeholder and final workshops organized by the project concluded that significant benefits had been achieved from the development of new technologies and strains of genetically improved tilapias in the Philippines. However, several issues and constraints emerged that could be addressed through public–private partnerships.

Stakeholder workshop

Several recommendations were made by participants in the stakeholder workshop to encourage effective, efficient, and equitable distribution of genetic research products and benefits to end-users.

- Public- and private-sector institutions need to work together to deliver improved tilapia breeds and technology to achieve the maximum benefits of genetic research. These links and partnerships are needed for effective, efficient, and equitable distribution of products and benefits.
- Based on geographical areas, socioeconomic conditions, and other factors, farmers' needs and how these are being met, require evaluation. Although the public sector caters to the needs of small farmers in general, it is essential that government line agencies place greater emphasis on providing services and focus on the small-scale, poor, and geographically isolated farmers, and those who do not have access to private-sector hatcheries, to ensure that they are not marginalized and have access to improved tilapia breeds.
- There is a need for public-sector policy that will: allow recognition and promote greater awareness by the public of all improved tilapia breeds available in the country; and target public-sector dissemination efforts on poor and geographically isolated farmers. Effective implementation

of such a policy should minimize competition between the public and private sectors.
- Breeding nucleus stations (private and public) should be responsible for providing the necessary technical services for effective management and maintenance of seed quality of improved tilapia breeds. Private-sector breeding nucleus stations, in partnership with the public-sector institutions, should also extend the specialized extension services needed by the multipliers and the grow-out farmers. The public sector has to continue providing the traditional type of extension services needed by small-scale hatcheries and the grow-out farmers, especially those not reached by existing distribution systems for genetically improved seed. The private-sector breeding nucleus stations can also act as a conduit for traditional types of extension information.
- The public sector should ensure that existing policies for conserving biodiversity, and safe-guarding the tilapia industry, are implemented and, where necessary, develop new policies for effective implementation.
- The government should take the lead in collecting, monitoring, and disseminating information on markets and prices of fingerlings and table fish. An effective mechanism needs to be established for collecting and disseminating this information to the producers. As well, the Philippine government should establish a fish-seed certification system.

Final project workshop

Based on project findings, and discussions of the issues that emerged, the participants in the final project workshop held in the Philippines in January 2004 formulated these recommendations for sustainable public–private partnerships in tilapia genetics research and the dissemination of research outputs.
- *Sustainable mechanisms for funding research.* Long-term investigation of traits for selection and transfer of the benefits of genetic-improvement research both require substantial amounts of capital. Public funds alone are usually insufficient or not available to finance these initiatives. The Philippine government should develop a policy to allocate a certain percentage of R&D budgets to tilapia research, create a policy to permit line agencies to use income from the sale of research products for research, and increase efforts to obtain international and bilateral funding.
- *Policy framework for public–private research collaboration.* Given the current stage of the tilapia industry in the Philippines, there is: inadequate incentive for the private sector to engage in collaborative research; a lack of mutual trust; and risk associated with competition between public- and private-sector breeding institutions. Policies are needed (e.g. tax incentives) to encourage private-sector investment in research. There should be delineation of public- and private-sector dissemination

activities to minimize competition, increase trust, and encourage research collaboration.
- *Tracking of investments on R&D.* The absence of financial information and values may contribute to difficulties in negotiating public–private partnerships in R&D and in commercializing R&D outputs. With the exception of the GIFT Foundation and GenoMar, none of the breeding institutions under the Tilapia Science Centre have systems for documenting the costs and investments made on tilapia R&D. Each institution should recognize what products they have within the scope of their research. Institutions should also make a fair assessment of the value of each product to be prepared to consider commercialization or licensing (e.g. historical investments, accounting practices, and value to others).
- *Diversity of improved and wild strains for future use.* The private sector generally has short-term objectives and will not maintain gene banks. Therefore, it should be a public-sector responsibility, but there are no long-term resources for this purpose. Genetic diversity is not receiving much attention in the public sector and present efforts are ad hoc and uncoordinated. The Philippines is a good site for coordinated effort. The Tilapia Science Centre should formulate a proposal for a 'tilapia germplasm trust' for long-term maintenance of farmed and wild tilapia strains.
- *Marketing.* There is inequitable distribution and inaccessibility by poor farmers in remote areas. Competition exists between public and private sectors in some areas, while other locations are not being served effectively. The government should continue to provide extension services and should develop innovative delivery systems suitable for small-scale farmers. Dissemination strategies should be formulated in consultation with stakeholders, and widely communicated to all sectors. The government should also concentrate on the production and distribution of broodstock; whereas, the private sector should concentrate on production and dissemination of fingerlings. The government must continue to distribute fingerlings for grow-out in areas not being served by the private sector.
- *Access to technical advice and assistance.* Extension services and technical assistance are necessary to facilitate transfer of technology to end-users. Without such support mechanisms, it is likely that targeted sectors of the industry will be marginalized and not benefit from technological change and innovation. Training programmes should be conducted with participation of the private sector for technology transfer. New models for delivering technical assistance and services should also be developed.
- *Protection of biodiversity (wild and agro-biodiversity).* There should be responsible transfer of tilapia germplasm in and out of the country. The government should strictly implement existing laws on fish export

and import and the regulations that protect aquatic biodiversity. The government should also set up a system to monitor movements of tilapia. Practical ecological risk-assessment procedures should be developed to determine the impact of improved tilapia. Biodiversity must also be considered when forging agreements with commercial private-sector companies.
- *Regulation and registration.* An effective way must be found to ensure the quality and integrity of genetically improved strains (both domestically and internationally bred). As well, efforts are needed to ensure that research into developing these strains is not negated through institutionalized regulations and registration mechanisms. The government should take the lead by developing such regulations. Consultation meetings among stakeholders on a fish-seed certification system should be convened, taking into account the lessons learned from other sectors (e.g. crops). A feasibility study on the applicability and workability of a seed-certification programme for tilapia should also be conducted.

Lessons learned

The programmes for genetic improvement of tilapia in the Philippines have undergone transformations and changes that featured various actors and organizations whose roles evolved over time. The experience of the breeding institutions under the Tilapia Science Centre as they sought to commercialize the products of genetic-improvement research (improved strains of tilapia) has important implications for the tilapia industry in the Philippines. Furthermore, it provides important lessons for the Philippines and for other developing countries that may be at a similar stage of growth and anticipate more private-sector involvement in their breeding programmes.

Foster an 'enabling environment' for public–private partnerships

The growing involvement of the private sector in genetic improvement of tilapia and fish-seed dissemination in the Philippines underscores the need to identify strategies that will enhance partnerships both among the various actors in the public and private sectors and between the two sectors for mutual achievement of their objectives. A major challenge is for both the private and public sectors to find ways to collaborate to transfer the products of genetic-improvement research and provide benefits to a larger section of the society.

Tilapia-breeding programmes in the country are now commercializing the products of genetic-improvement research. However, support programmes and policies that will create a favourable environment for partnerships in the dissemination and commercialization of research outputs are still lacking. Support programmes, clear policies, and institutional mechanisms and frameworks must be put in place to pave the way for strategic partnerships between the public and private sectors. This project has demonstrated that, similar to crops, private-sector companies will only be encouraged to invest in the commercialization of research products developed by public-sector breeding institutions if policy (e.g. protective technology or seed certification) is developed to guarantee proprietary protection. Public-sector institutions must also have established policies that will specify the conditions under which they should collaborate or engage in alliances with the private sector.

Define the roles of the public and private sectors

Most of the concerns and issues that were identified by the project are due in part to lack of clarity about the roles of the public- and private-sector institutions engaged in genetic improvement of tilapia and dissemination of research outputs. Effective partnerships between the public and private sectors can only be facilitated if the roles of the various players are clear. The stakeholder and final workshops organized by the project recommended that public- and private-sector institutions in the country must work together for effective delivery of improved tilapia breeds and technology to end-users. These workshops also assessed and identified the roles of the various players in the overall programme for genetic improvement and dissemination, and noted how these relate to the on going debates and issues surrounding this activity.

Harmonize activities of the public and private sectors

Strategic partnerships are essential to generate cooperation among the major players. One key factor is to ensure that problems and visions are shared, and that partners work together to find solutions to the problems.

The present alliances that involve public- and private-sector breeding institutions in the Philippines have spawned competition because they developed different improved strains and targeted the same market niche. Dialogue is crucial to help the present alliances to address the gaps within the public and private sectors and harmonize activities that will bring benefits to the tilapia industry.

Endnotes

1. This study was a collaborative effort of: the WorldFish Centre, Penang, Malaysia; the Freshwater Aquaculture Centre, Central Luzon State University; the Philippines National Freshwater Fisheries Technology Research Centre, Bureau of Fisheries and Aquatic Resources, Philippines; and the GIFT Foundation International Inc., Philippines.
2. Tilapia Science Centre is a collaboration of institutions that have been involved in research on various aspects of tilapia aquaculture and have been at the forefront in the development and dissemination of improved

strains of tilapia. These institutions, all located in the Science City of Muñoz, Philippines, are: the Central Luzon State University through its Freshwater Aquaculture Centre and College of Fisheries, the Philippine Department of Agriculture's Bureau of Fisheries and Aquatic Resources through its National Freshwater Fisheries Technology Centre, Phil-Fishgen, and the GIFT Foundation International, Inc.
3. The institutions involved include: International Centre for Living Aquatic Resources Management (ICLARM); Freshwater Aquaculture Centre (FAC-CLSU); Rockefeller Foundation (RF); Agricultural Research Organization (ARO), Israel; Philippine Council for Agricultural Resources and Research Development (PCARRD); University of the Philippines-Marine Science Institute (UPMSI); University of Houston-Clear Lake (UHCL); United States Agency for International Development (USAID); International Development Research Centre (IDRC); University of Wales (UW), Swansea; National Freshwater Fisheries Technology Centre, Bureau of Fisheries and Aquatic Resources (NFFTC-BFAR); Overseas Development Administration (ODA); AKVAFORSK Genetics Centre; Asian Development Bank (ADB); United Nations Development Programme (UNDP); University of the Philippines in the Visayas (UP Visayas); Department of Agriculture-Bureau of Agricultural Research (DoA-BAR); WorldFish Centre, FishGen Ltd., Department for International Development (DFID).
4. PHP53 = US$1 (2002 figures).

References

Abella, T. (2004) Role of public sector in genetics research and its partnership with private sector. *Workshop on public–private partnerships in tilapia genetics and dissemination of research outputs.* 21–23 January, Tagaytay City, Philippines.

Acosta, B.O. and Gupta, M.V. (2004) Public–private partnerships for tilapia genetics research in Philippines: case study on GIFT and lessons learned. *Workshop on public–private partnerships in tilapia genetics and dissemination of research outputs.* 21–23 January, Tagaytay City, Philippines.

Eknath, A.E. and Acosta, B.O. (1998) Genetic improvement of farmed tilapia project final report (1988–1997). *International Centre for Living Aquatic Resources Management* (ICLARM), Manila, Philippines.

GIFT (1997) 'Strategic Plan', GIFT Foundation International Inc., Philippines (unpublished document).

Guerrero, R.D. (2004) Public–private partnerships in genetic research and its importance to the tilapia industry in the Philippines: an assessment. *Workshop on public–private partnerships in tilapia genetics and dissemination of research outputs.* 21–23 January, Tagaytay City, Philippines.

Gjoen, M.H. (2001) GIFT programme continues: distribution of fast-growing tilapia to expand. *The Advocate*, December.

Gupta, M.V. and Acosta, B.O. (2001a) Development of global partnerships for fish genetics research: a success story. *Technical workshop on methodologies, organization and management of global partnership programmes.* 9–10 October, Rome, Italy. Doc. No. GFAR/GPP/01/10d.

Gupta, M.V. and Acosta, B.O. (2001b) Networking in aquaculture genetics research. in Gupta, M.V. and Acosta, B.O. (eds) Fish genetics research in member countries and institutions of the International Network on Genetics in Aquaculture. *ICLARM Conference Proceedings 64,* International Centre for Living Aquatic Resources Management (ICLARM), Manila, Philippines.

Huang, J., Pray, C., and Rozelle, S. (2002) Enhancing the crops to feed the poor. *Nature,* 418, 678–684.

James, C. (1996) Agricultural research and development: the need for public–private sector partnerships. *Issues in Agriculture* Number 9. Consultative Group on International Agricultural Research (CGIAR), Washington, DC.

Klotz-Ingram, C. and Day-Rubenstein, K. (2003) The changing agricultural research environment: what does it mean for public-private innovation? *AgBioForum,* 2(1). (http://www.agbioforum.org/v2nl/v2m1a05-klotz-htm)

Lee, W.J. (2003) A DNA tool accelerating genetic gains in tilapia breeding. Abstracts. *Symposium of International Association on Genetics in Aquaculture,* December. Chile.

Macaranas, J.M., Taniguchi, N., Pante, M.J.R., Capili, J.B., and Pullin, R.S.V. (1986) Electrophoretic evidence of extensive hybrid gene introgression into commercial *Oreochromis niloticus* (L.) stocks in the Philippines. *Aquaculture and Fisheries Management,* 17, 248–258.

Pinstrup-Andersen, P., Pandya-Lorch, R., and Rosegrant, M.W. (1999) World food prospects: critical issues for the early twenty-first century. Food Policy Report, *2020 Vision,* International Food Policy Research Institute (IFPRI), Washington, DC.

Philippine Department of Agriculture. (2002) A master plan for the tilapia industry of the Philippines, *Philippine Department of Agriculture,* Manila, Philippines.

Pullin, R.S.V. (ed.) (1988) Tilapia genetic resources for aquaculture. *ICLARM Conference Proceedings* 16, International Centre for Living Aquatic Resources Management (ICLARM), Manila, Philippines.

Pullin, R.S.V. and Capili, J.B. (1988) Genetic improvement of tilapias: problems and prospects, in Pullin, R.S.V., Bhukaswan, T., Tonguthai, K., and Maclean, J.L. (eds). The second international symposium on tilapia in aquaculture. ICLARM *Conference Proceedings* 15, Department of Fisheries, Bangkok, Thailand, and International Centre for Living Aquatic Resources Management (ICLARM), Manila, Philippines.

Rodriguez, B.M. (2002) Dissemination strategies for GIFT. *Steering Committee Meeting,* International Network on Genetics in Aquaculture (INGA), Bangkok, Thailand.

Rodriguez, B.M. (2004) Generating resources to continue tilapia genetic improvement R&D through public–private sector partnerships in the Philippines. *Workshop on public–private partnerships in tilapia genetics and dissemination of research outputs.* 21–23 January, Tagaytay City, Philippines.

Sevilleja, R.C. (2004) Effects of evolving partnerships on access to and uptake of tilapia genetic improvement technologies and their products: results of survey and policy implications. *Workshop on public–private partnerships in tilapia genetics and dissemination of research outputs.* 21–23 January, Tagaytay City, Philippines.

CHAPTER 8
Learning by networking with multinationals: A study of the Vietnamese automotive industry[1]

Tran Ngoc Ca

Abstract

This research examines the Vietnamese automotive industry to better understand how learning has taken place at the national level. This study sought to determine if Vietnamese firms could gain knowledge by collaborating with multinational actors in their networks, and to understand if intellectual property rights are a barrier to learning and innovation by firms. The study demonstrates that learning was encouraged through networks and links established with foreign multinational companies, that learning readiness of Vietnamese firms was extremely weak in the automotive sector, and that concerns over intellectual property rights discouraged investment by foreign multinational companies to upgrade technology. The authors conclude that the national policy environment does little to attract innovation-related investments, such as research and development, by foreign multinational companies. There is no clear evidence that intellectual property rights are a barrier to learning for Vietnamese firms.

This research sought to understand how Vietnam has responded to the challenges of globalization by building technological capability in the automotive sector. The objective was to contribute to a broader understanding of appropriate policy development. The project identified the policy measures that enable Vietnamese enterprises to overcome trade barriers, such as issues related to intellectual property rights (IPRs), and to integrate successfully into the international production networks. The focus was on learning and capacity building related to innovation; therefore, the study was also able to address some issues raised in the learning and innovation literature.

The study examined how Vietnamese companies, as active learners in the international economy, were able to close the knowledge gap while doing business with their counterparts. It also identified policy measures that support the learning process. The production network within the automotive industry in Vietnam was used as a case study. The key components of this learning and innovation system include: learning from multinational companies; upgrading learning capability by networking with foreign partners; attracting research and development (R&D) capability; and addressing the challenges posed by increasingly strict IPRs regulations and trade regimes. Small- and medium-size enterprises (SMEs) in Vietnam are the central actors of the national and sectoral systems of innovation, and their behaviour in an enabling policy and institutional (both technological and financial) environment was the main target of this research.

The twin objectives of the research were to: clarify some practical issues related to learning and innovation and related IPRs issues, and to recommend ways to improve the knowledge-policy environment in Vietnam; and contribute empirical experiences from a small developing economy to the literature on learning and innovation.

Linking with foreign partners as a learning strategy

The knowledge and technology gap between developed and developing economies is well known, and much of the research discourse and policy debate has been spent on the issue (Fransman, 1995; Lall, 1990; Perez and Soete, 1988). One approach to linking to broader knowledge communities (international, global, and regional) is for developing countries to become an active part of wider networks – networks of producers, technology suppliers and providers, marketers, and buyers (Ernst et al., 1999; Nelson, 1993).

Both theoretical and empirical studies have shown that multinational companies (MNCs) play an important role in 'spillover phenomena' in many developing economies. For some developing economies, especially from East and Southeast Asia, experience shows that active participation in international production networks of foreign direct investment (FDI) and technology transfer has been an effective and affordable way to learn and to close the knowledge gap (Hobday, 1995). More specifically, the spillover effects of FDI and joint R&D programmes can be crucial in allowing the host developing country to gain technology expertise and to develop a pool of knowledge (Blomstrom and Koko, 1998; Coe et al., 1997). International flows of technology contribute to learning and innovation in host economies in different ways – as embodied technology (machinery, equipment, and hardware) and as technological knowledge (both tacit and codified, and software).

However, it is not an automatic process. It depends on many factors, including host-countries policies. The concept of industrial upgrading and global value chains has recently become the focus of research on the role of transnational companies (TNCs) and developing countries (Gerefi, 2005). Many participants from developing countries have had the opportunity to learn by participating in global production networks. However, in the context of developing countries, this potential depends on many circumstances. The type of value chain also shapes learning potential and behaviour (Gerefi et al., 2005). These factors have implications for studying the behaviour of Vietnamese firms.

As a small economy attempting to integrate into the global economy, Vietnam must enhance its technological capability. To achieve this goal in the face of a widening knowledge gap, there is great urgency for Vietnam to work with the international community not only in terms of capital flows, but more so in the creation and use of knowledge. In practice, this approach is not easy and success should not be taken for granted.

Several problems hinder Vietnam's efforts. First, attracting FDI to Vietnam is no longer an easy task because of scarce global financial resources, increased competition among developing countries, poor infrastructure, and the current legal and policy environment. Second, even when the country has been successful in attracting FDI, foreign affiliates in Vietnam tend to do business within their own circle, which means that spillover to domestic firms may not happen or happens very slowly. Third, when they are given the opportunity to create links, few domestic firms have the 'learning readiness' to take their chance. Fourth, IPRs barriers created by many international and regional trade regimes (e.g. WTO – World Trade Organization, and WIPO – World Intellectual Property Organization) alter the nature of the learning approaches that domestic firms could employ.

Reviews of some emerging industries in Vietnam (e.g. electronics and apparel) reveal an extreme imbalance in the technological capabilities of industrial firms. These imbalances were evident in existing production methods and in the management of minor technical change, which are factors associated with early and entry-level technological capability. In contrast, little evidence was found of technological capability in major areas of technical change and marketing. This is not surprising given the long history of a 'command and control' approach to industry in Vietnam, and the nature of the recent transition to a more competitive economy. Indeed, this imbalance has been attributed to a lack of the learning opportunities that come from competitive pressure, and the consequent lack of a need to engage in marketing or product innovation. The most developed technological capabilities are in technical production. The linkage capability, which is instrumental in learning and especially for cooperating with MNCs, is still not well developed.

Among learning mechanisms, learning by doing is most common. Because the dominant activity of the majority of domestic firms is production, learning happens mainly in production capabilities but rarely in other areas such as marketing, design, and technical change. MNCs only create learning conditions for domestic firms when it is in their own interests to do so, and even then, domestic companies rarely make the most of their chances to learn. Domestic firms generally do not know how to use partnership arrangements with foreign firms to acquire technological capability. This passive approach needs to be replaced with a conscious and creative strategy by individual firms to exploit the potential for technology learning. Institutional factors (e.g. the vast difference in the traditions of state-owned enterprises (SOEs) and foreign firms, legal and regulatory regimes, and financial impediments) may also contribute to this situation in Vietnam.

Intellectual property rights: Pros and cons for learning

The protection of IPRs is very important for disclosing and diffusing new technology and knowledge, and for generating new knowledge. Indeed, effective protection of intellectual property will encourage creation and innovation by firms. With the appropriate benefits, firms will spend more money on R&D activities, and that means more inventions, new products, and new processes will be created. Technology and knowledge are improved and developed and make positive contributions to the economy and society. Ordover initially considered ways to adjust the patent system that would help both to provide returns to the inventor and to encourage the diffusion of the innovation in the economy. Later, Ordover (1991) argued that strong patent protection may not necessarily be conducive to growth. For example, in a strong intellectual property regime, R&D investment by one firm can significantly raise the costs of doing R&D for other firms and potentially discourage them from making their own investments.

From a developing country perspective, the impact of IPRs on learning is a controversial issue. In general, a loose IPRs regime could open up more room for reverse engineering and other learning activities, but it might also discourage foreign firms from transferring their advanced and appropriated technology to affiliates in the host countries. A strong IPRs regime would limit some learning approaches, but it might help to promote FDI and technology transfer.

The issue is more controversial because the impacts of a specific IPRs regime on learning are usually 'sector specific' and depend very much on labour quality, competition, S&T infrastructure, culture, and many other factors. Many studies have found that the importance of patents varies widely among industries (Scherer, 1959; Taylor and Silberston, 1973). Patents are viewed as a critical inducement to R&D investment only in a few industries – pharmaceuticals, specialty chemicals, and some mechanical engineering lines (Kaufer, 1983). In these industries, patents are not used for bargaining purposes, but simply to secure greater returns from investment research. Therefore, strong protection of IPRs is not absolutely necessary in every case, and for every industry. In many traditional sectors, which have so far been the main target of FDI in Vietnam, a strong IPRs regime would not make much difference to the behaviour of foreign investors with regard to technology transfer.

First, these sectors are not affected decisively by IPRs. Second, the technology decisions of an FDI project in these sectors usually depend on other general issues such as the global strategies of the parent firms, the comparative advantage of the host countries, and the regulatory environment. As such, a strong IPRs regime in accordance with international standards might not promote FDI and technology transfer in traditional sectors, while it might place a burden on the whole economy. A strong IPRs regime is usually the compromise that a developing country makes during the negotiation process to join international and regional trade regimes (such as WTO).

Unlike developed countries, IPRs systems in most developing countries are weak or not enforced in practice. There are different points of view on whether or not this is good for poor countries. For the rich, poor countries need to establish strong IPRs because they help to foster growth by stimulating domestic innovation, boosting foreign investment, and improving access to new technologies. However, for the poor, patents hurt, rather than help, domestic industries, which are often based more on copying than on innovation.

Both these points of view are true and reasonable. Without an IPRs system with strong enforcement, a developing country cannot attract FDI and this creates difficulties in accessing advanced technology, leads to less innovation, and causes the poor to become poorer (Verspagen, 1999). However, some argue that patents are obviously bad for poor countries. In this context, rich countries could provide more open access to their domestic IPRs systems by providing discounted fees and subsidized technical assistance. It is also suggested that rich countries should help poor countries to set up their own IPRs systems without saddling them with rich-world standards until they are ready to benefit from them.

The most important factor is the awareness of the country itself to deal with its problems. That is what India, China, and South Korea have been attempting with some success. India has a strategy to develop its own intellectual property by reversing the brain drain to foreign firms. Many experts who have worked for foreign companies come back to India to start their own businesses or research laboratories. Others, while doing research for foreign firms, conduct parallel R&D activities in India. Indian firms and individuals who undertake contract work with foreign firms also invest venture capital. These attempts to establish R&D capability in India have had some success. India has also developed policies to encourage innovation by small- and medium-size enterprises, and provides support to obtain patents. Although the IPRs system has been strengthened, India still faces problems related to expensive medicines and IPRs as they relate to plants, animals, and genes. Korea has been successful using a model of copying followed by innovation. Today, Korea has developed quite a strong IPRs system without support from rich countries or international organizations. Korea has established its own innovation capability and can compete internationally in some industries.

Overall, the importance of IPRs and associated policies in host countries is recognized, but their extent and application raise many issues and debates. There is no consensus on how this issue should be dealt with in the current trade and investment discourse on globalization. However, it cannot be denied that IPRs have played an important role in the transfer and diffusion of technology and knowledge, which are the foundations for the development of economies and societies.

Innovation: Developing country perspective

Thinking of and trying new and better ways of doing things is nothing new, and in this sense, innovation 'is as old as mankind itself' (Fagerberg, 2004). However, the meaning of innovation is interpreted differently in different contexts. One important feature distinguishes innovation from other similar concepts such as invention. Invention is the first creation of an idea for a new product or process; whereas, innovation is the first attempt to carry the idea forward into practice. As such, innovation is a continuous process that usually happens within firms (Fagerberg, 2004). To make the concept more operational, the OECD has proposed that the novelty of innovation should be seen in the context of firms. This is particularly relevant for developing countries.

For decades, there have been attempts to deal with innovation in economic literature. Marx realized that: 'The relative production of surplus value represents the real subsumption of the labour process by capital, and presupposes a change in the intensity or the productivity of labour. This requires technological development, which through successful innovations, reduces the necessary labour time' (quoted in Asheim and Haraldsen, 1991). Schumpeter later defined innovation as 'new combinations' of existing resources and pointed out that it required enormous effort by 'entrepreneurs' to fight against inertia.

Innovation is now widely accepted as the main force of economic growth. Baumol (2002) wrote: '...it can be argued that virtually all the economic growth that has occurred since the eighteenth century is ultimately attributable to innovation.' Lundvall (1992) argued that 'innovation is a fundamental and inherent phenomenon; the long term competitiveness of firms, and of national economies, reflects their innovative capability and, moreover, firms must engage in activities which aim at innovation just to hold their ground.' He also emphasized that 'technological progress is not regarded as a goal in itself. The main reason why national governments engage in innovation policy is the assumption that innovation is a key element in national economic growth.'

The complex and holistic nature of innovation makes it difficult to formalize, and this is probably the main reason why it was treated as a 'black-box' in neo-classical economics, despite the important role of technological innovation in economic development. This may also be the reason why innovation studies have been conducted by so many disciplines of social sciences. In the last two decades, many efforts have been made to formalize innovation into economic analysis under a branch of economics known as 'new growth theories' or 'endogenous growth theories'; however, in practice and for policy purposes, innovation should be looked at holistically.

It is important to distinguish between different kinds of innovation because they can have different impacts on the economy, and different expertise and policy measures may be required to make each happen. Innovation can be classified into product innovation and process innovation. According to Edquist

(2004): 'product innovations are – new or better – material goods as well as new intangible services. Process innovations are new ways of producing goods and services. They may be technological or organizational.' Another important classification is between radical innovation and incremental innovation, which has very important implications for the developing world.

Innovation is not necessarily linked to new science or original R&D. Many innovations result from new combinations of existing knowledge. The shortcoming of what is called 'the linear model' is that it assumes that innovation is applied science, and as such, research must come first. In reality, many innovations have occurred simply because the entrepreneurs believed there were opportunities to make profits from doing new things based on their experience and knowledge. R&D is called upon only when necessary, and in many cases, it does not involve original research, but applied research that might be resolved somewhere else.

To have successful innovation (the effective introduction of a new product to the market or the application of a new process in manufacturing), enterprises must undertake different activities, at different levels, depending on the essence of the innovation. Using the classification suggested by the OECD, these activities include: (1) acquisition and creation of new knowledge (new to the enterprises) such as R&D, acquisition of not-embedded technology, and adapting technology embedded in equipment; (2) manufacturing preparation activities such as tooling-up, industrial design, and acquisition of machinery; and (3) marketing. Innovation not only includes various kinds of activities but requires continuous improvement during the application process, which includes learning activities essential to the effective working of the technology system.

Recently, the majority of R&D activities in developed countries have been conducted by enterprises, especially large multi national enterprises. The economic power of these enterprises, and the critical role of technology in competition, have allowed and pressed these enterprises to invest intensively in large R&D projects. These projects are very well organized and employ leading scientists and engineers working in state-of-the-art laboratories. R&D efforts by these enterprises have created many significant innovations that have changed the landscape of the world economy.

However, many types of innovations do not require intensive R&D; they require a wise combination of existing knowledge and good vision. In this context, developing countries have hope. The majority of firms in Vietnam are SMEs, and their innovation relies very much on their flexibility and diversity and the effectiveness of their internal communication. These characteristics enable them to explore opportunities left by large firms, respond quickly to external changes, and develop unique ideas. Given the uncertain nature of innovation activities, the flexibility of SMEs is a significant advantage. In the past, we have witnessed the birth and dramatic growth of many influential SMEs based on their unique innovations. However, to convert good ideas into innovation, SMEs face important constraints such as limited financial power, poor managerial and technical skills, and a lack of R&D and testing facilities.

It is this conceptualization of innovation by SMEs that drives much of the discussion on policy design to support innovation by SMEs in more developed countries. In the developing world, and especially in Vietnam, policy discussions on SMEs have been mainly in the fields of private-sector development, job creation, and business services development. There are few studies of innovation by SMEs in the developing world, but what we know from these studies is that innovation by SMEs in the developing world is very different from the innovation discussed in the literature. What is called 'innovation' is, in fact, simply the firm doing something 'new'. This concept of innovation still has an important role in the developing world because it can significantly improve the performance of SMEs. However, it seems obvious that the issues have not been well addressed by researchers and policymakers in developing countries, and the theoretical framework to address this type of innovation is not very well developed.

Adapting the system of innovation approach

Since the term 'system of innovation' was coined (Freeman, 1987; Lundvall, 1992; Nelson, 1993), an enormous amount of literature has emerged. Edquist (2004) pointed out that a system of innovation is about determinants of, or factors influencing, innovation processes; however, the concept may have different meanings depending on the specific determinants that have been singled out. Although various players certainly have an important role, it is the interaction of players that makes the system alive. The interactions can be market- or non-market-based and include competition, transactions, and networking (Edquist, 2004). For firms in the developing world, given their small size and their limited capability, much of their innovation activities must rely on these types of interactions. Therefore, a system of innovation approach might be a good analytical framework to study innovation by firms in the developing world.

The system of innovation approach has been used in several studies in Vietnam, many of which were conducted in response to the need to reform the science and technology (S&T) sector. However, the majority of these studies concentrated too much on measures to link the S&T and production sectors without seriously investigating the kinds of support the firms needed and the traditional habits and practices the firms used to solve their innovation obstacles. This supply-side approach has not brought much progress to the reform of the S&T sector, and research into the innovation practices of firms in the developing world is required. Relationships with customer, supplier, and other producers (commercial relationships), especially with foreign partners, are important learning channels for enterprises. Enterprises that establish links with foreign partners have more chance to learn and develop.

Given the weakness of the S&T sector, inefficient financial markets, and underdeveloped technical services in Vietnam, commercial relationships (including competition) become the dominant interaction within the system of innovation. In this context, it is not surprising that S&T institutions have been locked out of the system. To solve this problem, a more appropriate specification of the innovation system must be developed. Figure 8.1 represents a (sectoral) innovation system in which commercial interactions assume a dominant role and the focus on SMEs is explicit.

The diamond in the diagram represents the interaction between SMEs and their business partners and competitors. SMEs buy capital goods and raw materials from suppliers, sell their products to customers, compete with larger firms, and sometimes sub-contract to these larger firms. Suppliers and customers of the SMEs also have some interactions. Customers, especially foreign ones, might request that producers buy capital goods from reliable suppliers to guarantee their quality. Suppliers might have to link firms with foreign customers so that they can sell their capital goods. The circle around the diamond in Figure 8.1 indicates that these commercial interactions are dominant, and that to various extents, financial institutions, public S&T research institutions, other service providers, and the government are locked out (the closer to the diamond, the greater the interaction between these institutions and the elements of the diamond).

Learning from linking up with foreign partners is not only the job of domestic firms, it is also the job of various agencies, both government and non governmental organizations. By providing appropriate support and

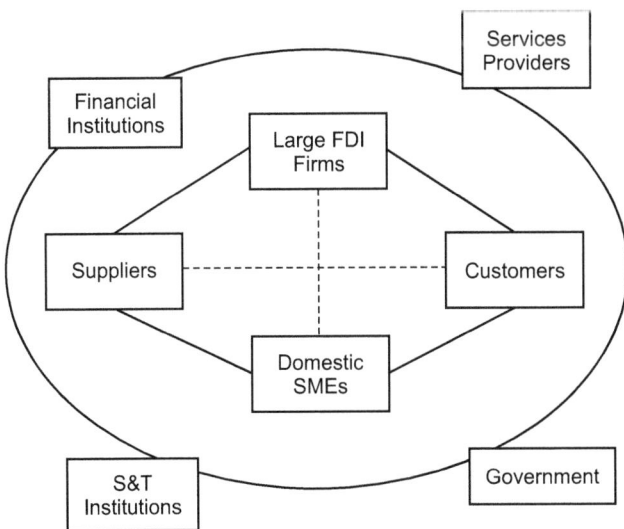

Figure 8.1 Innovation system showing the dominant role of commercial interactions

networking, they can speed up the learning process significantly. In this aspect, studies on policy measures, policy-making processes and the coordination and collaboration of various supporting organizations are badly needed.

Research questions

This research examined the following hypotheses:
- Weak learning readiness is the main constraint to Vietnamese firms participating in, and using, networks with foreign firms to upgrade their technological capability and climb the learning ladder.
- IPRs issues, posed by the new international context, are hindering the learning and innovation efforts of Vietnamese SMEs, which do not receive sufficient support from the government in terms of a suitable knowledge policy and incentive system.
- The overall macro-policy environment of the host economy is not encouraging multinational and foreign actors (suppliers, providers, and buyers) to foster learning efforts among Vietnamese SMEs, and thus, is not promoting learning.

To clarify the research issues, two research questions were examined:
- Can Vietnamese firms gain knowledge and close the knowledge gap by collaborating with the multinational actors (sellers, providers, and suppliers) in their networks?
- What IPRs barrier, among other things, do Vietnamese firms face in this process, and how could they deal effectively with this issue?

One expected outcome of the study was to provide recommendations on policy measures that would improve the policy environment for learning and would help Vietnamese firms cope with the IPRs barrier in their efforts to close the knowledge divide. Changes in domestic policy and organizational institutions are proposed. This includes all actors within the national and sectoral systems of innovation, such as R&D institutes, universities, technology intermediaries, and other organizations dealing with consulting, information, standards, and quality control. Market institutions (i.e. financial and banking), because they are crucial elements in the innovation system, were also examined.

Automotive industry in Vietnam

Within the automotive industry, the motorcycle industry is very important in Vietnam. Therefore, the industry provides a good case study of the impacts of FDI on learning by domestic firms. Research on the motorcycle industry will both benefit policymaking related to the industry, and provide insights into policy arrangements relevant to FDI, local enterprises, and S&T institutions. The automobile industry was also studied, but to a more limited extent.

Emergence of the motorcycle industry

The motorcycle has been an important means of transportation in Vietnam since the country's unification in 1975. After unification, used motorcycles were traded from the South to the North, and they became a new mode of personal transportation. From 1975 to 1987, a significant number of East European motorcycles entered Vietnam as Vietnamese, who had worked overseas under a labour export deal between Vietnam and former socialist countries, returned home. A large number of Vietnamese academic staff also worked in the education sector in Africa. They earned foreign currencies, and many sent home new Japanese or French motorcycles. These new motorcycles became a symbol of prosperity in Vietnam, and this attitude remains today.

From 1988 to 1992, the sector was dominated by Japanese motorcycles. This was caused partly by changes in policy and partly by the availability of new sources of supply. During this period, every person travelling overseas could import two motorcycles duty free. Given the huge gap between the world price and domestic price, the product became profitable for overseas travellers. However, new sources of supplies were emerging. First, significant quantities of second-hand motorcycles accumulated in Japan and their prices were very attractive. Second, many international flights that linked Vietnam to the world were routed through Bangkok, the region's motorcycle manufacturing and trading centre. The legendary Honda Dream II was imported from Thailand as luggage. Due to trade barriers and short supply, motorcycle prices were relatively high, and only middle-income families could afford a motorcycle. Very few families could afford to have more than one motorcycle.

By 1992, being an important means of transportation, the accumulated number of registered motorcycles in Vietnam had reached 2,846,000. However, in spite of a huge mechanical sector, which included many large SOEs, the manufacturing of motorcycle spare parts remained the business of small production units (mainly mechanical cooperatives). The motorcycle industry literally did not exist at that time. The production of spare parts was based on the use of outdated machinery, and the quality of products was generally low.

Since 1992, the development of the motorcycle industry in Vietnam has undergone incredible growth. The first FDI Law in 1987, and its subsequent amendments, made way for the entry of foreign motorcycle makers into Vietnam. The first products from these FDI enterprises were introduced in 1994, and they developed quickly in terms of models and quantities in subsequent years. Considered as an import-substitute industry, high tariffs were applied to imported motorcycles, which created favourable conditions for these FDI enterprises to explore local markets (at the cost of consumers). The motorcycle industry became a flagship industry in Vietnam considering both the size of the market and its rapid expansion.

The motorcycle market in Vietnam has grown briskly since 1999 (Table 8.1). By the end of 2003, there were 52 motorcycle assemblers operating in Vietnam,

Table 8.1 Motorcycle production in Vietnam (1999–2004)
Sources: Traffic Police Department and Ministry of Public Security

Year	CKD	FDI	Local	Total
1999	163,881	211,676	178,975	554,532
2000	65,775	294,697	1,507,052	1,867,524
2001	14,852	325,704	2,079,963	2,420,519
2002	24,137	769,914	988,149	1,782,200
2003		809,957	602,906	1,412,863
2004		1,005,602	895,309	1,900,911

(CKD Complete Knock Down; FDI Foreign Direct Investment)

of which 22 were state-run (42.3%), 23 were private (44.2%), and 7 were foreign-invested (13.5%) enterprises. In addition to these assemblers, there were about 200 parts makers, many of which were FDI firms. Measured by the number of vehicles produced, Vietnam now ranks eighth in the world motorcycle market.

Because per capita income growth has been relatively steady at about 7% in recent years, the critical factor behind the rapid growth of the Vietnamese motorcycle market was a dramatic price decline. The price dropped from about US$2,200 on average in 1998 to $630 in 2001 due to the penetration of low-priced motorcycles assembled from Chinese components. The market segment for high-priced products (more than $1,000) increased only slightly; whereas, the market for low-priced products (less than $1,000) expanded dramatically (Figure 8.2). The trend has reversed in recent years, but low-price motorcycles

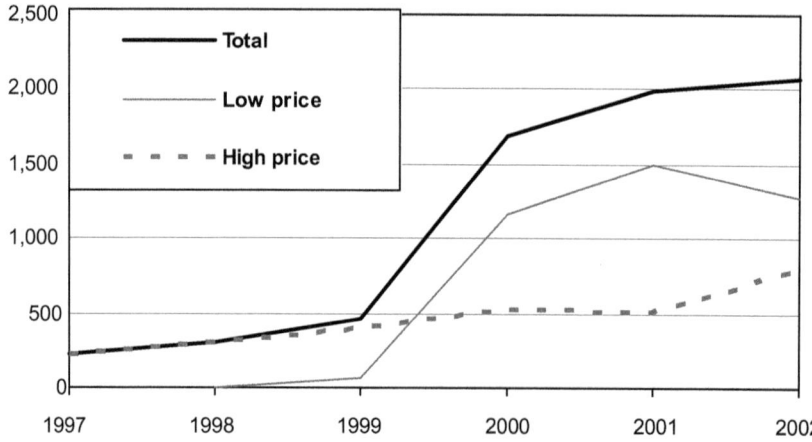

Figure 8.2 Motorcycle sales (in thousands of units) in different market segments in Vietnam. Sales are greater than the number of licensed motorcycles because of the existence of unlicensed motorcycles
Source: Ministry of Trade, Ministry of Industry, and Ministry of Public Security

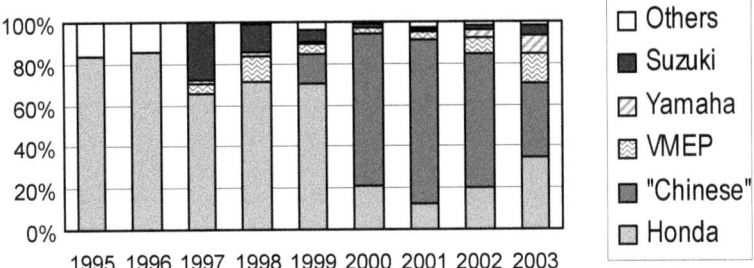

Figure 8.3 Shares in the Vietnamese Motorcycle Market
Source: Ministry of Trade, Ministry of Industry, and Ministry of Public Security

still dominate the market. However, now the FDI assemblers dominate with their low-price models. Figure 8.3 illustrates the fluctuation of market share since 1995.

The continued expansion of production volume is the premise for healthy growth of the Vietnamese motorcycle industry. Because Vietnam is in the early years of the development of the motorcycle industry, the importance of production volume cannot be overemphasized. Assuming that this premise is met, there is a potential for the development of parts suppliers in Vietnam. As larger production volume draws more suppliers to Vietnam, localization should progress more rapidly. Over time, FDI assemblers and suppliers are likely to let local suppliers undertake the manufacturing and production of some parts. As a consequence, supporting industries will begin to emerge.

Policy issues

The development of the Vietnamese motorcycle industry was boldly impacted by policy. The import prohibition on completed motorcycles from the mid-1990s, and measures to promote component production in Vietnam since 2000, are worthy of special mention. The main policy tools for regulating the motorcycle industry have been taxation and import quotas. A progressive import tax based on the ratio of local content was applied to encourage domestic parts production (the higher the local content, the lower the component tariffs).

Local content was defined as the proportion of locally produced components in a motorcycle in terms of value. Taxation based on local content has had a strong influence on the formation of subcontracting networks by motorcycle manufacturers. The quota on importing parts was another significant policy measure to control the motorcycle industry and protect domestic production. The import quota for each company was based on its capital, production capacity, and local content ratio. Besides taxation and import quotas, requirements related to the environment and transportation also aimed to decrease imports of components and promote or protect the domestic motorcycle industry. These policies intensified cooperation within the Vietnamese motorcycle industry.

The impacts of FDI on technology advancement in the industry are obvious. Being the largest motorcycle assemblers, FDI establishments also invested in making selected parts using relatively advanced technology. Influenced by the local content policy, these FDI establishments were under pressure to look for locally made parts from local parts makers.[2] As a result, local producers were also forced to improve their technology and management. FDI also intensified and created competition among local assemblers, who were forced by the local content policy to buy parts locally. Although the quality requirements of these assemblers were not as strict as the FDI establishments, their orders created a large market for parts makers, which allowed them to make necessary investments.

The presence of FDI motorcycle assemblers in Vietnam also attracted international parts makers who supply parts globally. In 2001, there were only 7 FDI motorcycle assemblers; however, the number of FDI firms in the motorcycle industry was 84 (Table 8.2). Table 8.2 also indicates that assemblers from one country usually bring with them parts suppliers from the same country. The production network based on country of origin helped to develop the industry quickly; however, it also raised barriers for domestic parts makers to enter the market.

The local content policy also had some negative impacts on the development of the industry. After it was implemented, the policy revealed many complications and became a hot topic for debate, not only between the authorities and motorcycle assemblers, but among government bodies. The policy was criticized because the methods used to calculate local content were not appropriate and, given the lack of an effective monitoring system, the policy created room for rent-seeking activities. The threshold of local content for applying privileged import duty was 40%; whereas, in 2000 almost all local assemblers reported only 20% local content, at most, in their Chinese motorcycles.

In 2001, when the policy came into effect, all of these assemblers claimed that they were successful in raising the local content of their Chinese

Table 8.2 FDI in the Vietnamese motorcycle industry (1992–2001)

	1992	1993	1994	1995	1996	1997	1998	1999	2000	2001	Total
China							1			7	8
Japan				2	5	5	2		1		15
Korea		1		1				1	1	1	5
Taiwan	2	1	12	2	1		4	5	8	10	45
Thailand					1	1		1		2	5
Other	1				1	2				2	6
Total	3	2	12	6	8	7	7	7	10	22	84

motorcycles to the threshold level of 40%, an amazing effort if this were real. However, later investigations showed that firms used many tricks to increase the local contents artificially.

The majority of domestic motorcycle assemblers were originally trading firms. They became involved in motorcycle trading first. When the trade barrier was raised, they switched to assembling activities using the simplest technology without making any major investments in the production of parts and components. The 40% local content requirement was a strong force designed to encourage assemblers to cooperate with local parts suppliers or to invest in making parts. However, given the weak position of the parts-making sector at the time, and the huge capital required for investment in parts making, the firms found a quicker way to satisfy the authorities.

Given the widespread smuggling activities at the Vietnam–China border, motorcycle parts were being smuggled into Vietnam. Once in Vietnam, these smuggled parts were registered as locally made. Later investigations showed that there are about 400 firms registered as local parts makers, but in fact, they were trading firms without any significant investment in production. Many of them were set up specifically to meet local content requirements. As a result, the local content policy, which was supposed to develop the motorcycle industry, became a paradise for rent-seeking activities.

Policy debate resulted in many modifications to the local content calculation methods and verification requirements during 2001. Investigations during this period created chaos in the motorcycle industry. Failures in the transportation infrastructure to cope with the motorcycle boom made things go from bad to worse. Enterprises blamed the government for inconsistency, government bodies blamed each other, and government offices were busy seeking appropriate solutions. In the end, the debate was ended by abandoning the local content policy. The government introduced new mechanisms to regulate the industry by establishing production quotas and other demand-side measures such as restrictions on motorcycle registration.

Automobile sector

Similar to the motorcycle sector, the automobile sector emerged with the entry of FDI assemblers. From 1989 to 2002, 14 automobile assembly projects were given licences with total registered investment of $889.6 m. However, three licences were withdrawn, so effectively 11 enterprises with a total registered capital of $571.7 m were set up (Table 8.3).

The 11 FDI projects involved 22 foreign firms and 11 Vietnamese firms. Among the foreign firms, there were 13 Japanese firms (Toyota Motors, Suzuki Motors, Hino Motors, Daihatsu Motors, Isuzu Motors, Mitsubishi Motors, Sumitomo Corp, Nichimen Corp, Mitsubishi Corp, Nissho Iwai Corp, Kanematsu Corporation, and Saeilo Nachinery), 1 Singaporean firm, 1 Philippino firm, 1 Malaysian firm, 2 Indonesian firms, 2 Korean firms, 1 German firm, and 1 United States firm. All 11 Vietnamese firms were

Table 8.3 Performance of FDI firms in the automobile sector (up to 31 December 2002). Capital and sales figures are in thousands of US dollars

Firm	Year of entry	Ratio Vietnam/foreign	Registered capital (US$)	Implemented capital (US$)	Accumulated sales (US$)	Vehicles assembled
Isuzu	1989	30/70	50,000	23,920	43,814	1,958
Mekong Auto	1991	30/70	35,995	35,995	127,976	5,529
VMC	1991	30/70	58,000	25,000	215,679	16,313
VIDAMCO	1993	0/100	32,229	28,217	203,616	11,816
VinaStar	1994	25/75	50,000	53,000	201,181	6,454
Mercedes-Benz	1995	30/70	70,000	22,500	155,027	4,814
VIDANCO	1995	33/67	32,000	12,914	32,265	2,782
Suzuki	1995	30/70	34,175	38,863	279,000	3,124
Ford	1995	25/75	102,700	72,000	395,027	18,812
Toyota	1995	20/80	89,609	110,627	169,001	6,340
Hino	1999	33/67	17,031	8,111	9,147	452
Total	–	–	571,739	419,854	1,831,933	78,394

state-owned enterprises (3 by the Ministry of Industry, 5 by the Ministry of Transportation, and 3 by provincial governments).

Since 1990, the government has launched various measures to attract FDI to help develop the automobile sector. For example, prohibitive import duties were applied to imported cars, a ban was placed on the import of used cars, and various import duties were used to encourage investment in more complicated productive activities (e.g. painting, finishing, and testing). However, the multi-purpose nature of these policies made it difficult to be consistent. It aimed at nursing the infant automobile sector by creating a trade barrier to protect local production. However, duties applied to imported and locally made automobiles are an important source of budget revenue. After almost 15 years of protection, local production is limited to assembling activities of foreign affiliates. There is little value added, and this poor result is paid for by the tax burden placed on consumers.

Up to 2002, not a single enterprise had achieved the rate of local content indicated in their investment licences. Some enterprises are prepared to increase this rate. For example, Toyota Vietnam is investing in a new workshop to produce car frames and bodies to fulfil its local content requirement. However, the local content level is still very modest within the industry as a whole. Most enterprises have not achieved the required localization rate indicated on their business licences. Total design capacity of the 11 enterprises was about 148,000 products of various types; however, the number of vehicles assembled in 2002 was only 26,706 (17.6% of design capacity), which was the highest percentage of design capacity compared with previous years (9.5% in 2000 and 13.5% in 2001).

Although implemented capital has reached 74% of total registered capital, the assembly activities of almost all enterprises are limited to complete knock down (CKD2) (except Hino Vietnam). Selective investment in simple assembly activities, combined with high-tariff protection rates, are believed to allow six FDI enterprises (out of 11) to make a profit even at very low rates of production. Five of the other enterprises are operating at a loss, including serious losses by Mekong Car. Since 2000, business performance has improved due to a boom in car consumption.

Learning in the automotive sector

Survey methodology

To obtain a more solid understanding of the learning activities of domestic firms in the automotive sector, a survey of domestic firms that had been making automotive parts was undertaken. Starting with a list of parts makers supplied by the Ministry of Industry in 2002, the research team developed an updated list of more than 200 firms, which is believed to include almost all automotive parts makers in Vietnam. These firms were concentrated around Hanoi and Ho Chi Minh City, where the main assemblers were located. About half of the firms were domestic, and half were firms with foreign investment. Because this research sought to understand learning activities of domestic firms that were linked to foreign firms, these firms became the research population.

A research tool questionnaire was developed using knowledge gained from a literature review and preliminary interviews. After pre-testing, the questionnaire was revised and used during the interviews of the firms. This is not a sample survey. All firms in the research population (112 domestic automotive parts makers) were contacted for face-to-face questionnaire-based interviews. The research team successfully interviewed 87 firms, mainly in the North and South; however, only 56 of the completed questionnaires were of good enough quality to be included in the dataset construction.

Firms in the dataset

Among the 56 firms in the dataset, 60% were established since 1999, the year considered to be the starting year of the boom in the sector (Table 8.4). Most firms (75%) were set up for the purpose of making automotive parts; whereas, a few started by making something else before switching to making automotive parts (Table 8.5).

With regard to firm type, Table 8.6 shows that the majority of the firms were limited liability firms (74.6%). There were only two state-run firms (3.6%). Because the research population included only domestic firms, by definition there were no FDI firms in the dataset. The dominance of non-state-run firms in the automotive parts market indicates the dynamics of this sector, regardless of the fact that the majority of Vietnamese partners in FDI automotive assembly projects are state-run enterprises.

Among the 56 firms, 46 (82%) made parts exclusively for the motorcycle sector, 7 (12.5%) made parts solely for the automobile sector, and only 3 (5.4%)

Table 8.4 Years in which firms were established (total percentages exceed 100 due to rounding)

Year	Number	Percentage	Cumulative percentage
1960	3	5.4	5.4
1978	1	1.8	7.2
1987	1	1.8	9.0
1990	3	5.4	14.4
1992	1	1.8	16.2
1994	4	7.1	23.3
1995	3	5.4	28.7
1997	3	5.4	34.1
1998	3	5.4	39.5
1999	5	8.9	48.4
2000	8	14.3	62.7
2001	8	14.3	77.0
2002	5	8.9	85.9
2003	2	3.6	89.5
2004	6	10.7	100.2
Total	56	100.2	

Table 8.5 Time lag (in months) between time of establishment of firm and production of parts (total percentages exceed 100 due to rounding)

Time lag (months)	Number	Percentage	Cumulative percentage
0	40	75.5	75.5
1	4	7.6	83.1
2	1	1.9	85.0
5	2	3.8	88.8
6	3	5.7	94.5
36	2	3.8	98.3
41	1	1.9	100.2
Total	53	100.2	

Table 8.6 Types of firms that participated in the survey

Type of firm	Number	Percentage	Cumulative percentage
Limited-liability	41	74.6	74.6
Joint-stock	5	9.1	83.7
Private	5	9.1	92.8
State-owned	2	3.6	96.4
Other	2	3.6	100.0
Total	55	100.0	

made parts for both sectors. With regard to the types of parts made by these firms, Table 8.7 shows that mechanical components are produced by 44.6% of the firms, plastic and rubber components by 26.8%, and electrical and electronic components by 17.9%. Although engine components are normally included in the mechanical group, they were considered to be a separate category in this analysis because they require more sophisticated technology. The fact that only 3 firms (5.4%) make engine components illustrates that most domestic firms enter the market to produce simple parts and that more complicated parts (engine components) are still imported or manufactured by FDI firms.

The entry level of the parts makers is reflected in what these firms considered to be important to allow them to successfully participate in the automotive parts market. Firms were asked to rank three capabilities in their order of importance (1: most important, 2: second most important, and 3: third most important) from a list of 12 capabilities. It was hypothesized that different levels of sophistication would require different capabilities for success. For example, making simple standard automotive parts might require only production capabilities such as machinery, stable quality, and low cost; whereas, making more complicated, advanced parts might require capabilities in advanced technology and International Property Rights (IPRs). Table 8.8 shows the evaluations provided by the firms with regard to these issues.

Several observations can be made. First, having stable quality, reasonable cost, and machinery were reported with the highest frequency and were very concentrated as both the most important and the second most important factors (Table 8.8) for entering the market. Second, having access to advanced technology and having IPRs were reported with the lowest frequency among all 12 capabilities. Third, marketing capabilities and distribution channels were ranked only at a moderate level. This pattern supports our arguments that the majority of domestic firms entered the automotive parts market at the entry level with simple products. At this level, it is not surprising that production capabilities, such as having machinery and being able to maintain stable quality and low cost, are more important than having access to advanced technology or IPRs.

Table 8.7 Types of parts manufactured by domestic firms in the automotive sector (total percentages exceed 100 due to rounding)

Types of components manufactured	Number	Percentage	Cumulative percentage
Engine	3	5.4	5.4
Mechanical	25	44.6	50.0
Electrical and electronic	10	17.9	67.9
Plastic and rubber	15	26.8	94.7
Other	3	5.4	100.1
Total	56	100.1	

This analysis suggests that the most important factor for local suppliers in Vietnam is to establish skills for mass production. The ability to conduct R&D will surely become important in the future, but that is not what FDI assemblers currently expect from local parts makers. For survival, and to be competitive in the increasingly open economy, skills in mass production are far more crucial. In addition, local suppliers in Vietnam must be able to cut costs while maintaining uniformly high quality. Suppliers in Vietnam must also be prepared to assume the same active role as suppliers in Thailand and Indonesia to enhance the competitiveness of the Vietnamese automotive

Table 8.8 The first, second, and third most important capabilities required to enter the automotive parts market (total percentages exceed 100 due to rounding)

Capability	Number	Percentage	Cumulative percentage
Most important			
Machinery	9	16.1	16.1
Quality sample product	3	5.4	21.5
Stable quality	17	30.4	51.9
Reasonable cost	17	30.4	82.3
Working capital	2	3.6	85.9
Qualified workforce	1	1.8	87.7
Marketing capability	1	1.8	89.5
Established reputation	3	5.4	94.9
Strategic business relationship	2	3.6	98.5
Distribution channel	1	1.8	100.3
Total	56	100.3	
Second most important			
Machinery	8	14.3	14.3
Quality sample product	4	7.1	21.4
Stable quality	15	26.8	48.2
Reasonable cost	12	21.4	69.6
Working capital	4	7.1	76.7
Qualified workforce	2	3.6	80.3
Marketing capability	3	5.4	85.7
Established reputation	1	1.8	87.5
Strategic business relationship	3	5.4	92.9
Distribution channel	3	5.4	98.3
Advanced technology	1	1.8	100.1
Total	56	100.1	
Third most important			
Machinery	5	8.9	8.9
Quality sample product	4	7.1	16.0
Stable quality	4	7.1	23.1
Reasonable cost	8	14.3	37.4
Working capital	6	10.7	48.1
Qualified workforce	7	12.5	60.6
IPRs	3	5.4	66.0
Established reputation	6	10.7	76.7
Strategic business relationship	9	16.1	92.8
Distribution channel	4	7.1	99.9
Total	56	99.9	

industry as soon as possible. Daily efforts on the factory floor to learn by doing are very important for mass production. As a final step toward the development of suppliers in Vietnam, R&D ability will be required. This means there is a need to develop the ability to propose new or improved part designs to assemblers.

In terms of the labour force, the firms were small and medium size (Table 8.9). Among the 45 firms for which labour data were available, 93.3% had a labour force of less than 300 people. The percentage of firms having fewer than 150 people was 77.3%. Firms are also very concentrated in automotive parts. Among the 31 firms for which data were available, 20 firms (64.5%) were solely automotive parts makers. Only 4 firms (12.9%) reported that their proportion of automotive parts sales was less than 35% of total sales during their peak year (Table 8.10).

Firms were also asked in which market segments they sold their products. Four market segments were provided and the survey results revealed that sales to domestic assemblers and in the free market accounted for the majority of sales. On average, 41.9% of parts were sold to domestic assemblers and 33.1% were sold on the free market; whereas, only 5.4% were exported and 20.19% were sold to FDI assemblers. Of those who sold to FDI assemblers, only one firm sold exclusively to FDI firms, 6 firms sold more than 75% of their total sales to this market, and 33 firms sold less than 30% of their total sales to this market (Table 8.11). These statistics mean that even for those firms that are

Table 8.9 Firm size in term of number of workers during peak year

Firm size	Number of workers	Percentage	Cumulative percentage
≤ 50	7	15.6	15.6
51–150	26	57.8	73.4
151–300	9	20.0	93.4
301–1,000	2	4.4	97.8
< 1,000	1	2.2	100.0
Total	45	100.0	

Table 8.10 Proportion of sales that automotive parts contributed to total sales during peak year

Proportion of automotive parts sales (%)	Number	Percentage	Cumulative percentage
10	2	6.5	6.5
20	1	3.2	9.7
35	1	3.2	12.9
80	1	3.2	16.1
90	1	3.2	19.3
95	2	6.5	25.8
98	1	3.2	29.0
99	2	6.5	35.5
100	20	64.5	100.0
Total	31	100.0	

Table 8.11 Percentage of sales that go to FDI firms (total percentages exceed 100 due to rounding)

Percentage of sales	Number	Percentage	Cumulative percentage
0	13	24.5	24.5
5	7	13.2	37.7
10	9	17.0	54.7
15	5	9.4	64.1
20	7	13.2	77.3
25	3	5.7	83.0
30	2	3.8	86.8
75	1	1.9	88.7
80	3	5.7	94.4
90	2	3.8	98.2
100	1	1.9	100.1
Total	53	100.1	

able to serve FDI assemblers, domestic assemblers and the free market are still their most significant markets.

As a main theme of this research, it was believed that linking with foreign partners would provide more chances for domestic firms to learn. Because being able to export, or to supply FDI assemblers, could be regarded as a link with foreign partners, those firms were considered to be the 'linked' group; whereas, those without this ability were considered the 'not linked' group. There were 40 firms (77%) (out of 52 firms with appropriate data) in the linked group and 12 firms (23%) in the not linked group. Further analysis was done to compare these two groups of firms.

Learning by domestic firms

Although they can enter the automotive parts market at the entry level with simple products, domestic firms must still learn to cope with many new obstacles and problems. Understanding the kinds of problems that these firms have experienced, and the channels they have employed for learning, are crucial for policy design.

Table 8.12 shows the obstacles that firms experienced in learning to make automotive parts. For both groups of firm, lack of resources for overseas visits was reported most often (75% of not linked firms and 72% of linked firms). This result reflects both the desire of domestic firms to go overseas for learning and the poor local learning environment (forcing firms to go overseas for training).

The availability of technical documentation in Vietnamese is problematic for both groups, but it is more serious for the linked group (68%). Again, this is an indication of a poor learning environment. From an innovation system perspective, this is a serious problem because the system fails to provide

Table 8.12 Obstacles that firms experience in learning to make automotive parts

Obstacles	Not linked		Linked	
	Number	Percentage	Number	Percentage
Standards for parts	6	50	23	57
Access to testing equipment	5	42	24	60
Consultants for technical problems	6	50	15	38
Technical documentation in Vietnamese	6	50	27	68
Intellectual property data	5	42	2	5
Production equipment	3	25	6	15
Funds for trial production	7	58	13	33
Copying or imitation	1	8	4	10
Resources for overseas visits	9	75	29	72
Efficiency of Internet use	5	42	23	57
Labour force skills	4	33	7	17
Design capability	3	25	3	7

innovative firms (innovative in the sense that they make something new to them) with appropriate technical reference documents. It is even more serious because it is happening not in an advanced sector, but in a relatively mature sector like simple automotive parts.

Also related to technical documents is the problem of standards for automotive parts. Standards are important technical documents that normally include valuable information that can guide firms in how to make specific products appropriately. A lack of standards for a specific part means that firms must learn about technical specifications from other sources, which is not always easy. An FDI motorcycle assembler said that when they were looking for local parts suppliers, many suppliers could make a geometrically exact copy of sample parts; however, their material, physical, and mechanical characteristics were not in accordance with the samples provided. Standardization of automotive parts in the Vietnamese Standards System is underdeveloped.

Lacking technical documents or standards for reference, parts makers must learn through experimentation. This creates a demand for testing and analysis services. Given the small size of the firms, and low frequency of use by a single firm, investing in this equipment does not make sense for individual firms. Therefore, they expect technical services in this field. However, a high proportion of firms in both groups (60% in the linked group and 42% in the not linked group) reported obstacles in accessing testing equipment. This indicates that this kind of technical service is not well developed and that services from the public sector are not effective. Having difficulties in accessing consultants for technical problems is another indication of poor technical services. This obstacle was reported with high frequency in the not linked group, and was considered even more important than access to testing equipment by this group.

Table 8.12 also reveals that obstacles related to design capabilities and copying or imitation were reported with low frequency. This could be interpreted to be a consequence of low IPRs protection in this field[3] because firms do not have many problems copying or imitating products. Under these conditions, design capabilities are not a big problem because firms do not have to deal with new products. Obstacles related to production equipment and skills of the labour force were also reported with relatively low frequency, especially by the linked group.

Because they lack technical knowledge in codified form (technical documents and standards), it was to be expected that learning by firms would rely more on their interaction with other organizations in the system. Table 8.13 reports on the importance of different organizations to learning by firms. The scale used in the questionnaire was a Likert scale from 1 to 4, with 1 standing for negative impacts, 2 insignificant, 3 positive impacts, and 4 very significant impacts (2.5 was the mean, or average score, of the scale).

Several observations can be made from these data (Table 8.13). In general, firms in the linked group evaluate contributions by various organizations to their learning processes more positively than those firms in the not linked group. It seems that pressure from links with FDI assemblers has accelerated the interaction between firms and other organizations.

Looking at the evaluations provided by both groups, it is easy to see that organizations in the public sector, such as government agencies, chambers of commerce and industry, and customs and tax authorities, were evaluated as not having made much of a contribution – although the score is significantly higher in the linked group than in the not linked group. Organizations related to technical services, such as universities and colleges, R&D institutions and government laboratories, international institutions and nongovernmental agencies, information agencies, local consultants and engineers, and foreign consultants and engineers, were all evaluated with low scores (lower than the average score). This result is consistent with the earlier analysis that technical services have not been well developed in either the private or public sectors. The relatively high score given to vocational schools and centres is not a surprise because making simple automotive parts requires workers with practical skills and training, not necessarily a university or college education.

The organizations that made a positive contribution to learning were the firms' business partners (Table 8.13). For the not linked firms, sales outlets in a free market were rated most highly (3.36), local automotive assemblers and banks and financial institutions were both rated 3.09, and local vendors and foreign vendors were rated 2.91 and 2.73, respectively. The two organizations with the highest scores for the not linked group were their main customers. Because FDI automotive assemblers are not customers of these firms, a low score was to be expected. However, such a low score (2.09) was quite surprising. This result indicates that if firms do not sell to FDI assemblers, it is difficult to learn from them.

Table 8.13 Contributions of various organizations to the learning processes of firms

Type of organization	Not linked	Linked
Chambers of commerce and industry	2.00	2.67
Automotive associations	2.55	3.17
Government agencies	2.09	2.40
Customs and tax authorities	2.09	2.77
Banks and financial institutions	3.09	3.36
Universities and colleges	2.27	2.33
Vocational schools and centres	2.91	3.10
R&D institutions and government laboratories	2.00	2.05
International institutions and NGOs	2.00	2.00
Information agencies	2.09	2.33
Local construction and engineering firms	2.45	2.13
Foreign construction and engineering firms	2.18	2.17
FDI automotive assemblers	2.09	3.13
Local automotive assemblers	3.09	3.45
Local vendors	2.91	3.36
Foreign vendors	2.73	3.08
Sales outlets in free market	3.36	3.25

For the linked group, FDI automotive assemblers received a much higher score (3.13). Selling parts to FDI automotive assemblers appears to open significant learning opportunities. However, it is local automotive assemblers who received the highest score (3.45), followed by local vendors and banks and financial institutions (both 3.36), sales outlets in the free market (3.25), and automotive associations (3.17). It seems that links with foreign partners not only offer direct learning opportunities, but facilitate interactions with other organizations and additional learning.

This analysis confirms that customers and vendors are important sources of learning. However, working with them involves many problems, some of which could restrict learning. Table 8.14 reports some of the problems firms experienced when trying to learn from customers and vendors.

Table 8.14 Problems firms experienced when working with customers and vendors

	Not linked		Linked	
Type of problem	Number	Percentage	Number	Percentage
Lack of parts' design	1	9	10	25
Client did not help with expert	5	45	21	53
Did not know client's needs	0	0	6	15
Unstable orders	9	82	29	72
Restricted in selling to others	1	9	7	17
Vendor did not help with expert	0	0	4	10
Vendor did not give full documentation	1	9	16	40
Failed to explore vendor fully	8	73	31	78

With regard to customers, many firms in both groups reported that their clients did not provide experts to help with their orders. This is problematic, and it is more serious in the linked group, in which 53% of firms reported this problem, compared with 45% in the not linked group. In many industrial sectors in developing countries (e.g. textiles and footware), foreign clients usually provide technical support at the early stage of development by providing advisors or supervisors. These experts are an important source of practical knowledge and offer many advantages over other types of learning. The automotive parts sector seems not to enjoy this luxury.

Table 8.14 points to another problem – unstable orders from customers. This problem is more serious in the not linked group (82%) than in the linked group (72%). Further investigation showed that few supply contracts between parts makers and their customers, especially non-FDI customers, are long term. As a result, it is very difficult for parts makers to plan any serious investment, including investments in learning. FDI customers tend to enter more long-term contracts, while rent-seeking activities provoke short-term approaches by domestic customers. Efforts to prevent rent-seeking opportunities should support long-term relationships between parts makers and automotive assemblers.

The loose relationship between parts makers and their customers is also reflected in the low proportion of firms that are restricted in selling to others. Only one firm in the not linked group (9%) was restricted; whereas, 7 firms in the linked group (17%) reported restrictions. During the interviews, some firms said that their FDI customers put sales-restriction conditions on the negotiation by using the IPRs-protection argument.

The earlier analysis indicated that machine and production skills (to maintain stable quality and low cost) were considered the most important factors for entering the parts market. In this regard, vendors are expected to be a source of knowledge. Although access to experts and documents from vendors was not considered a big problem, failure to fully explore vendors was problematic for 73% of the not linked firms and 78% of the linked firms. Interviews with the firms revealed that most had not properly explored vendors in advance. They only realized their errors after the deals had been done, and if they had to do it again, they would approach their negotiations differently.

The importance of different channels or approaches that firms used for their learning was also measured (2.5 was the mean value of the scale). Table 8.15 reports the average scores for the two groups of firms. Recruiting technicians with know-how was the most important learning channel for firms in both groups. The learning channels with the highest scores were those that reflected self-efforts by firms in terms of learning by visiting others and trial and error. Other methods such as learning from customers and learning from vendors were also important. Scientists, S&T organizations, and consultants are not important learning channels for automotive parts makers. These results are consistent with how the firms evaluated the contributions of different organizations to their learning.

Table 8.15 Importance of different learning channels to automotive parts makers

Learning channel	Not linked	Linked
Visits to other firms in Vietnam	3.40	3.50
Going overseas for learning	3.45	3.56
Recruiting technicians with know-how	3.64	3.60
Trial and error	3.00	3.25
Learning from customers	2.91	3.20
Learning from vendors	2.64	2.52
Cooperation with scientists and S&T institutions	2.20	2.10
Attending training courses	2.40	2.45
Referring to technical documents	3.27	3.02
Using consultants	2.00	2.17
In-house R&D	2.42	2.34

The policy environment plays an important role in how firms learn. Interactions among macro-environmental factors and firm-level micro factors have an important influence on learning and technological accumulation. Although they seek to promote the automotive industry, policy measures are not consistent. Incentives (mainly tax measures) to promote localization of production activities have been created, but support (especially technical support) has not been adequate or effective, and other regulations have had negative impacts.

Firms were asked to evaluate the impacts of policy on their learning activities (Table 8.16). The results show that local content policy and support from the government in all forms are welcomed by both groups of firms. This indicates that, although the local content policy has been criticized for its implementation, in general, it is considered to have a positive influence by domestic parts makers.

The fact that favourable conditions for FDI are appreciated by linked firms, but not by not linked firms, provides some evidence that the linked firms receive some benefits from FDI assemblers. There is also a large difference between the two groups with regard to regulations on loans. Firms in the linked group highly appreciate the regulations (3.73); whereas, the not linked firms provided a much lower rating (2.42). It appears that links with FDI assemblers help parts makers access loans.

Policy also has some drawbacks. All restrictions on R&D, training, and technology acquisition are considered to have a negative impact on learning. Further investigation showed that tax regimes do not consistently support learning. Low import taxes applied to automotive assemblers encourage them to buy parts locally, which opens opportunities for local parts makers; however, restrictions on expenditures that can be deducted from taxable corporate income for R&D, training, and technology acquisition limit learning activities and do not allow firms to fully benefit from such opportunities.

Table 8.16 Impact of policy issues on learning activities of firms

Policies and regulations	Not linked	Linked
Local content policy	3.58	3.63
Support from government in all forms	3.09	3.77
Favourable conditions for FDI	2.36	3.08
Restrictions on R&D	1.82	1.98
Restrictions on training	2.00	1.98
Restrictions on technology acquisition	2.18	2.42
Regulations on loans	2.42	3.73
Regulations on IPRs	1.82	2.08

Case studies

The analysis of the survey results revealed many general issues related to the learning activities of automotive parts makers. To better understand the interactions among different players with regard to learning, several case studies were conducted. These cases included firms in both the linked and not linked groups. In addition, FDI assemblers were also studied to better understand the learning opportunities that emerge from their operations.

Honda Vietnam

Honda Vietnam (HVN) was established in 1996 as a joint venture between the Honda Group (70% in total, in which Honda Motor Co. Ltd. holds 42% and Asian Honda Motor Co. Ltd. holds 28%) and the Vietnam Engine and Agricultural Machinery Corporation (VEAM, a state-owned enterprise). The legal capital of the joint venture is $31.2 million, in which the Vietnamese partner contributes the value of the land-use rights, and the foreign partner contributes the capital. The majority share in the joint venture, and the contribution of capital and technology, provides Honda with managerial control over the operation.

The factory is located in Vinh Phuc province, about 30 km from Hanoi on the road that links Hanoi and Haiphong. The operation was started in 1997 with the production of Honda's legendary Dream model (which is named Super Dream in Vietnam). The design capacity of the factory was 450,000 motorcycles per year and it has been extended several times. By 30 October 2001, the accumulated investment was about $134.4 million. By January 2002, HVN had 1,143 labourers and a capacity of 450,000 motorcycles per year. By April 2002, it had expanded to a capacity of 600,000 motorcycles per year with about 2,000 labourers. However, restrictions on motorcycle registrations in large cities the following year had negative impacts on the whole sector, including HVN. In 2005, this restriction was removed, and HVN reached sales of 620,000 units. From 1996 to the end of 2005, HNV sold 2.5 million motorcycles and is a profitable FDI business in Vietnam.

As a leading motorcycle manufacturer, there is no doubt about the superiority of Honda technology. Honda has selected Thailand as its headquarters in Southeast Asia for R&D and engineering. Affiliates like Honda Vietnam focus mainly on production, assembly, and marketing. The factory was constructed in accordance with the development plans and engineering priorities of Honda. The technology that has been transferred was process technology, which includes the equipment and skills needed to operate and control production processes. Product technology is not transferred fully because design and product development capacity is centralized in Honda R&D and in Honda's factories located in Thailand. Learning within HVN focuses on production technology, in which assembly is central, and marketing concentrates on the domestic market and the development of reliable distribution channels, safe-drive programmes, and many other promotional activities.

In terms of machinery and production structure, HVN had six production workshops by the end of 2000: (1) Pressing Workshop – using a 200 t and two 400 t pressing machines and a computer numerical control (CNC) pipe-framing machine to make frames, gasoline tanks, chain boxes, and other precise parts; (2) Welding Workshop – using 5 robots to ensure productivity, precision and quality of components; (3) Plastic Object Workshop – using computer-controlled machines, which allow high productivity, while providing endurance and aesthetics of plastic parts; (4) Painting Workshop – using state-of-the-art technology to ensure the greatest surface protection for metal parts; (5) Assembling Engines and Frames – the assembling line is modern, has a relatively high level of automation, and is equipped with on-line testing facilities that allow quality to be checked at every step of the production line; and (6) Quality Control Workshop – equipped with state-of-the-art modern Japanese testing equipment operated by overseas trained staff. HVN also manages a 500-m test runway, which is the longest in ASEAN. Recently, HVN has started to invest in the local manufacturing of engine components.

HVN started by assembling standard models that combined some parts produced and sourced locally with sophisticated components (such as the engine) sourced overseas through Honda's procurement network in the region. The establishment of HVN also brought with it many foreign parts and accessory makers, which created a group of satellite companies around HVN. The next step in the development of HVN is to produce sophisticated components in Vietnam. Although the capabilities to operate the production system might be upgraded, there is little evidence that R&D, design, or engineering capabilities will be developed locally.

This technology was transferred mainly through staff training. Before starting production, HVN built a core staff of engineers and technicians who were sent to Japan and Thailand for training. A 6-month course was provided to production-line managers, and a 3-month course was given to managers at lower levels. In total, 100 people received this type of training. After production started, Honda sent its own supervisors on a regular basis to oversee operations and provide guidance on production activities.

Besides overseas training, on-the-job training has been provided since the start of the operation in the form of short training courses provided by Japanese lecturers. This type of training is targeted at specific problems and issues realized during the operation of the new venture. The training curriculum is based on Honda's Foundation Course, a programme used only within Honda. Teaching methods include classroom lectures, role-playing, and scenario building.

HVN recruits local residents who have successfully completed their secondary education to be operational workers. Because many of them have an agricultural background, it takes extra effort to train them as industrial workers. This is one of the challenges Honda must overcome to make its operations in Vietnam a success. Almost all training is in production skills, operational management, and quality management. There is little design training.

The entry of Honda into Vietnam had a strong impact on the development of the motorcycle industry. The local content policy and other commitments forced HVN to develop a network of suppliers in Vietnam. This network is made up of domestic suppliers, who were selected and given technical support by HVN, and other FDI enterprises that in many cases are regional suppliers for Honda. By 2004, Honda had 20 local suppliers. The majority of these suppliers were joint ventures of Japanese parts makers with local firms or 100% foreign-invested firms. To date, there are only six domestic firms in this network. Honda itself has entered into two more joint ventures with other local partners to produce motorcycle parts.

The process of seeking local domestic suppliers has had an important impact on the awareness of many local firms. By negotiating with Honda, they have learned more about quality requirements and management. Those who failed to become a supplier for Honda learned why they had failed and what they had to improve. Those who did succeed improved to meet Honda's requirements. In many cases, they also received technical support from Honda, especially with regard to quality management, which proved to be very valuable.

The entry of Honda also brought about competition, which to some extent triggered learning. The late 1990s and early 2000s were marked by so-called Chinese motorcycles (because most of the components were made in China), and their prices ranged from half to a third of Honda's standard prices. In response, Honda launched a new model called the Wave Alpha, which was aimed at the low-end market. This move by HVN drove the cheap, unreliable Chinese motorcycles out of the market and forced domestic assemblers to produce better quality models.

VMEP

VMEP was the first FDI company to invest in the Vietnamese motorcycle industry. This 100% Taiwanese-owned enterprise came to Vietnam in 1992 and started production in 1994. For its operations in Vietnam, all machines, equipment, and technology were transferred from Taiwan, and all motorcycle models were made from designs (detailed drawings and illustrations, and descriptions of manufacturing processes) supplied from the parent firm in Taiwan.

Beginning with models from abroad and using imported parts, VMEP modified some specifications to address the specific requirements of Vietnamese customers (e.g. reducing the noise and shake of the engine). Over time, VMEP has invested in more machines and equipment to produce components for its assembling activities. In the beginning, the machines were simple, but now they include CNC machinery. By 2005, sophisticated engine components were being manufactured at the factory in Dong Nai province. Local staff control production technology, although CNC machines are still programmed in Taiwan. Recently, in a move to make VMEP into Sanyang's Centre in Asia, the technological capability of VMEP has been strongly improved. In an effort to improve design capability, new models are partly designed in Vietnam (although comprehensive design and testing are still carried out in Taiwan). Equipment critical to design and design training has been acquired, and 20 engineers are being trained in Taiwan.

Similar to the case of Honda Vietnam, investment by Sanyang in Dong Nai encouraged many Taiwanese parts makers to set up factories in Vietnam. Together they have changed the landscape of the industrial zone in Dong Nai by making it into a cluster in the motocycle sector. VMEP has also worked with local parts makers to out source some work. The process of searching for suitable partners revealed weaknesses in the local motorcycle parts sector. VMEP reported that in the 1990s it was extremely difficult to find local firms that could make simple motorcycle parts of stable quality. During these early days, VMEP worked with some large well-equipped mechanical factories from the Ministry of Defence, but they also failed to meet quality requirements. The problems were not related to technology (because it is quite simple) but to quality management and the reliability of mass production. Lack of standards on motorcycle parts was another problem. As a result, the same part was made with different materials by different parts makers. This situation drove VMEP to rely more on its Taiwanese partners and on its own production capabilities. Later, some of its former engineers set up their own firms and became parts suppliers for VMEP.

With regard to learning, the VMEP case reveals many opportunities for learning and demonstrates the need to develop a non-stop process of learning. Technologies were acquired step by step on the basis of technology transfers between the parent firm and VMEP. By 2004, the manufacturing technology for 18 motorcycle models had been transferred, 117 employees (equivalent to 10,930 people-days) had been trained abroad, and 152 foreign experts had come to Vietnam to provide technical support (1,606 people-days). The total cost of technology transfer was estimated to be $8.7 m, of which $7.4 m was paid. Many local staff benefited from this training, and some left the firm to become entrepreneurs.

Lien Ha private company

Lien Ha is one of the suppliers of motorcycle seats in Vietnam.[4] The production site is part of a sports shoe manufacturer located in the outskirts of Hanoi. The company was officially established in 2002, after implementation of the Private Companies Law. However, business started unofficially in 1992 when the present owner and director, after retirement, decided to start the business with a group of friends. The director, the former CEO of a state-owned automobile company, expressed great pride in his company because he has never required a bank loan or any state financial support to operate his company. He attributed his success to: his network of contacts; recognition of domestic and foreign markets in terms of consumer needs and supplier possibilities; awareness of the operations of local institutions and the legal system; and great entrepreneurial spirit and a belief in the company.

The company started with 50 employees and now has 200 employees during the peak season. Given the broad contacts of the owner in the automobile industry, the initial plan was to produce seats for Toyota cars; however, this plan failed because Toyota decided to use imported seats. The company then turned to the production of seats for sofas sold in the domestic market. In the last few years, given the implementation of the local content policy in the motorcycle industry, and suggestions from potential customers, the company has expanded to manufacture motorcycle seats. Its customers include 70% Vietnamese motorcycle assemblers and 30% foreign-invested companies in Vietnam, such as Honda and Toyota.

The technology applied is quite simple in terms of the equipment required and the skills of the workers employed on the production line. Small second-hand plastic pressing machines (which were made in 1990) were imported from Korea and Japan and require only a single operator. Product designs are based on foreign models available in the market, although the company claims that modifications to their product make it more durable than competitors' seats. Moulds are made locally by mechanical companies, including IMI (Industrial Machinery Institute); whereas, the materials (mainly polyurethane) are imported entirely from the United States (through a Taiwanese distributor).

Based on our observations at the production site, there is no doubt about the operational capability of the company in the sense that its workers can operate effectively and productively. However, many things need improvement. First, the factory should be better organized. It is quite messy, which will affect productivity. Furthermore, we did not see any evidence of Total Quality Management (TQM) at the site. Second, although second-hand machines are inexpensive, breakdowns are more likely and the rejection rate is quite high (about 10%). When the machines break, common problems can normally be fixed by the company's technical staff, but in some cases, external help is required. Given the lack of formal technical support from machine manufacturers, this help must come from technicians or engineers at research institutes and universities, or other companies or even individual technicians.

These people can usually make the machines work again, but repairs take time, and in some cases they cannot solve the problem properly.

There is little to discuss about adaptation of machines. Adaptation has instead focused on materials. Specific types of material and sometimes their combinations are critical to the durability of the product. The company has a good knowledge of materials, and it is able to produce an appropriate combination for its product.

The company claims to have some design capability and to be able to produce a product with an advantage over competitive products. However, this is only a minor change to designs available in the market. The key issue is how to make a durable product using the least amount of material, and this is where the company's capability lies.

Song Cong Ltd. Co.

Song Cong Mechanics was established in January 1995 at the site of a mechanical cooperative. Located in Ha Dong, Hatay province, just 20 km from the centre of Hanoi, it is considered a flagship of the mechanical sector in the province. Its traditional products are motorcycle replacement parts for second-hand bikes, a huge market in the 1980s and early 1990s. Being in this business for quite a long time, the company has developed good relationships within the wide-ranging distribution network in Hanoi.

As a result of the local content policy, it has expanded to manufacture various components for both the domestic and FDI motorcycle assemblers. It was a major supplier for VMEP's Hatay's factory before this Taiwanese company started its own production facility in Dong Nai. For the last 3 years, Song Cong has been supplying many Chinese-based domestic assemblers with different kinds of simple components. Surprisingly, this is usually not based on long-term contracts but on meeting short-term needs created when domestic assemblers fail to buy smuggled components from China. With better control of smuggling since 2002, the company has seen more stable orders from domestic assemblers. In 2004, Song Cong employed about 600 people working one shift. This represented a doubling of the number of workers since 2000 due to the opening of a new factory using second-hand Japanese machines.

Except for the new factory, Song Cong's production is based on multipurpose machines modified for production of specific components. Most of these machines are second-hand Japanese ones, and some are Russian. The majority of the machines are old, and their precision is no longer high.

Regardless of its inferior machinery, Song Cong has managed to produce many kinds of motorcycle components, some of which are quite sophisticated. The company's approach is to change its old, multi purpose machines into specialized productive machines with simple innovative accessories. Some of these accessories are inventions of the company; whereas, others are copied from factories in Taiwan. This approach allows the company to obtain productivity and reasonable precision at relatively low cost, which is sufficient to meet the requirements of domestic assemblers. However, this does not allow the company to become a supplier to FDI assemblers, which require higher quality and stability. Investment in a new factory would be needed to overcome this limitation.

Technical knowledge is obtained mainly through learning by doing and learning by watching. Business tours organized by the Vietnam Chamber of Commerce and Industry (VCCI) to Taiwan have proven to be valuable because Song Cong acquired technical information that allowed it to innovate successfully. Feedback from distribution agents is an important source of information, which allows the company to modify its products or launch new ones.

Regardless of the many technical problems that must be addressed, the company tackles these by itself. Relationships with S&T organizations are considered to be of no help because of high costs and the ineffectiveness of these organizations. The manager of Song Cong believes that people from S&T organizations cannot become involved deeply enough to be able to find solutions to the very specific problems of the company. He believes it is better to let engineers who must face the problems every day be in charge of finding solutions. However, S&T organizations are quite helpful for testing services because the company does not own any measurement equipment.

Thang Long Metalware Company

Thang Long Metalware was established in 1968 as a state-owned enterprise that belongs to the Hanoi Industrial Department. Thang Long's headquarters are in Sai Dong, 10 km from the centre of Hanoi. Thang Long has three factories: one in Hoixa, Gialam, Hanoi, producing moulds and motorcycle components; one in Lang Yen, Hanoi, producing water tanks and eating utensils; and one in Ho Chi Minh City, producing fabricated metal products – oil-cookers, table lamps, and candle lamps; stainless steel utensils; and motorcycle components.

In 2001, Thang Long employed 1,059 people, which included 100 engineers and others with Bachelor's degrees, and more than 200 skilled workers. Many retired experienced workers were invited to work for Thang Long, and they have contributed remarkably to the success of the company, which has several important customers such as Honda Vietnam and IKEA of Sweden.

With regard to motorcycle components manufacturing, Thang Long's technology is superior to Lien Ha's and Song Cong's. Its products are sold to Honda Vietnam, which has high requirements for quality and stability. The machinery and equipment used by Thang Long is more sophisticated than what is used by the other two companies. It has many large-scale, brand-new computer-controlled machines. Being able to operate these machines to produce various kinds of products for different customer demands demonstrates the company's operational capabilities.

Although it has operated since 1969, the learning activities of the company only started in 1989. This period has been marked by heavy investment in machinery and human resource development. Thanks to various sources of capital, especially the profits gained from its joint venture with Honda and Goshi Giken in Goshi Thang Long Auto Parts, the company has been able to expand its operation into many fields based on improved quality and productivity. The company has also expanded geographically with its under-construction factory in Ho Chi Minh City.

To be able to meet the fast-changing demands of customers, the company also invested in a mould-making factory using brand-new CNC machines. This gave it full control of the moulds needed to manufacture different kinds of products and components. It also provided opportunities for some innovation within the company. However, the mould factory and CNC machines also represent a test of the company's engineering capability because programming of CNC machines for different jobs is a rare skill. So far, the manufacturing of motorcycle components for Honda Vietnam and fabricated metal products for IKEA is based on these customers' designs. The CNC machines are programmed accordingly, and the company does not have much input. Special training for computer-aided design and computer-aided manufacturing (CAD and CAM) technology is badly needed if the company wants to develop its engineering capability.

The company has demonstrated its ability to choose appropriate technology for its needs. The pressing machine is an example. After a time-consuming period of consultation, the company decided to choose a Taiwanese vendor. The decision was based on the argument that the machine made by the Taiwanese combined all the desirable features of the Japanese design, used German materials (steel), and was flexible in component selection, which gives the best value for money. This approach could not have been used without a thorough understanding of the technology embedded in such a machine.

Learning by solving problems and learning from working with customers are the main learning channels employed by Thang Long. Disappointed with support from S&T institutions, the company arranges for its staff to work with selected scientists and technicians to address issues that emerge from innovation activities. Technicians from customers and vendors of foreign machines have proven to be valuable sources of technical information.

Observations and policy proposals

Observations

Several general observations can be made from the survey and case studies: Vietnamese producers have obsolete levels of technology, both in engineering and management; design capability is weak and relies on input from FDI firms or on imitation; and there is a lack of cooperation and coordination among local firms.

There are obstacles to relationships between Vietnamese producers and foreign firms. FDI firms usually impose restrictions on local firms in terms of production volumes and also have strict requirements for quality and delivery time. In addition, the same products supplied to FDI firms quite often cannot be sold to third parties. FDI firms tend not to invest directly in local producers. Instead, they usually send in experts to supervise quality and to support operational management. FDI firms also tend not to buy from a small number of firms, but prefer to use many suppliers.

FDI has positive impacts on the development of local industry in general and technology in particular. However, FDI operations tend to concentrate on production activities and use proven technology to take advantage of cheap labour or markets protected by high trade barriers. This mode of investment determines the type of investment and knowledge transfer that occurs between the parent firms and their affiliates in Vietnam. Investment in production technology is the main type of resource transfer. Training is also concentrated on production management. There are few activities in terms of design or more sophisticated engineering work. Some FDI firms are just starting to develop design capability and more advanced skills in their work forces. There is little room for S&T organizations to get involved in activities of FDI firms.

For local firms, the results of this research indicated that innovation does not result in product breakthroughs, but rather investment is generally directed to new production facilities. The study also showed that links with the business community play a much more important role than links with the academic community, as both a source of innovation ideas and a channel for problem solving. Within the business community, foreign or FDI partners are the main channel for learning, not only for technical issues, but also for issues related to product and inputs markets. Large firms seem to better manage technology than SMEs, and they also have a better chance of joining the production networks of foreign and FDI firms.

The firms surveyed, especially SMEs, are not totally ready for learning. Even in positive learning environments, such as the alliance between Honda Vietnam and its local suppliers, not all firms can use this opportunity to learn. As a result, the kinds of products produced by Vietnamese SMEs are still simple, and most of the core components of the operations of MNCs are still imported despite the local content policy. It is also clear that IPRs issues created more concern for MNCs than for local firms, and this has resulted in less enthusiasm by foreign firms to upgrade to more sophisticated technology.

The overall policy environment, although recently improved, still does not provide sufficient support to firms in terms of specific learning and incentive systems. Moreover, the macro-policy environment does not sufficiently encourage multinational and foreign actors (suppliers, providers, and buyers) to support learning efforts by Vietnamese SMEs. Most of the progress made during the last few years to promote foreign investment has not included specific measures to encourage learning.

Regardless of the disadvantages of being small, SMEs do manage to survive through creative innovations or 'no-innovation'. One important lesson learned from the SMEs cases is that innovation must suitably match the capability of the firm; otherwise, the firm may face bankruptcy. The case studies also show that innovation requires many types of learning, some of which are industry-specific and common among local firms. It would be a waste of efforts if each firm tried to address these problems individually. However, cooperation between competitive firms is not easy and interventions by the government and S&T institutions are needed. These are areas in which the government should support cooperation between firms and S&T institutions, which may also provide opportunities for fruitful international cooperation.

Firms must clarify what they need to learn and how they need to learn. Their needs will depend on their business orientation and strategies. As a coherent part of their business plan, firms must identify what is required for each period and specific context and which kinds of knowledge are needed. They must then decide how to acquire this knowledge and tailor their learning efforts accordingly. Instead of learning on an ad-hoc basis, learning must become a key and permanent means for firms to become more competitive. A conscious approach to invest in, plan, and organize learning activities is necessary for learning to take place within firms.

Vietnamese firms are generally still not active enough in augmenting their learning activities. The government should play a role, but firms must also be more active in taking the lead. They should introduce new initiatives in their relations with the government to lobby for policies that are conducive to learning. To side-step the serious funding shortage, firms also need to devise flexible learning mechanisms that do not require heavy levels of funding, e.g. the barter or exchange of knowledge and training courses, and the organization of mutually beneficial services.

The use of connections and networks with foreign firms, especially MNCs, is especially important for Vietnamese firms. Firms must be more aware of the advantages and disadvantages of this mechanism and become more active in pursuing opportunities. They must stop relying passively on receiving knowledge and consciously engage in intelligence gathering while working with their foreign partners. Firms should seek opportunities to jointly implement different kinds of technical improvements, and use them as chances to learn how foreign companies handle technical change. The firms can take the same approach to learning marketing skills. By becoming part of a larger network of producers and suppliers, such as the Japanese manufacturers in East and Southeast Asia, firms may be able to learn more about marketing. Different foreign sources could be used in combination to create new expertise among firms.

A consistent strategy is required to expand technological competence. Vietnamese firms must distinguish between those actions that contribute to meeting their long-term strategy, and those that only meet their tactical or short-term ends. With regard to IPRs concerns, firms should balance the short-term gains and long-term benefits when they are deciding how far to pursue IPRs protection.

In addition to the efforts of individual firms, support and intervention by the government are also necessary. As the policymaker, the government should create the general framework in which industries can develop – a framework that includes regulations related to macroeconomic stability and the generation of favourable social conditions such as more business-friendly attitudes among government officials, especially toward private entrepreneurship. Among other things, the government should create more conducive conditions for firms and provide more learning resources for firms involved in R&D, training, and education. Possible initiatives include promoting technological development by issuing S&T policies for the whole country, devising plans suitable for each sector, and providing incentives for firms to do business and to learn.

Policy proposals

Although this study examined the automotive industry, the findings are common to many other sectors. For this reason, these policy proposals may be applicable to many SME-dominated sectors in Vietnam. The policy proposals are grouped into: measures to promote links between local firms and international business networks; measures to develop an SME-oriented innovation system; and measures to maximize the benefits from IPRs.

Linking SMEs to national and international business networks

This research showed that FDI assemblers would like to buy parts from local parts suppliers, but it was not easy for local firms to become reliable partners. Among other things, good business management, good quality management, and good behaviour with regard to IPRs are key issues. If they were equipped with such knowledge and capability, local firms would have more chance to integrate into national and international production networks.

> *Proposal 1: Publish and disseminate a manual on good practices in standard business management and quality management and a code of conduct on intellectual property rights for SMEs. These documents should be sector specific.*

Overseas learning is highly appreciated by firms, but a lack of funds for this purpose is a major concern. This is definitely an area in which both the central and local governments could assist. Each year the government allocates funds for foreign study tours. However, under the current arrangement, it is very difficult for local private SMEs to access such funds. Trade promotion is more popular; however, learning promotion should receive more attention.

> *Proposal 2: Governments at both the central and local levels should allocate an exclusive proportion of their budgets for international cooperation to support overseas learning by innovative SMEs.*

One reason FDI assemblers prefer to work with international parts makers is their reliability. High reliability helps to minimize transaction costs, which may offset the higher cost of these international partners. Local parts makers can offer low-cost products, but doing business with these firms can incur high transaction costs. This research also indicates that learning from FDI assemblers is not free of obstacles. Only when local firms have proven themselves as good partners can they tap into the knowledge pool of their international partners. Policy measures that reduce transaction costs could effectively promote links between FDI assemblers and local firms, which in the long term could benefit all parties.

> *Proposal 3: Expenditures made by MNCs and FDI enterprises to provide technical assistance to local SME suppliers should be deducted from taxable income or partly reimbursed.*

> *Proposal 4: Allow local governments to use their own budgets to pay part of the training costs that SMEs incur to meet their requirements as sub contractors or suppliers to FDI enterprises and MNCs.*

> *Proposal 5: Within the framework of ODA, develop programmes that promote business links between local firms and foreign or FDI firms from donor countries.*

The ability to recruit technicians with appropriate knowledge is key for technology learning by local firms. The case studies show that some parts makers were former staff of FDI firms who left to set up their own businesses to supply their former employers. The FDI firms seem to prefer working with these spin-off firms because transaction costs can be reduced. Measures to support this kind of entrepreneurship are desirable.

> *Proposal 6: Capital, land, and other incentives should be provided directly to SMEs that are established by former FDI workers, either to compete with, or to supply, that FDI enterprise.*

SME-oriented innovation system

The lack of technical documentation in Vietnamese is an obstacle to learning by firms. Knowledge generation is a function of the innovation system; however, from a Vietnamese perspective, codifying knowledge in Vietnamese and making it accessible to SMEs should be seen as important, or even more important, than knowledge creation.

> *Proposal 7: It should be a priority to codify technological knowledge in Vietnamese for each industry and professional field, especially those in which SMEs are in the majority. Technological knowledge available in Vietnamese should be compiled in different ways to make it easily accessible to all SMEs.*

> *Proposal 8: Efforts should be made to compile and diffuse technical standards appropriate for SMEs in each industry and field of technology, including the compilation and diffusion of technical manuals.*

Worker training should receive more attention, and local governments should be more active in supporting vocational training. This training should also be flexible and include participation by both local and FDI firms.

> *Proposal 9: Develop vocational schools, with the participation of local SMEs, to provide short- and medium-term courses appropriate to local needs. FDI enterprises should be encouraged to provide vocational training for their workforce.*

> *Proposal 10: Within the framework of multilateral and bilateral cooperation, build exchange programmes that allow technicians from advanced countries to work in local SMEs and technicians from SMEs to go overseas to work in counterpart firms.*

Technical services provided by public organizations (e.g. universities, laboratories, and technology information centres) are not very effective in supporting learning by firms. Measures to improve this situation need to be considered.

> *Proposal 11: Increase the budget, authority, and responsibilities of S&T departments at the local level to allow them to be better and more proactive in implementing and acquiring R&D and other S&T services to address the demands of local firms.*

> *Proposal 12: Develop a programme that gives local firms coupons they can use to acquire, either free of charge or at a discounted rate, different kinds of technical services from national laboratories, laboratories at universities, or ministries.*

> *Proposal 13: Develop a network of not-for-profit technical-service providers to support innovation and learning by local firms. The requirements for specific services should be decided by local authorities in consultation with local firms.*

Intellectual property rights for the benefit of all parties

Although this research found little evidence of the direct impact of IPRs on learning, it is believed that IPRs can benefit both local and FDI firms.

> *Proposal 14: Laws concerning intellectual property rights (IPRs) should be compiled in different formats and at different levels to promote better understanding of IPRs among all parties, including the SMEs community, the S&T community, and state administrative officers.*

> *Proposal 15: SMEs should be continuously supported in their IPRs activities, and the impact of IPRs enforcement on SMEs should be studied and analysed to provide SMEs with sufficient time to adapt.*

Conclusion

Several conclusions can be drawn from this study. First, the learning readiness of firms is weak, especially among SMEs in the automotive industry. This is a general situation of most Vietnamese SMEs working with foreign companies. With regard to IPRs, it is not clear whether they prevent local firms from learning; however, they do discourage further investment by MNCs in upgrading technology. The policy environment does little to attract MNCs to invest in innovation-related activities, such as R&D or learning. However, significant progress has been made over the last few years with the enactment of IP Law by the National Assembly, and with the many commitments that have been made under bilateral trade agreements (BTAs) and during World Trade Organization (WTO) entry negotiations. This is an encouraging sign that conditions may soon be more favourable for learning.

Local firms have definitely gained considerable knowledge through working with MNCs such as Honda and VMEP; however, the knowledge they gained seems restricted to simple levels of production operations. Very little knowledge about innovation (R&D, design, or marketing) was gained. Moreover, this 'staying behind' status is true not only for SMEs, but for some larger firms and other institutions such as R&D institutes and universities. There is no clear evidence that IPRs are a barrier to learning. Most IPRs issues involve trade issues and trademarks on motorcycle models. Vietnamese SMEs seem to have two concerns about IPRs: in the long term how to avoid infringing on IPRs for fear of terminating their relationship with foreign companies; and how to bypass IPRs requirements, if any, to achieve short-term benefits. This means that IPRs are not an immediate issue for local SMEs.

Endnotes

1. The project team included: Tran Ngoc Ca, Deputy Director, NISTPASS; Nguyen Thanh Ha, Head, Science Policy Studies Department, NISTPASS; Vu Thi Thanh Huong, Senior Expert, Planning and Finance Department, MOST; Nguyen Vo Hung, Head, Technology Policy Studies Department, NISTPASS; Nguyen Thanh Tung, Senior Expert, Technology Policy Studies Department, NISTPASS; Nguyen Phuong Mai, Expert, Technology Policy Studies Department, NISTPASS; Le Quoc Phuong, Head, Information Department, NISTPASS; Tran Hai Yen, Hanoi Institute for Socio-Economic Development Studies, Hanoi Municipality; Nguyen Tai Vuong, Faculty of Economics, Hanoi Technology University; Nguyen Ngoc Anh, Senior Expert, America Department, Ministry of Trade; and Mai Thu Van, Senior Expert, Tax Department, Ministry of Finance.
2. Local content ranges from 42% to 64% among FDI assemblers.
3. In addition to weak enforcement of IPRs regulations, many automotive parts are simple products that do not have any IPRs protection.
4. Although the owner claimed a market share of 20%, this appears to be an overstatement given our knowledge of his production facility. We think a more realistic estimate is less than 5% of the market.

References

Asheim, B.T. and Haraldsen, T. (1991) Methodological and Theoretical Problems in Economic Geography. *Norsk geografisk tidsskrift*, 45, 189–200.

Baumol, W.J. (2002) *The Free-Market Innovation Machine – Analyzing the Growth Miracle of Capitalism*. Princeton University Press, Princeton, NJ, USA.

Blomstrom, M. and Koko, A. (1998) Multinational Corporations and Spill Over. *Journal of Economic Surveys*, 12, 247–277.

Coe, D.T., Helpman, E., and Hoffmaister, A.W. (1997) North–South R&D Spillovers. *The Economic Journal*, 107, 134–149

Edquist, C. (2004) Systems of Innovation: Perspectives and Challenges, in Fagerberg, J. (ed.), *The Oxford Handbook of Innovation*. Oxford University Press, Oxford, UK, pp. 181–208.

Ernst, D., Ganiatsos, T., and Mytelka, L. (eds) (1999) *Technological Capabilities and Export Success in Asia*. Routledge, London, UK.

Fagerberg, J. (2004) *The Oxford Handbook of Innovation*. Oxford University Press, Oxford, UK.

Fransman, M. (1995) Competitiveness and the Importance of Technology, Competence, and Strategy at Enterprise and National Levels: An Interpretive Survey of Literature on Developed and Less Developed Countries. *Institute for Japanese–European Technology Studies* (JETS), The University of Edinburgh, Edinburgh, UK. (mimeo).

Freeman, C. (1987) *Technology Policy and Economic Performance. Lessons from Japan*. Frances Pinter, London, UK.

Gerefi, G. (2005) The Global Economy: Organization, Governance and Development, in Smelser, N.J. and Swedberg, R. (eds.), *The Handbook of Economic Sociology*, Princeton University Press and Russell Sage Foundation, USA, pp. 160–182.

Gerefi, G., Humphrey, J., and Sturgeon, T. (2005) The Governance of Global Value Chains. *Review of International Political Economy*, 12(1), 78–104.

Hobday, M. (1995) *Innovation in East Asia: The Challenge to Japan*. Edward Elgar Publishing, London, UK.

Kaufer, E. (1983) *The Economics of the Patent System*. Harwood Academic Publishers, Amsterdam, The Netherlands.

Lall, S. (1990) *Building Industrial Competitiveness in Developing Countries*. OECD Development Centre, Paris, France.

Lundvall, B.-A. (ed.) (1992) *National System of Innovation. Towards a Theory of Innovation and Interactive Learning*. Frances Pinter, London, UK.

Nelson, R. (ed.) (1993) *National Innovation Systems: A Comparative Analysis*. Oxford University Press, New York, NY, USA.

Ordover, J.A. (1991) A Patent System for Both Diffusion and Exclusion. *Journal of Economic Perspectives*, 5(1), 43–60.

Perez, C. and Soete, L. (1988) Catching Up in Technology: Entry Barriers and Windows of Opportunity, in Dosi, G., Freeman, C., Nelson, R., Silverberg, G., and Soete, L. (eds) *Technical Change and Economic Theory*. Frances Pinter, London, UK.

Scherer, F.M. (1958) *Patents and the Corporation: A Report on Industrial Technology Under Changing Public Policy* (Second Edition). Harvard University, Boston, MA, USA.

Taylor, C.T. and Silberston, Z.A. (1973) *The Economic Impact of the Patent System: A Study of the British Experience*. Cambridge University Press, Cambridge, UK.

Verspagen, B. (1999) The Role of Intellectual Property Rights in Technology Transfer. Paper prepared for the *WIPO Arab Regional Symposium on the Economic Importance of Intellectual Property Rights*, Muscat, Sultanate of Oman, 22–24 February 1999.

CHAPTER 9
Conclusion

This book presents the outputs of the RoKS-supported research projects stemming from its inaugural competitive research-grant competition. These projects addressed the fundamental changes that are taking place in the funding of research in the public and private sectors and looked at how these changes are affecting the development of effective public policy.

The RoKS competition sought to develop a knowledge network to advance understanding of the shifting balance of public- and private-sector support to research for development. It was also envisioned that it would foster debate on possible policy responses at the institutional, national, and international level. Within this context, research projects focused on one or both of these themes: trends in funding, performance, and management of research and development; and policy options to stimulate research and development in, and for, developing countries.

In chapter two, Dr Daniel Chudnovsky and his team analyse productivity among Argentine manufacturing firms in the 1990s, in particular the policies introduced in that decade to foster innovation in the private sector. They identify several lessons for policymakers: R&D investment is a fundamental determinant of the probability of successfully introducing innovations; technological flows increase the magnitude of innovation output; large firms are more likely to engage in innovative activities; and firms consider R&D activities to be valuable, even during recessionary times. By extrapolation of these findings, public policies geared toward R&D promotion should have positive results. One such policy step would be to remove barriers that prevent SMEs from engaging in innovation. Additional research is required on the relationships between domestic innovative efforts and the acquisition of technology, and the impacts of new policies designed to foster private innovation.

In chapter three, Dr Qiu Haixiong and his team analyse the development of industrial clusters in South China to better understand how policies have been developed and implemented to encourage innovation. Over the decades, private enterprises have grown within these clusters. This growth was assisted by local governments and by links with foreign companies, which were instrumental in upgrading networks of suppliers and bringing in foreign expertise. Innovation centres have recently begun to create networks of enterprises, improve innovation capacities, and enhance communication with universities and research centres. In some districts, local government policy is to promote these innovation centres. Based on their study, the team conclude that 'marketized' research centres appear to have a greater probability of success than innovation centres due to their objective of selling products. Innovation centres were promoted during difficult economic times, when a need for better quality and higher priced products made sense in China. As such, innovation centres were mainly oriented toward servicing the local industry, rather than maintaining a competitive edge.

In chapter four, Drs Olman Quirós and Jorge Garza along with their two respective teams from Costa Rica and El Salvador examine partnerships within the agroindustrial research and development sector in both countries. There is little knowledge about how to create a public–private partnership that can respond to both public and private stakeholder needs. The teams found that public interests do not feature in partnerships as prominently as they should because the government sector often does not specify clearly how public money should be spent.

In chapter five, Ms. Juana Kuramoto and her team examine Peruvian institutional policies for innovation and R&D by assessing their effect on the performance of firms. Recognizing the importance of R&D and innovation is a recent phenomenon in Latin America (with the exception of Chile, Brazil, and Mexico), as seen by the low R&D expenditure in the region. Based on the study, the team recommends the strong need for investment policies that encourage: externality generating activities; complementary policies that facilitate both the dissemination of knowledge and the entry and exit of multinational companies (MNCs); free mobility of people and capital; links between firms and universities, and between industry and local research; and the development of funds for R&D.

In chapter six, Dr Samuel Wangwe and his team explore the trends in funding, institutional arrangements, and the relevance of R&D in Tanzania to better understand how policy is influencing both public and private support to R&D. They conclude that there has been: a decrease in the share of public R&D funding; a shift toward more private funding, especially in terms of public–private partnerships; and a dominance of donor funding, which has raised concerns over ownership and undue influence on the development agenda. Their recommendations include the need to: increase public funding to research in agriculture and health; pay greater attention to the continuity and predictability of R&D funding; diversify funding sources; enhance domestic ownership of the research agenda to reflect national development priorities; and improve monitoring of research outputs and dissemination of results.

In chapter seven, Ms. Belen Acosta and her team at the WorldFish Centre report on research to better understand the contributions of public–private partnerships in fish-genetics research in the Philippines. They note that public- and private-sector institutions worked together to deliver improved tilapia breeds and technology to achieve maximum benefits from genetic research. The key conclusion reached by the team underscored the importance of public- and private-sector harmonization by way of strategic partnerships to encourage cooperation among the major sectoral players. This cooperation ensured that problems and visions were shared and that partners worked together to find solutions to mutual problems.

Finally, in chapter eight, Dr Tran Ngoc Ca and his team examine the Vietnamese automotive industry to better understand how learning has taken place at the national level. They report that this learning was encouraged through networks and links established with foreign multinational companies. Intellectual Property Rigths (IPRs) were a special focus of this research project. The team determined that learning readiness of Vietnamese firms was extremely weak in the automotive sector, and that IPRs discourage investment by foreign MNCs in upgrading technology. Overall, the national policy environment does little to attract innovation-related investments, such as R&D, by foreign MNCs. There is no clear evidence that IPRs are a barrier to learning for Vietnamese firms.

Together, these papers present interesting insights into R&D funding and related policies in a range of institutional and government settings. They reinforce the need for additional research to further understand how R&D is best funded and managed, and to develop guidelines on how to support policy development that stimulates R&D and innovation for sustainable economic growth.

Index

References to tables, figures or appendices are in **bold**.

Argentina 3
   2001 economic crisis in 5–6
   as developing country 7–8
   infrastructure in **121**
   innovation surveys in 10, **11–14**, 14–16, 18–19, **21**, **23**, **26**
   innovation surveys in manufacturing firms in 3, 5–6, 9, 17–18, 25–7, 263
   policy recommendations 26
   R&D expenditures in **109–10**

CDM (Common Diagnostic Model) 7, 17, 19–20, 22, 34–5
Central America, policy recommendations 87
China 3
   industrial policy in 52
   and intellectual property 223
   promotion of innovation policy 39
   science and technology policy of 53
   support for private sector 50–1
   and Vietnamese automotive industry 233, 251
cooperative links 16–18, **18**, 21–2, **21**, **25**, **37**
copying 59
Costa Rica 3, 89–90
   agricultural sector in 264

   availability of ICTs 113
   economic growth in 109
   education system in 148
   innovation in 111
   organic coffee in 89–90, **97**
   organic coffee in
   potatoes in 91, **103–4**
   public-private partnerships in 92–3, **95**, **97–8**, **103–4**
   public-private partnerships in
   R&D expenditures in **109–10**
credit, in Latin America 119

Dachangjiang Group 46, 67–70, 76
Dachong 40, 54–5, 57–9, 62, 76–7
developing countries
   biotechnology and 193–4
   challenges of 160
   and hydrometallurgy 133
   industry in 244
   and innovation 9, 226
   and intellectual property 222–3
   links with foreign actors 128–9
   research and development in 1–2, 105, 122
   and technology transfer 45
   TIS in 147
donors, funding of R&D 91, 129, 171–4, 178, 187–8, 197

economic creativity 109–12, **111**
El Salvador 3, 89
   agricultural sector in 264
   innovation in 111

Ioroco in 89–91, **99–100**
public-private partnerships in 92, **96**, **99–100**
source of R&D expenditures **110**

foreign direct investment (FDI) **45**
  in Argentina 6
  Chinese legislation on 46
  in Guangdong 41–3, 47–8
  in innovation system **227**
  and intellectual property 222–3
  and Peru 149
  in Vietnam 220–1, 228–9, 232–5, **232**, **234**, 237–40, **240**, 242–5, **246**, 252–4, 256–7

government
  and economic planning 135
  as source of R&D expenditure 109, 119–20, 122
Guangdong
  bankruptcies 70
  future development of 47–8, 79–80
  government policies in 48–9
  history of investment in 41–2, **42**, 44–5
  productive systems in 42–4
  research and development in 44–7, 53–4
  support for industrial clusters 52
  technological learning in 44–7

HIV/AIDS 2, 51, 163, 169, 185
hydrometallurgy 130, 133, 137–9, 148

import-substitution industrialization (ISI) 10
India, and intellectual property 223
industrial associations 56, 58–9, 71–2

industrial clusters 3, **40**
  in China 39–41, 59, 66, 70–1, 76–7, 263
  creation and support of 50, 52
  development of 50, 55, 67, 70–1, 148
  and innovation centres 53
  types of 48–9, 75–6
information and communication technologies (ICTs) 39, 70, 112–13
innovation
  agroindustrial 88, 146
  in Argentina 263
  Chinese prioritisation of 53
  in copper hydrometallurgy 130, 133
  and economic growth 265
  in economic theory 224–6
  expenditure on 6, 9, **16–17**, 20–1, 27, **36**
  and FDI 223
  importance of to firm's performance 7
  indicators of 27, 112
  levels of expenditure on 6
  measurement of 9–10, 19
  and novelty 162
  and patents 222
  in Peru 264
  process of 7–8, **8**, 20, 22, 27, 107, 129, 226
  relationship with R&D 106–7
  and size of firms 226
  studies of 1, 7–11, 18, 20, 22
  and technology 112
  in Vietnam 228, 241, 255, 258
innovation policy 1, 3
  in Argentina 5, 28
  in China 39, 49–50
innovation centres (ICs)
  in China 56–8, 60–6, 77, 264
  creation of 52
  development of 76–7
  need for 72–3

in Peru   122, **124**, 144
  problems of   **78**
innovation clusters   148
innovation development   88, 91–2, **97**, **99–100**
Innovation, Policy, and Science (IPS) programme   1
innovation systems
  in China   39, 56, 63
  in economic theory   226–7
  in Peru   134, 136–8, 141, 147
  in Vietnam   219–20, **227**, 257
intellectual property rights (IPRs)
  in China   77
  in developing countries   223
  in Latin America   117, 147
  in Vietnam   219, 221–2, 228, 237, 242, 244, **246**, 258–9, 265
Internet, and innovation   112, 147

joint ventures (JVs)   **45**, 46

Korea, and intellectual property   223

labour productivity   14
labour skills   8, 20–1, 24–5
  in Latin America   116, 148
  in Peru   **127**
  in Vietnam   **241**, 258
Latin America
  characteristics of   146–7
  economic and political crises   105
  economic creativity in   111
  education in   116, **117**
  infrastructure in   **121**
  innovation in   112
  policy recommendations for   147–9
  R&D expenditures in   107
  supply of credit in   119
local content policy in Vietnam   232–3, 245–6, **246**, 248, 250–1, 254

local government
  in China   39, 41, 51, 56, 60–1, 72, 263
  in Peru   142, 144
  in Philippines   209
  responsibilities of   58, 77
  in Vietnam   256–8

Malaysia   3, 48, 149
maquiladoras (n6)   81
Medical   187
multinational companies (MNCs)   3
  in China   42
  in Peru   42
  in Vietnam   3, 219–21, 254–5, 257, 265

National Systems of Innovation (NSI)   7–8, 10, **21**, 27, 161–2

open economies, benefits of   119
original equipment manufacturing (OEM)   **45**, 46

patents   9
  in China   54
  importance of   222–3
  as indicator of innovation   9
  in Peru   **118**
Pengjiang   40, 66, 68–9, 76
Peru   3
  access to credit   119
  agriculture in   139–46
  availability of ICTs   **113**
  education in   116, 125–6, 136
  government in   115–16
  government of   115–16, 119–20, 122, 142–4
  impact of R&D   **131–2**
  infrastructure in   120, **121**
  innovation in   111, 113–14, 130
  institutional environment   117–19, **118**
  and Internet access   112

manufacturing firms in 137
mining sector in 130, 133–8
policy recommendations for 147–9
R&D and firm performance 129–30
R&D expenditures in 106–8, **109**
reforms of 1990s 105–6, 114, 119–20, 136–7, 139–40, 142, 147
relationships between firms 126, 128–9, 136, 139, 141–2, **143**, 145 research and technology institutions 122, 124–5, 135, 144
research and technology institutions **123**
size of firms 114–15
source of R&D expenditures **110**
Philippines 3
aquaculture sector in 193–6, 199–205, **205–6**, 207–12, **210**, 214–16, 264
cooperation between government and private sector 209
government of 200
policy recommendations for 212–14
public-sector research programmes in 197
policy recommendations 3, 26, 87, 147, 190
private sector
attitude to R&D 2, 89, 139
in developed countries 225
funding of R&D 159, 162, 174, 176, 182, 186–9, 196–7, 200–3, 206
links with academia 148
performance indicators of 8
in Peru 146
in Philippines 196–7, 200–4, 206, **211**, 213–14, 216
relationships with and within 126, 128
role in pursuing innovation 5, 28, 138
size of firms 5, 7–8, 10, **11**, 21, 42, 114, 126, 129, 148–9, 189, 220, 225–6, **239**, 263
subsidization of 93
in Tanzania 159, 162, 166, 174, 176, 182, 186–9
privatization
in China 52, 64
in Peru 105
public-private partnerships 3
in Central America 3, 87–9, 92–4, **101**–2, 264
in China 48
in Philippines 193–5, 203, 211, 215–16, 264–5
in Tanzania 166–7, 172, 174, 176–7, 188, 264
public sector
funding of R&D 159, 166, 170, 178, 181–2, 184, 188, 190, 197, 201–2
in Latin America 105
in Philippines 197, **198–9**, 201–2
in Tanzania 159, 166, 170, 178, 181–2, 184, 188, 190
in Vietnam 242

Qingxi 52, 70–2

research and development (R&D)
agroindustrial 89
and globalization 160
and innovation 225
and intellectual property 222
and technology acquisition 16, 20, 22
in Argentina 263

INDEX   271

in Central America 87–8, 90–1
in China 39, 51, 53–4, 71–2, 75, 80
comparative expenditure 107–8, **107**
continuity of 22–4, 26–7
intensity of expenditure on 15
medical 169, 184, 186–9
in Peru 106–7, 109, 129–30, 138, 264
in Philippines 195, 201–2, 214
relevance of 173
sources of funding 2, **110**, 148, 161–2, 169–70, **170**, 173, 178, 183, **184**, 187–8, 211–12, 265
in Tanzania 163–5, 172, 175, 178–80, **179**, **181**, 188–9, 264
in Vietnam 220, **245–6**, 247, 256, 259, 265
research centres
in China 50–2, 54, 56–7, 62, 69, 77, 80, 263
in Costa Rica 98
in El Salvador 96–7, 99
links to enterprises 54
marketization of 50–2, 64, 80, 264
in Peru 133
research funds, in Tanzania 185
research institutions
in Peru 109, 120, 137–8, 148
in Philippines 204
in Tanzania 162–4, 166–72, 174, 176–8, 180–1, 183, 186–8
in Vietnam 242, 250
Research on Knowledge Systems (RoKS) 1–3, 159, 263

sales, as innovation indictator 9
scale-effectiveness, and R&D 25, 207
science and technology (S&T)
institutions 106, 119, 227–8, 245, 253, 255

special economic zones (SEZs) 50, 79
sustainability 176, 182, 190, 193–4, 199

Taiwan 252
exports from China to 58
investment in China 41–3, 70
and OEM 46
and R&D in China 71
and Vietnamese automotive industry 248–9, 251–2
Tanzania 3
agricultural sector in 163, 165–6, 169, 172–7
background 160
economic reforms in 174–6, 178, 182
government of 168–9, 171, 176
health sector in 163, 168–9, 183–7, **185**
industrial sector in 163, 167–8, 178–83, **178**
institutional arrangements 189
policy recommendations 190
reforms in 160–1, 165
research funds in 160, 170–1, 175, 184
taxes 171
technology transfer in 166
Technological Innovation System (TIS) 113–14, 120, 147
technological learning 44–5, 47–8, 160, 221
models of **45**
technology
acquisition of 5–7, 15–16, 20, 23–4, 28
tangible and intangible 15–16, 24
transformative 1
technology transfer 220
in China 45, 73
and intellectual property 222

in Latin America 15, **96**,
   110–11, 122, 137
in Tanzania 166, 174–6
in Vietnam 220
technology transfer index 110–11
Thailand 48, 229, 238, 247
"Third Italy" 49, 52

Vietnam
   automotive industry in
      219–21, 228–33, **230–1**, 235,
      237–40, **236–8**, **241**, 243,
      245–6, 253–6, 258–9, 265
   case studies 246–53
   emerging industries in 221
   government policy in 234
   intellectual property in 222,
      228

investment levels in 46
policy issues in 231–2
policy recommendations
   255–8
science and technology sector
   226–7
size of firms in 220, 225–6

World Bank 48, 93, 171
World Trade Organization (WTO)
   42, 70, 221, 223, 259

Xiqiao 40, 59–62, 76–7

Zhongshan University 40, 73–5,
   74, 78–9

www.ingramcontent.com/pod-product-compliance
Ingram Content Group UK Ltd.
Pitfield, Milton Keynes, MK11 3LW, UK
UKHW021847140426
5217IPUK00022B/1641